My Neighbor Seki

Tonari no Seki-kun

9

Takuma Morishige

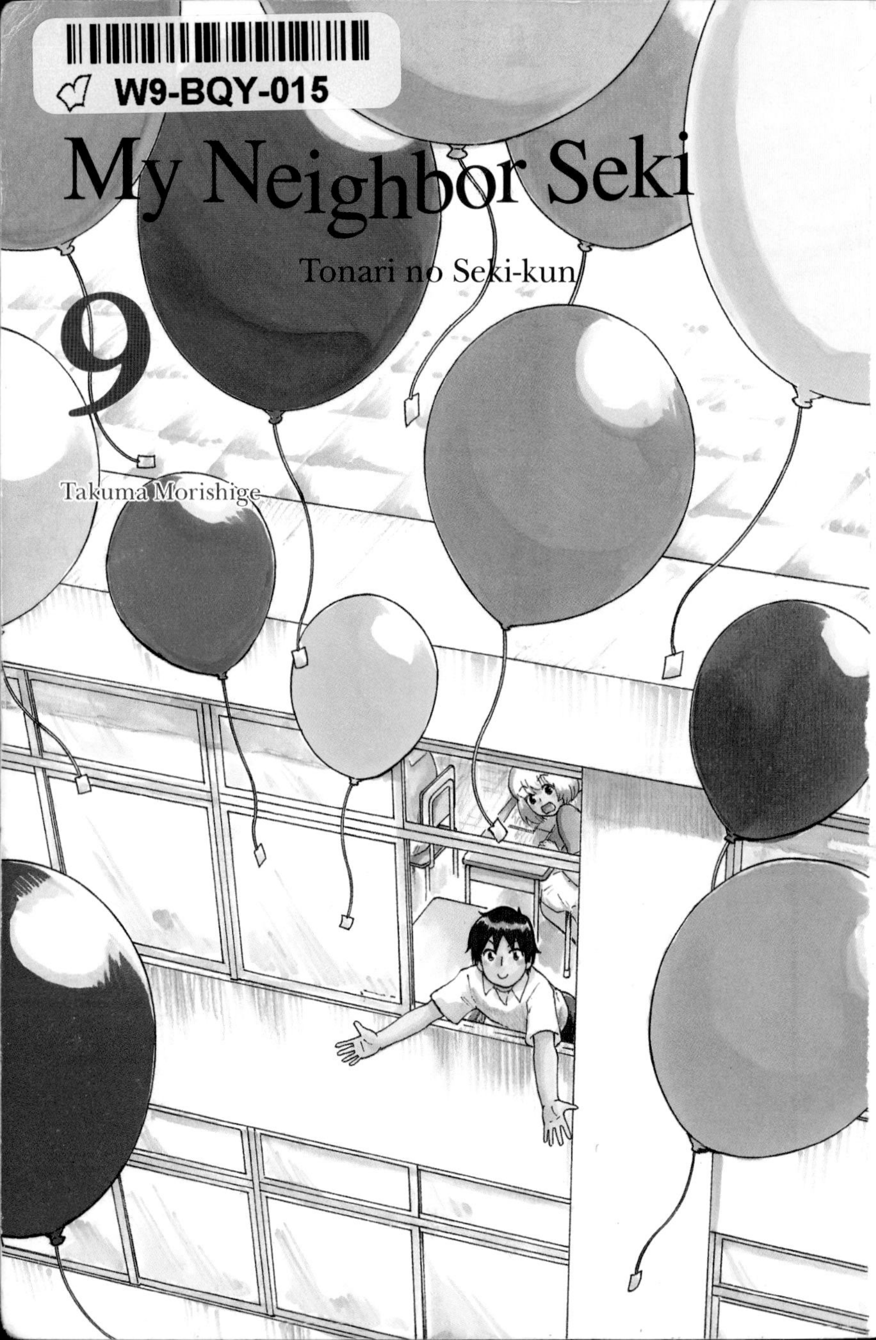

Schedule

My
Neighbor
Seki

9

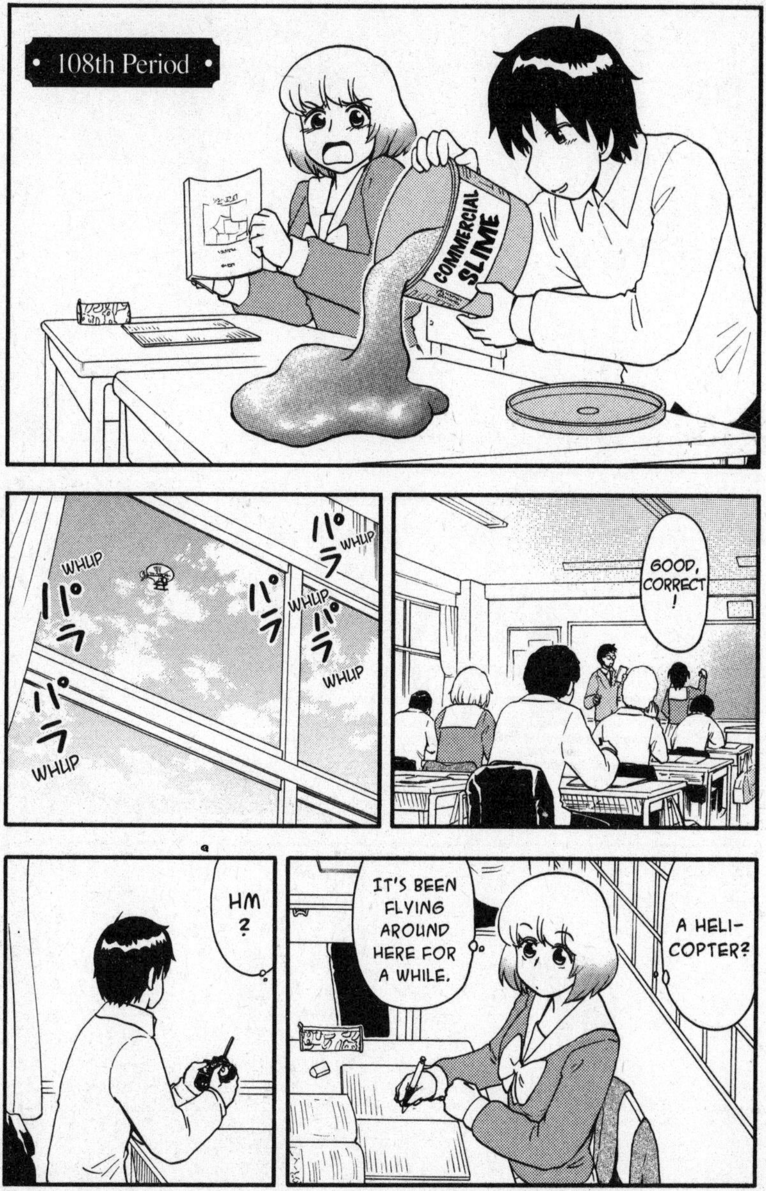
• 108th Period •
COMMERCIAL SLIME
GOOD, CORRECT!
パラ
WHUP
パラ
WHUP
パラ
WHUP
パラ
WHUP
パラ
WHUP
A HELI-COPTER?
IT'S BEEN FLYING AROUND HERE FOR A WHILE.
HM?

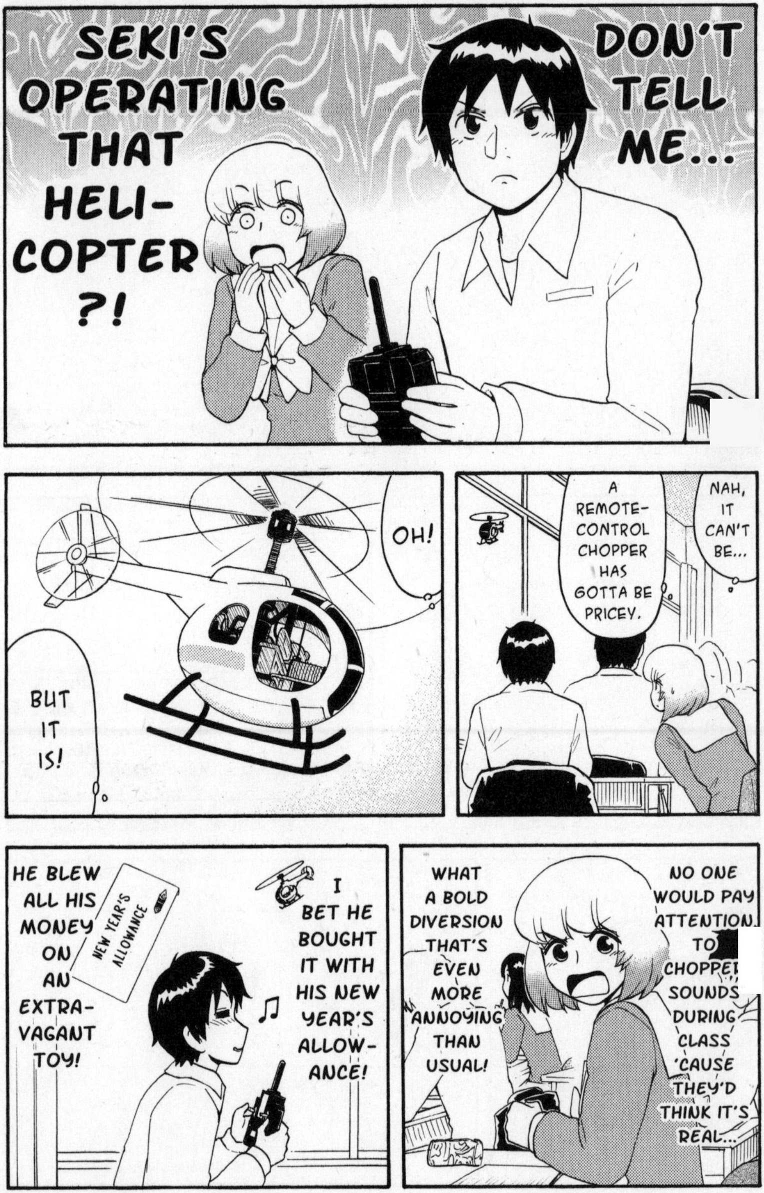
DON'T TELL ME...
SEKI'S OPERATING THAT HELI-COPTER?!
NAH, IT CAN'T BE...
A REMOTE-CONTROL CHOPPER HAS GOTTA BE PRICEY.
OH!
BUT IT IS!
NO ONE WOULD PAY ATTENTION TO CHOPPER SOUNDS DURING CLASS 'CAUSE THEY'D THINK IT'S REAL...
WHAT A BOLD DIVERSION THAT'S EVEN MORE ANNOYING THAN USUAL!
I BET HE BOUGHT IT WITH HIS NEW YEAR'S ALLOWANCE!
HE BLEW ALL HIS MONEY ON AN EXTRA-VAGANT TOY!
NEW YEAR'S ALLOWANCE

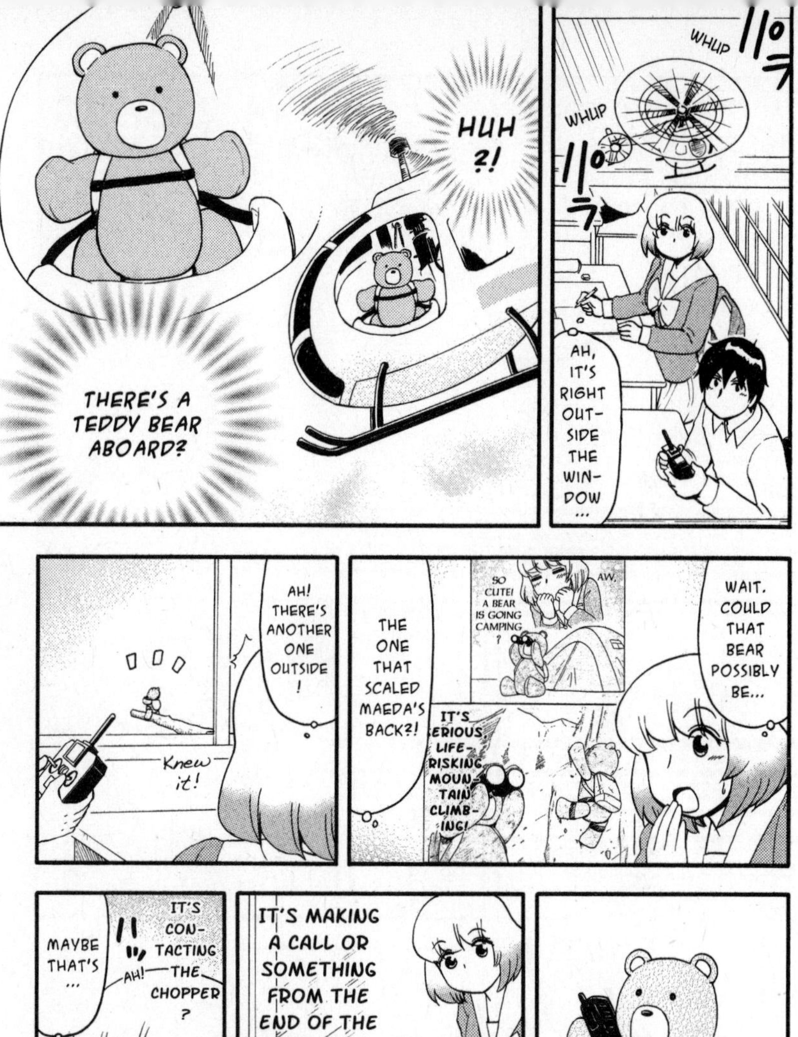
WHUP
WHUP
AH, IT'S RIGHT OUTSIDE THE WINDOW...
HUH?!
THERE'S A TEDDY BEAR ABOARD?
WAIT. COULD THAT BEAR POSSIBLY BE...
THE ONE THAT SCALED MAEDA'S BACK?!
AW.
SO CUTE! A BEAR IS GOING CAMPING?
IT'S SERIOUS, LIFE-RISKING MOUNTAIN CLIMBING!
AH! THERE'S ANOTHER ONE OUTSIDE!
Knew it!
IT'S MAKING A CALL OR SOMETHING FROM THE END OF THE BRANCH...
IT'S CONTACTING THE CHOPPER?
AH!
MAYBE THAT'S...

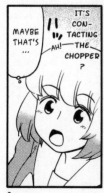

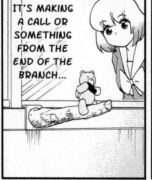

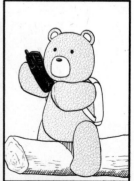

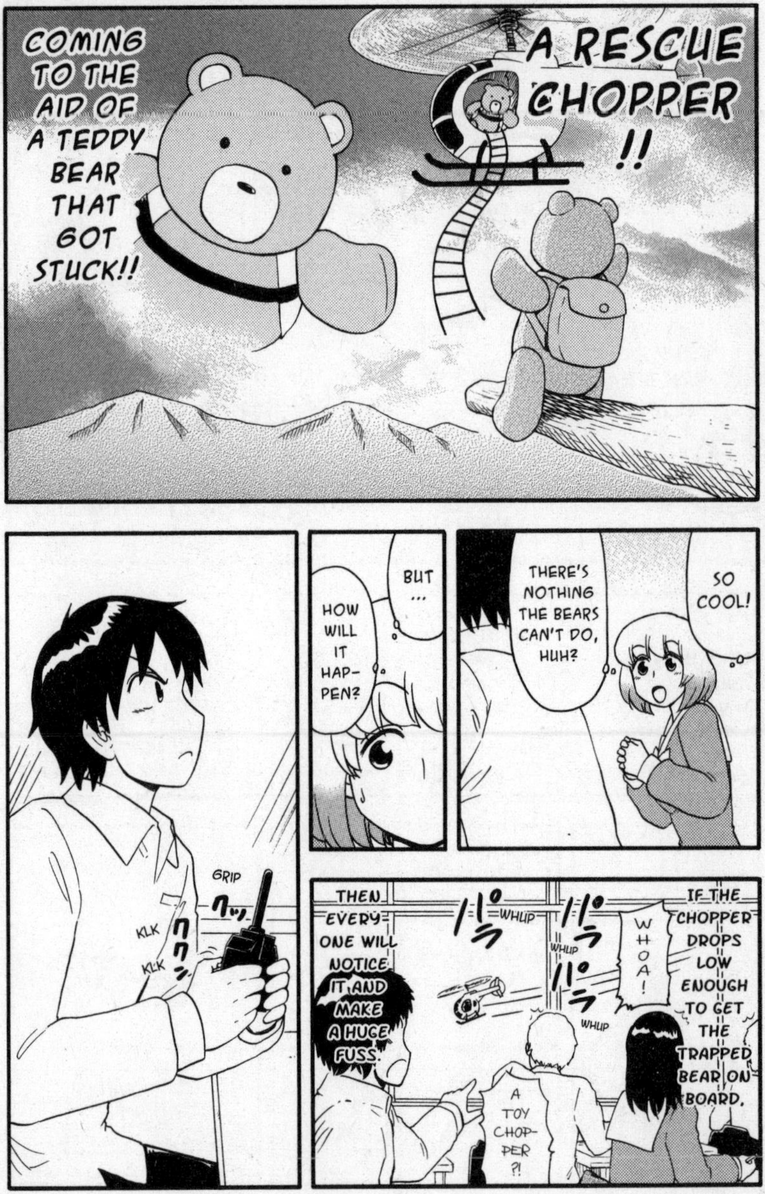
A RESCUE CHOPPER !!
COMING TO THE AID OF A TEDDY BEAR THAT GOT STUCK!!
SO COOL!
THERE'S NOTHING THE BEARS CAN'T DO, HUH?
BUT ...
HOW WILL IT HAPPEN?
IF THE CHOPPER DROPS LOW ENOUGH TO GET THE TRAPPED BEAR ON BOARD.
WHOA!
WHUP
WHUP
WHUP
A TOY CHOPPER ?!
THEN EVERYONE WILL NOTICE IT AND MAKE A HUGE FUSS.
GRIP
KLK
KLK

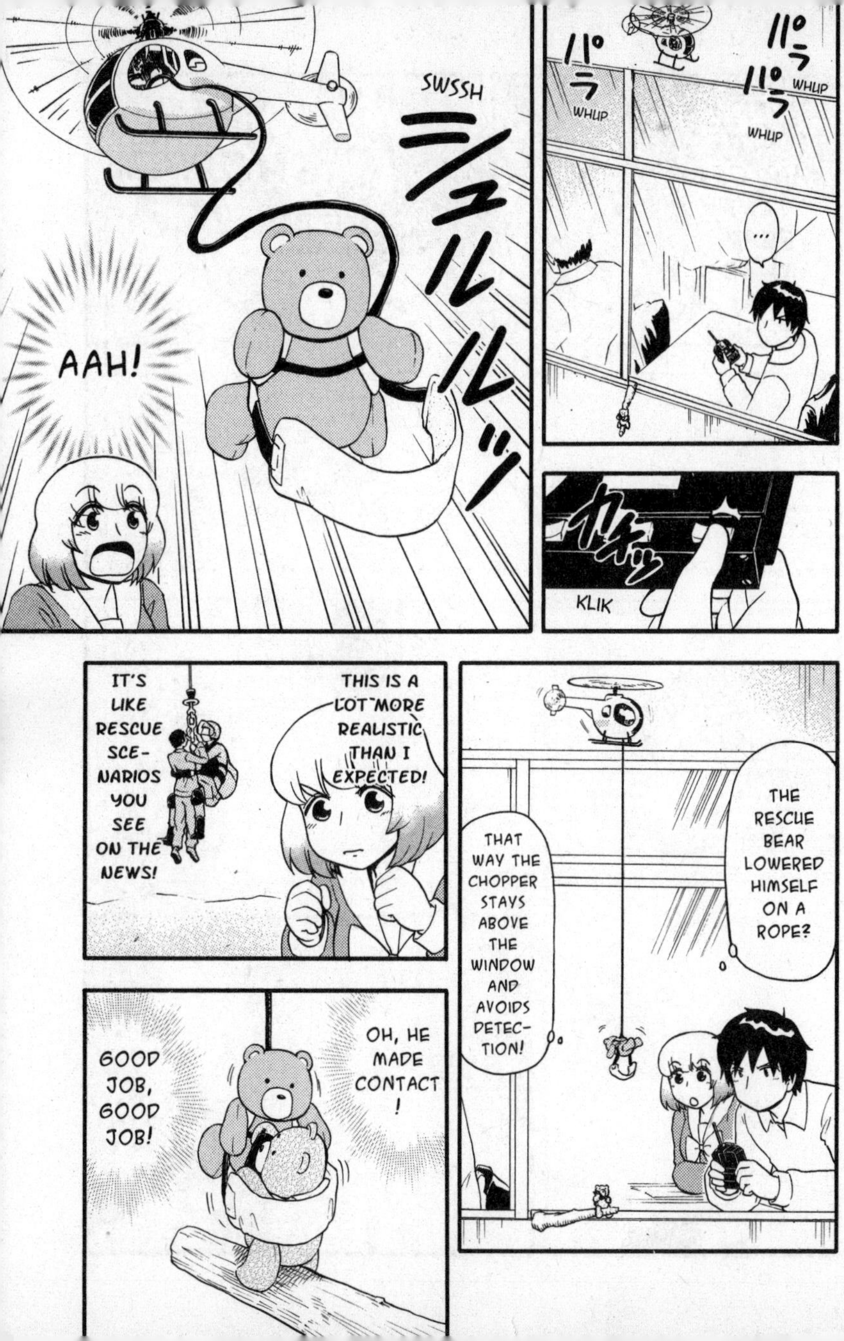

パラパラ
WHUP
WHUP
パラ
WHUP
...
カチッ
KLIK
SWSSH
シュルルッ
AAH!
THE RESCUE BEAR LOWERED HIMSELF ON A ROPE?
THAT WAY THE CHOPPER STAYS ABOVE THE WINDOW AND AVOIDS DETEC-TION!
THIS IS A LOT MORE REALISTIC THAN I EXPECTED!
IT'S LIKE RESCUE SCE-NARIOS YOU SEE ON THE NEWS!
OH, HE MADE CONTACT!
GOOD JOB, GOOD JOB!

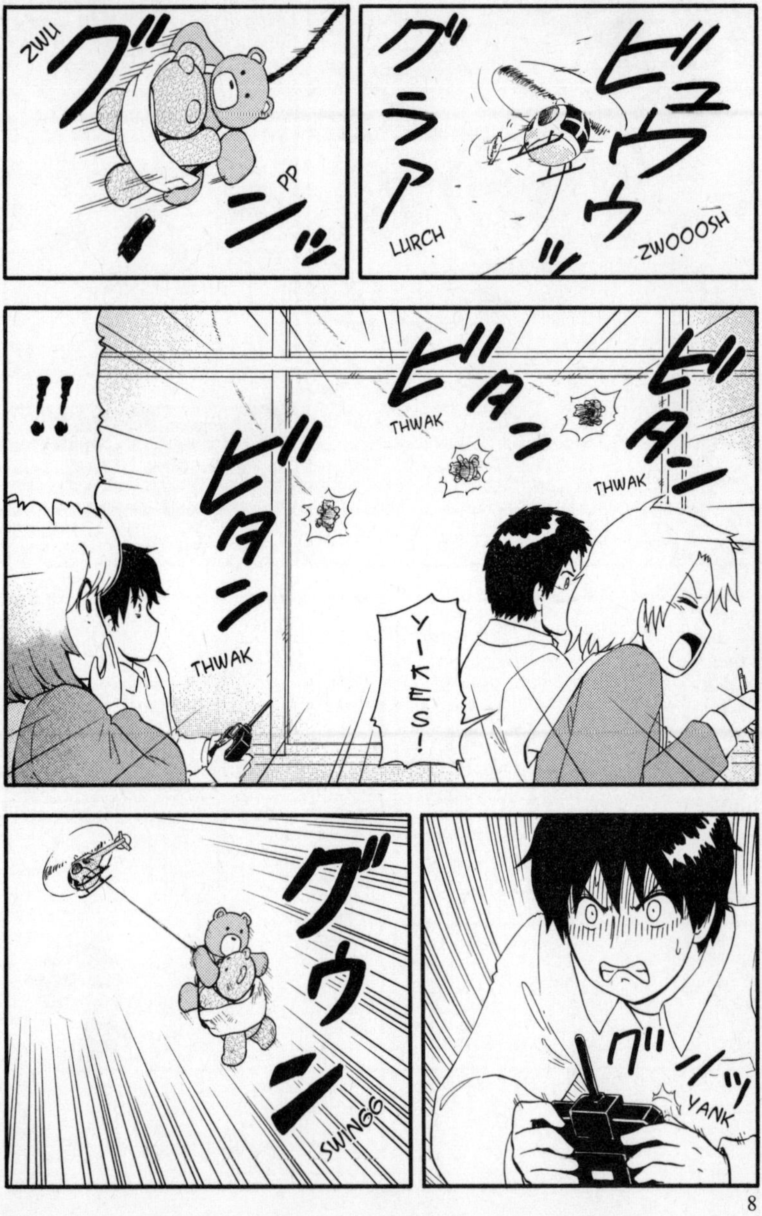
ビュウウゥッ
ZWOOOSH
グラア
LURCH
グンッ
ZWU
PP
ビタン
THWAK
ビタン
THWAK
YIKES!
!!
ビタン
THWAK
グンッ
YANK
グウン
SWINGG

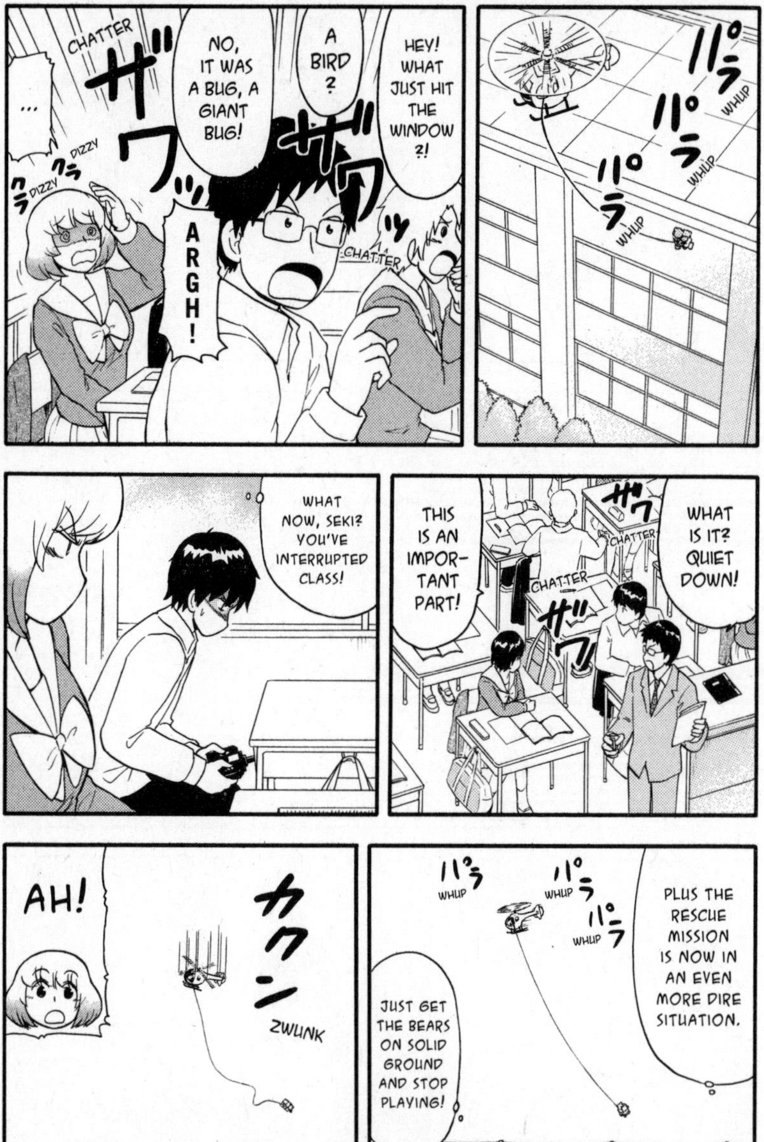
パラ WHUP
パラ WHUP
パラ WHUP
HEY! WHAT JUST HIT THE WINDOW?!
A BIRD?
NO, IT WAS A BUG, A GIANT BUG!
ザワッ
CHATTER
ザワッ
CHATTER
ARGH!
...
クラ DIZZY
クラ DIZZY
WHAT IS IT? QUIET DOWN!
ザワ
CHATTER
THIS IS AN IMPORTANT PART!
CHATTER
ザワ
WHAT NOW, SEKI? YOU'VE INTERRUPTED CLASS!
PLUS THE RESCUE MISSION IS NOW IN AN EVEN MORE DIRE SITUATION.
パラ WHUP
パラ WHUP
パラ WHUP
JUST GET THE BEARS ON SOLID GROUND AND STOP PLAYING!
カクン
ZWUNK
AH!

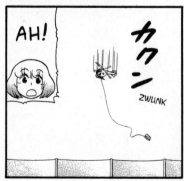

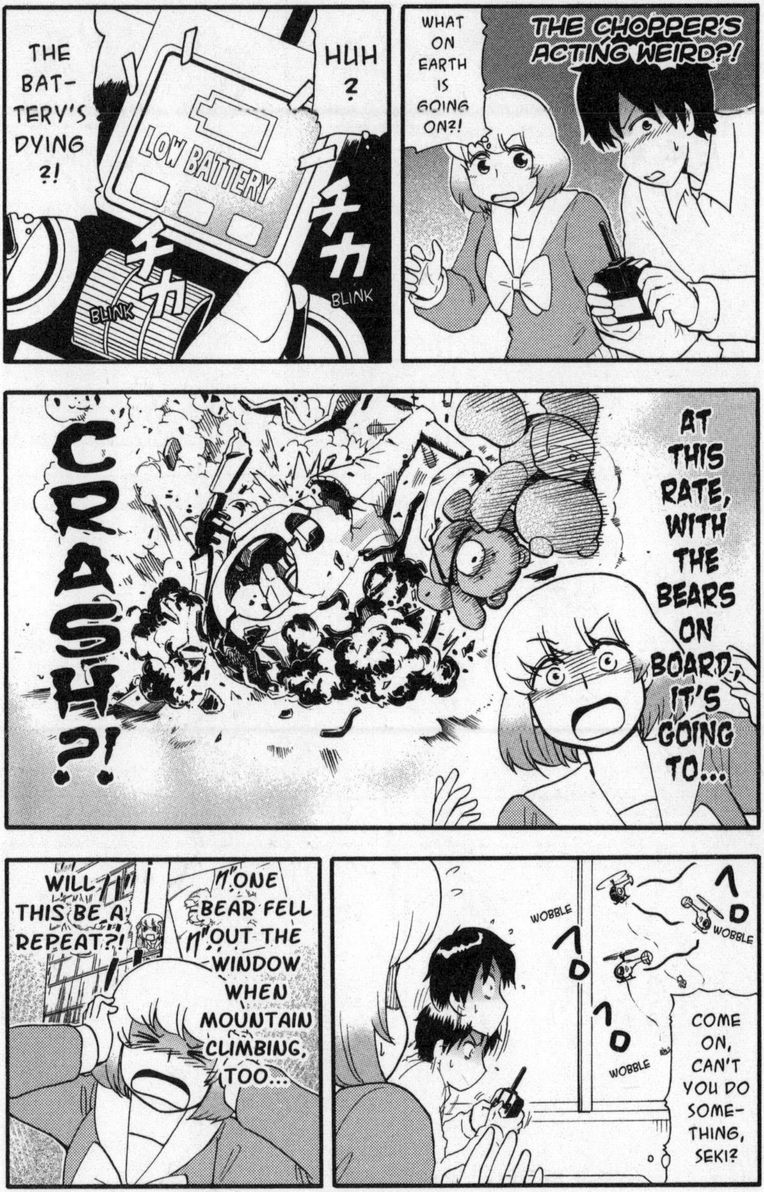
THE CHOPPER'S ACTING WEIRD?!
WHAT ON EARTH IS GOING ON?!
HUH?
THE BAT-TERY'S DYING?!
LOW BATTERY
チカ
BLINK
チカ
BLINK
AT THIS RATE, WITH THE BEARS ON BOARD, IT'S GOING TO...
CRASH?!
WOBBLE
WOBBLE
WOBBLE
COME ON, CAN'T YOU DO SOME-THING, SEKI?
ONE BEAR FELL OUT THE WINDOW WHEN MOUNTAIN CLIMBING, TOO...
WILL THIS BE A REPEAT?!

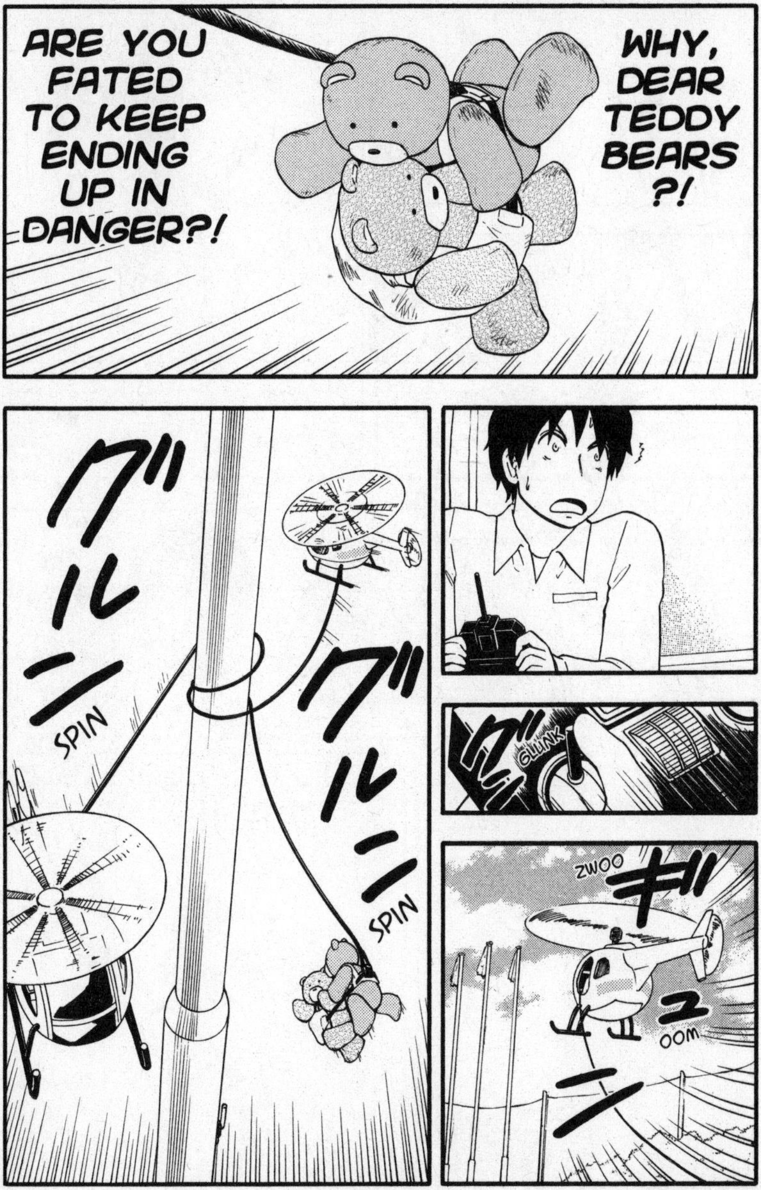

WHY, DEAR TEDDY BEARS?!
ARE YOU FATED TO KEEP ENDING UP IN DANGER?!
GLUNK
ZWOO
OOM
グルン
SPIN
グルン
SPIN

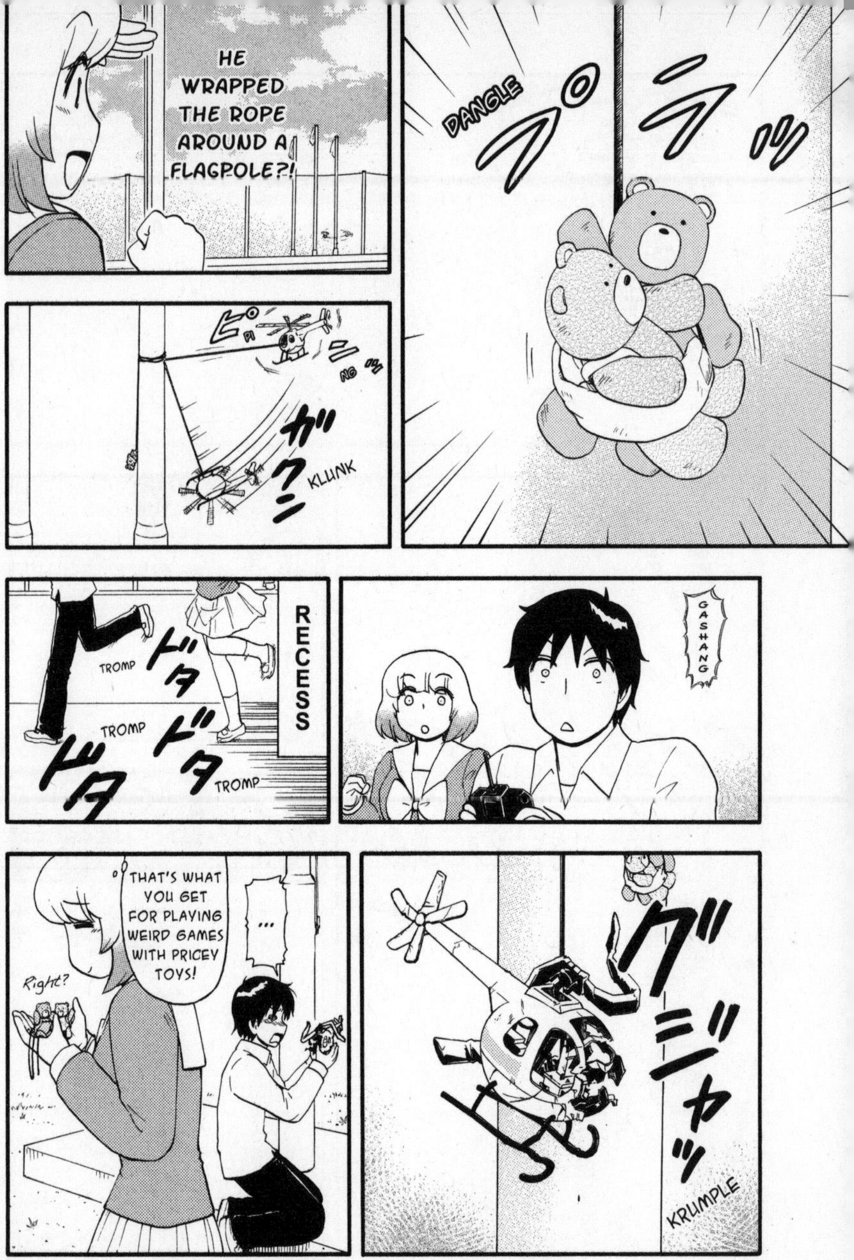
DANGLE
HE WRAPPED THE ROPE AROUND A FLAGPOLE?!
PI
NG
KLUNK
GASHANG
RECESS
TROMP
TROMP
TROMP
KRUMPLE
THAT'S WHAT YOU GET FOR PLAYING WEIRD GAMES WITH PRICEY TOYS!
...
Right?

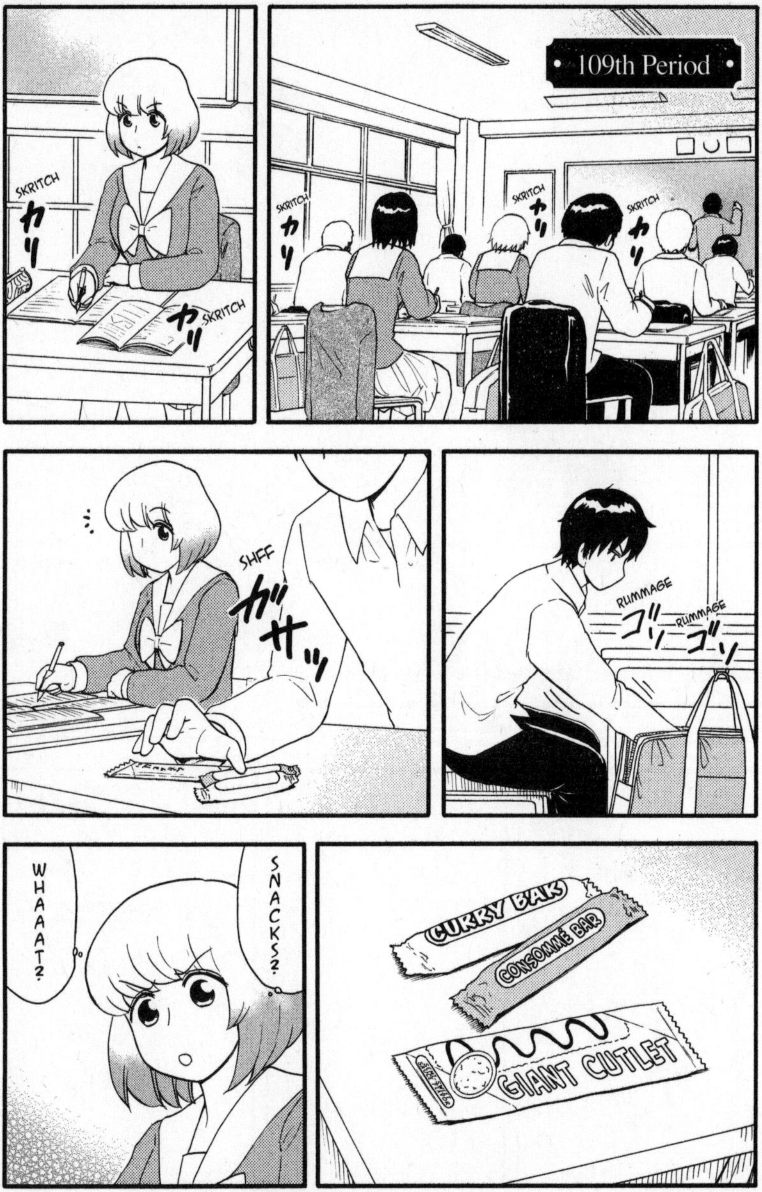
109th Period
SKRITCH
カリ
SKRITCH
カリ
SKRITCH
カリ
SKRITCH
カリ
カリ
SKRITCH
RUMMAGE
ゴソ
RUMMAGE
ゴソ
SHFF
ガサッ
CURRY BAR
CONSOMMÉ BAR
GIANT CUTLET
SNACKS?
WHAAAAT?

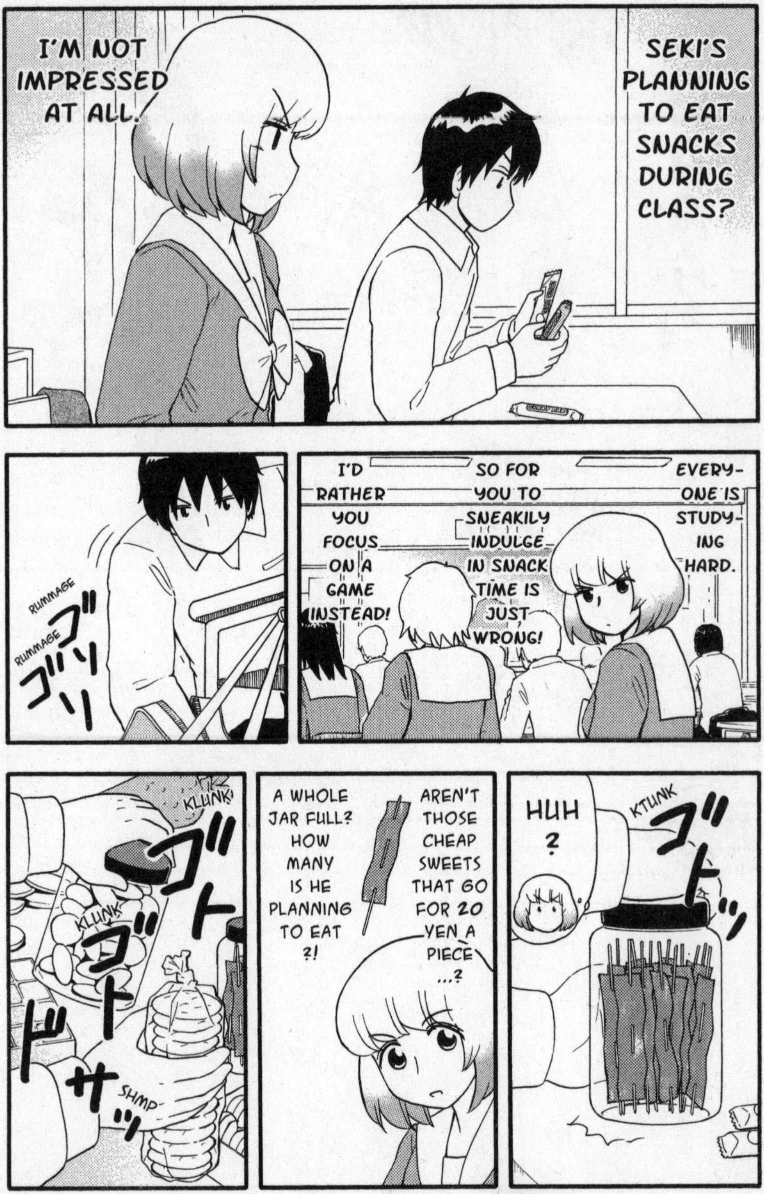
SEKI'S PLANNING TO EAT SNACKS DURING CLASS?
I'M NOT IMPRESSED AT ALL.
EVERY-ONE IS STUDY-ING HARD.
SO FOR YOU TO SNEAKILY INDULGE IN SNACK TIME IS JUST WRONG!
I'D RATHER YOU FOCUS ON A GAME INSTEAD!
RUMMAGE
RUMMAGE
ゴソゴソ
HUH?
KTUNK
ゴトッ
AREN'T THOSE CHEAP SWEETS THAT GO FOR 20 YEN A PIECE ...?
A WHOLE JAR FULL? HOW MANY IS HE PLANNING TO EAT?!
KLUNK
ゴト
KLUNK
ゴト
ドサッ
SHMP

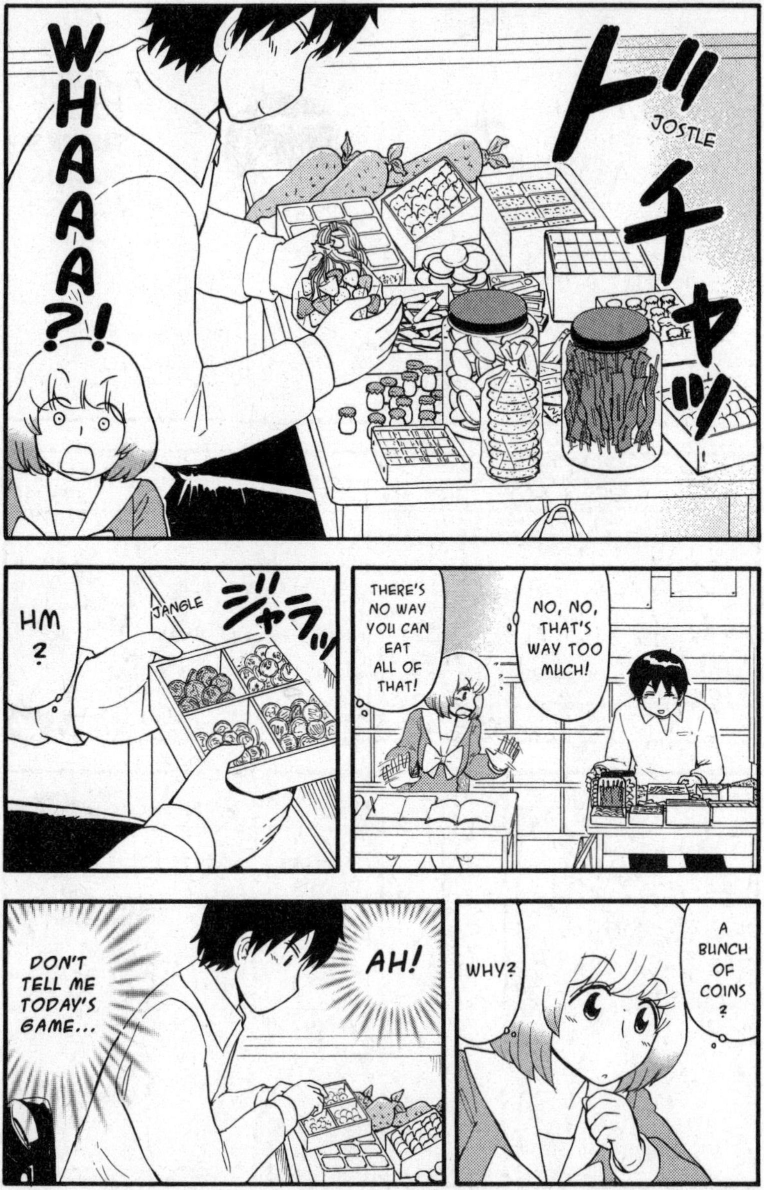
ドチャッ
JOSTLE
WHAAAA?!
NO, NO, THAT'S WAY TOO MUCH!
THERE'S NO WAY YOU CAN EAT ALL OF THAT!
ジャラッ
JANGLE
HM?
A BUNCH OF COINS?
WHY?
AH!
DON'T TELL ME TODAY'S GAME...

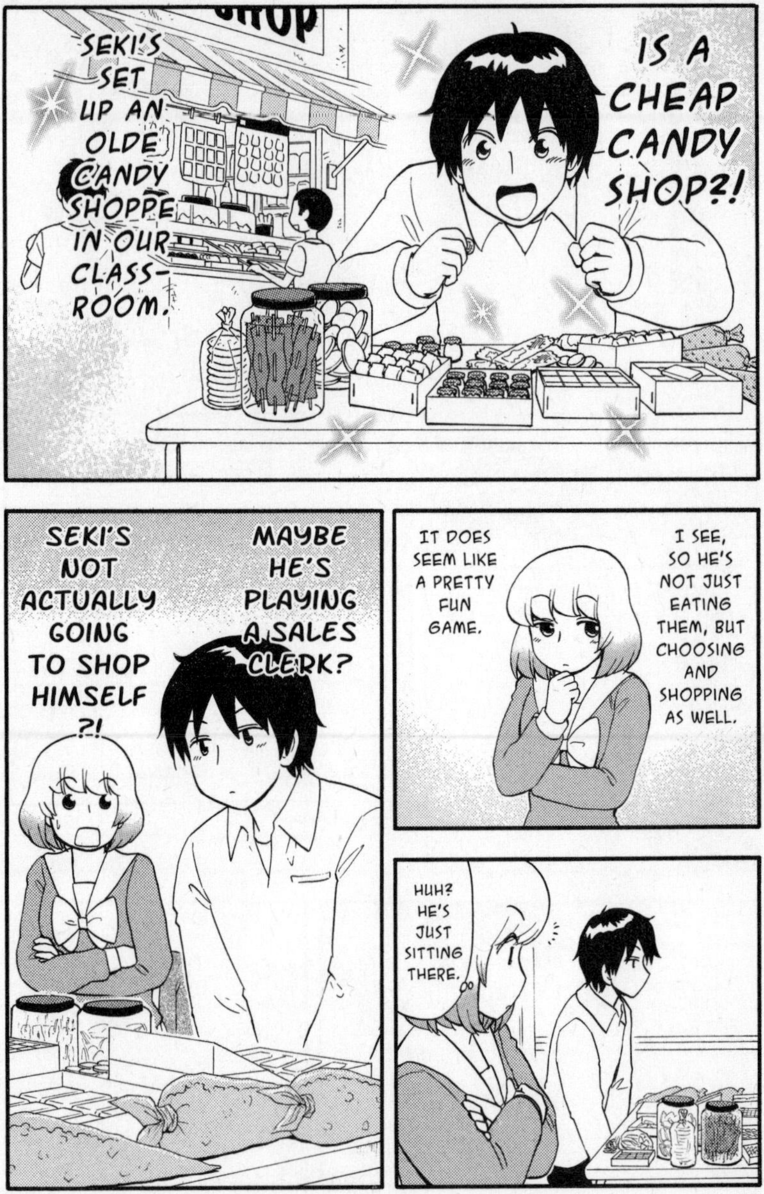
IS A CHEAP CANDY SHOP?!
SEKI'S SET UP AN OLDE CANDY SHOPPE IN OUR CLASSROOM.
I SEE, SO HE'S NOT JUST EATING THEM, BUT CHOOSING AND SHOPPING AS WELL.
IT DOES SEEM LIKE A PRETTY FUN GAME.
HUH? HE'S JUST SITTING THERE.
MAYBE HE'S PLAYING A SALES CLERK?
SEKI'S NOT ACTUALLY GOING TO SHOP HIMSELF ?!

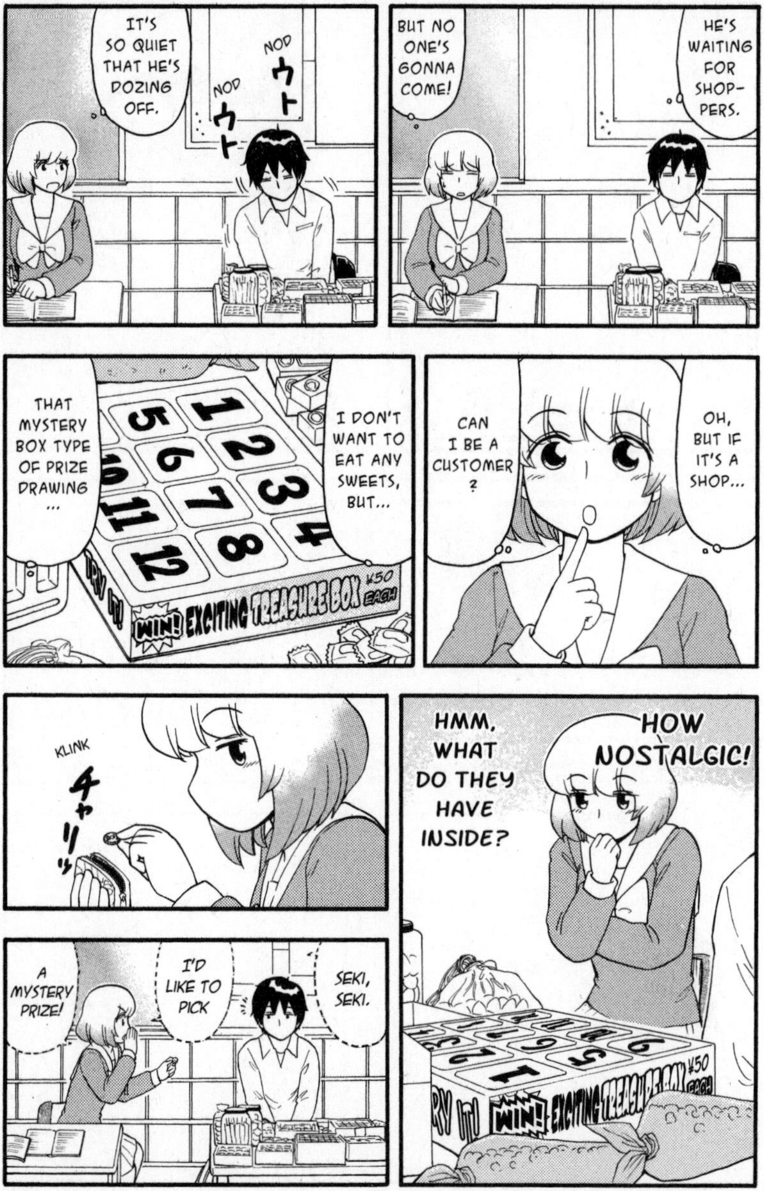

HE'S WAITING FOR SHOP-PERS.
BUT NO ONE'S GONNA COME!
NOD ウト
NOD ウト
IT'S SO QUIET THAT HE'S DOZING OFF.
OH, BUT IF IT'S A SHOP...
CAN I BE A CUSTOMER?
I DON'T WANT TO EAT ANY SWEETS, BUT...
THAT MYSTERY BOX TYPE OF PRIZE DRAWING...
1 2 3 4 5 6 7 8 10 11 12
TRY IT! WIN! EXCITING TREASURE BOX ¥50 EACH
HOW NOSTALGIC!
HMM, WHAT DO THEY HAVE INSIDE?
KLINK
チャリッ
SEKI, SEKI.
I'D LIKE TO PICK
A MYSTERY PRIZE!

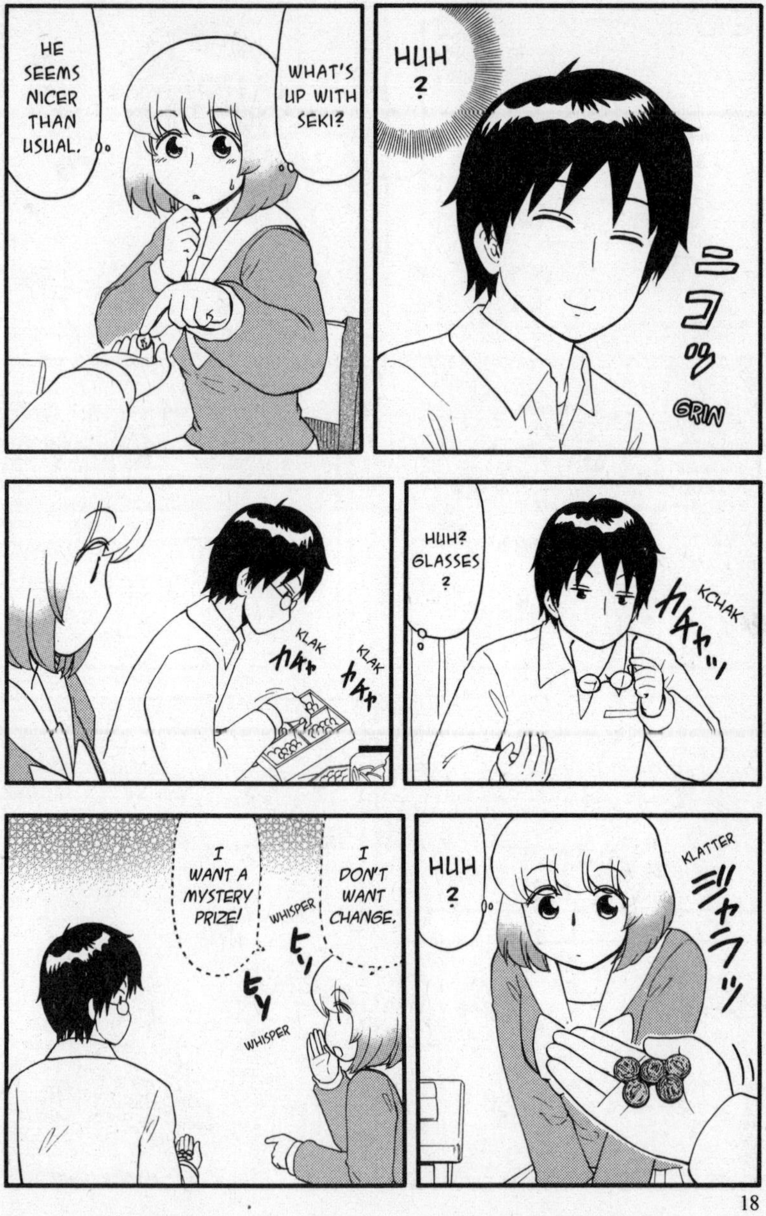

HUH?
ニコッ
GRIN
WHAT'S UP WITH SEKI?
HE SEEMS NICER THAN USUAL.
HUH? GLASSES?
KCHAK
カチャッ
KLAK
カチャ
KLAK
カチャ
HUH?
KLATTER
ジャラッ
I DON'T WANT CHANGE.
I WANT A MYSTERY PRIZE!
WHISPER
ヒソ
ヒソ
WHISPER

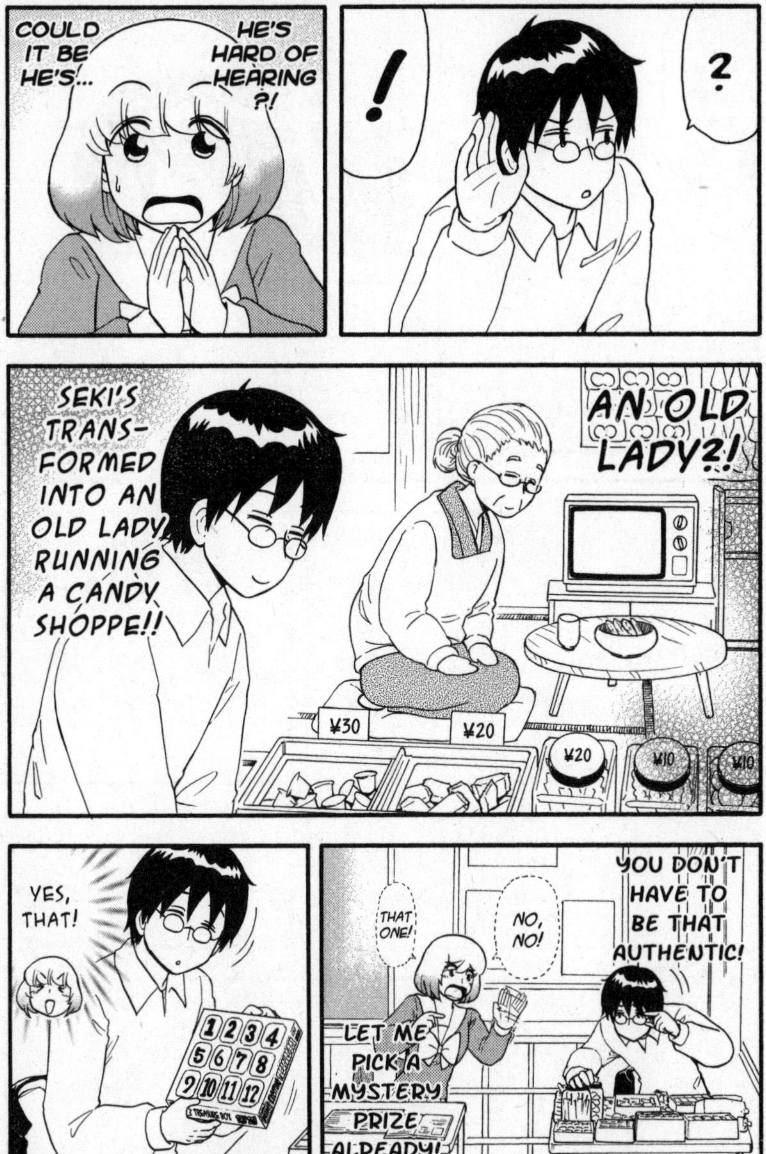
?
!
HE'S HARD OF HEARING ?!
COULD IT BE HE'S...
AN OLD LADY?!
SEKI'S TRANS-FORMED INTO AN OLD LADY RUNNING A CANDY SHOPPE!!
¥30
¥20
¥20
¥10
¥10
YOU DON'T HAVE TO BE THAT AUTHENTIC!
NO, NO!
THAT ONE!
LET ME PICK A MYSTERY PRIZE ALREADY!
YES, THAT!
1 2 3 4
5 6 7 8
9 10 11 12

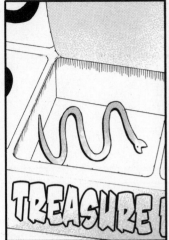

TREASURE !

GLANCE キョロ
GLANCE キョロ

°° THIS
ONE!

PEEL
ペリ
ペリ
PEEL

ぐ は〜 WILT

AWW...

I JUST
WASTED
MONEY!

DANGLE
ぴ
ろ
ん

...

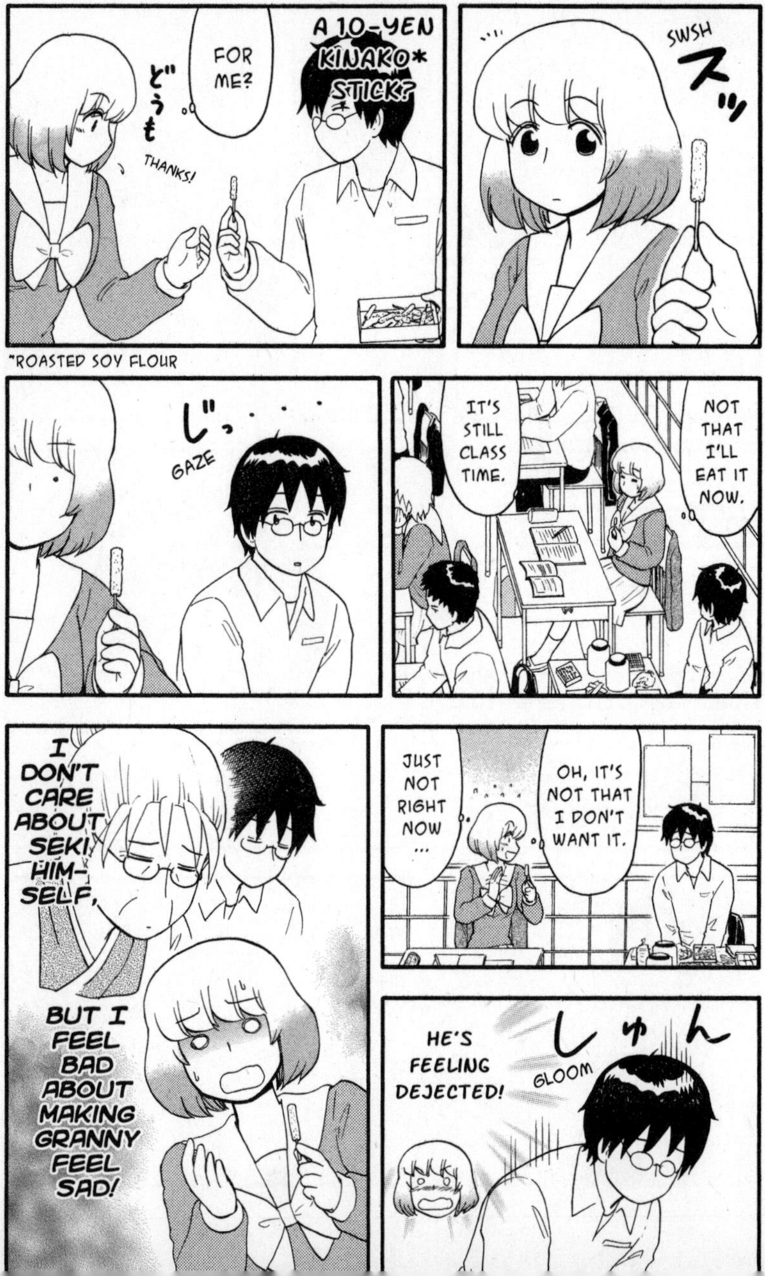
SWSH
スッ
A 10-YEN KINAKO* STICK?
FOR ME?
どうも
THANKS!
*ROASTED SOY FLOUR
NOT THAT I'LL EAT IT NOW.
IT'S STILL CLASS TIME.
じっ
GAZE
OH, IT'S NOT THAT I DON'T WANT IT.
JUST NOT RIGHT NOW...
しゅん
GLOOM
HE'S FEELING DEJECTED!
I DON'T CARE ABOUT SEKI HIMSELF,
BUT I FEEL BAD ABOUT MAKING GRANNY FEEL SAD!

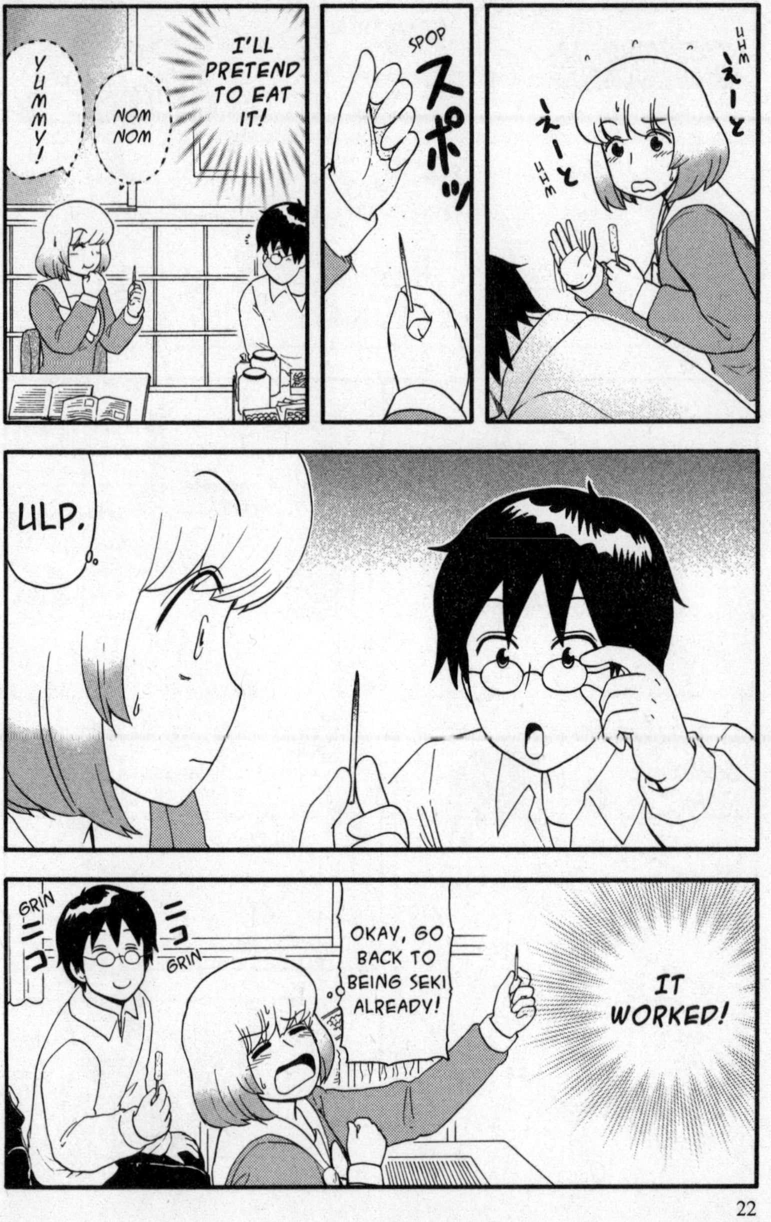
UHM
えーと
えーと
UHM
SPOP
スポッ
I'LL PRETEND TO EAT IT!
NOM NOM
YUMMY!
ULP.
IT WORKED!
OKAY, GO BACK TO BEING SEKI ALREADY!
ニコ
GRIN
ニコ
GRIN

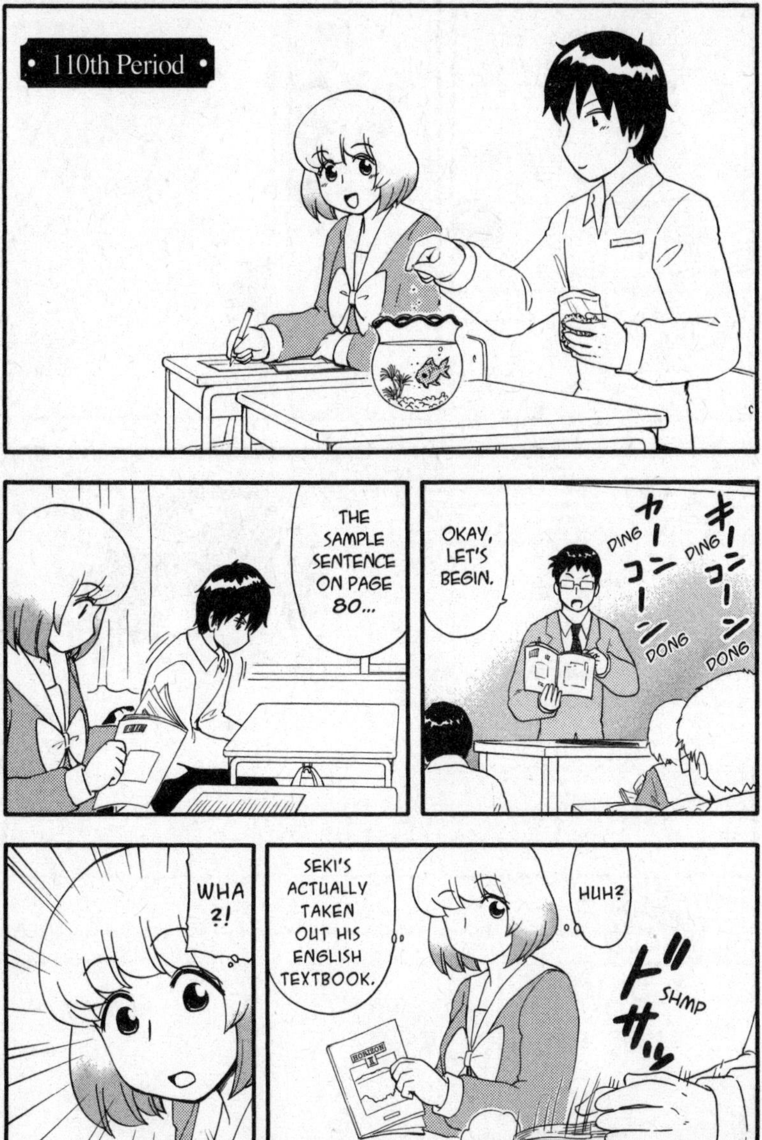
• 110th Period •
OKAY, LET'S BEGIN.
キーンコーン
DING DONG
カーンコーン
DING DONG
THE SAMPLE SENTENCE ON PAGE 80...
HUH?
SEKI'S ACTUALLY TAKEN OUT HIS ENGLISH TEXTBOOK.
ドザッ
SHMP
WHA ?!

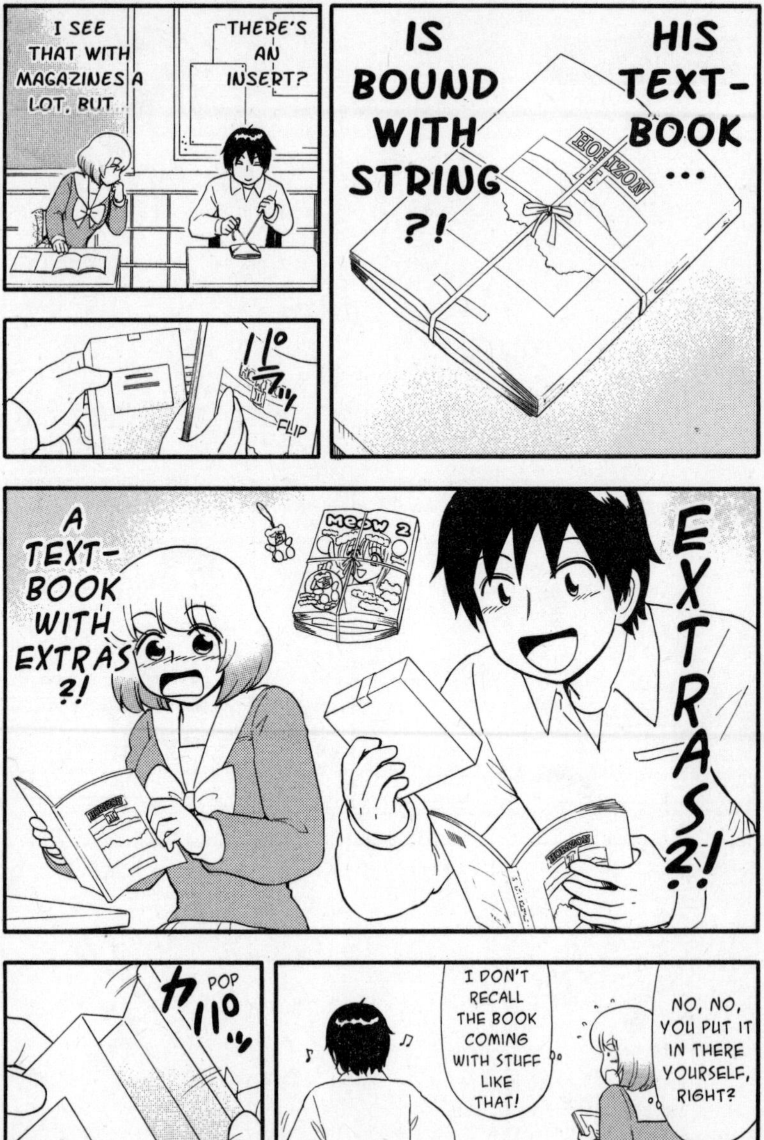
HIS TEXTBOOK...
IS BOUND WITH STRING?!
THERE'S AN INSERT?
I SEE THAT WITH MAGAZINES A LOT, BUT...
パラッ
FLIP
EXTRAS?!
MEOW 2
A TEXTBOOK WITH EXTRAS?!
NO, NO, YOU PUT IT IN THERE YOURSELF, RIGHT?
I DON'T RECALL THE BOOK COMING WITH STUFF LIKE THAT!
カパッ
POP

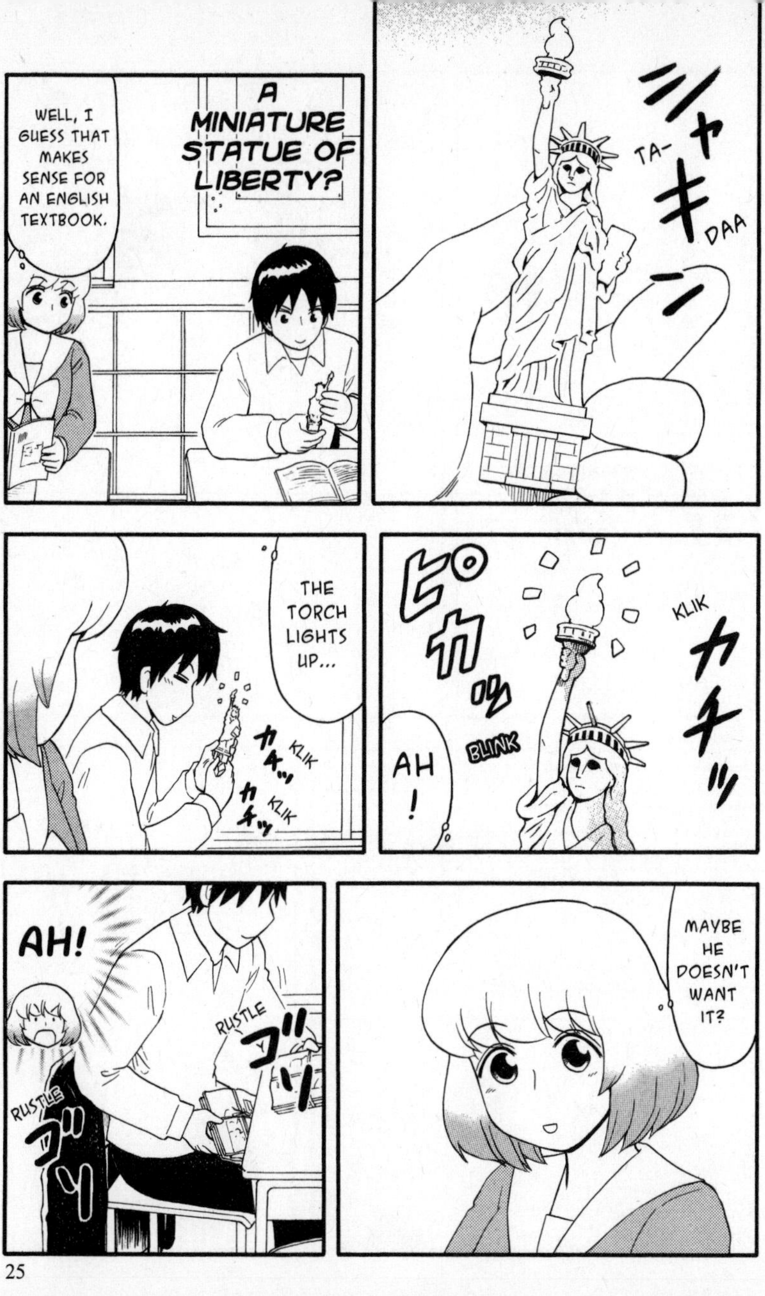
シャキーン
TA-DAA
A MINIATURE STATUE OF LIBERTY?
WELL, I GUESS THAT MAKES SENSE FOR AN ENGLISH TEXTBOOK.
KLIK
カチッ
ピカッ
BLINK
AH!
THE TORCH LIGHTS UP...
KLIK
カチッ
KLIK
カチッ
MAYBE HE DOESN'T WANT IT?
AH!
RUSTLE
ゴソ
RUSTLE
ゴソ

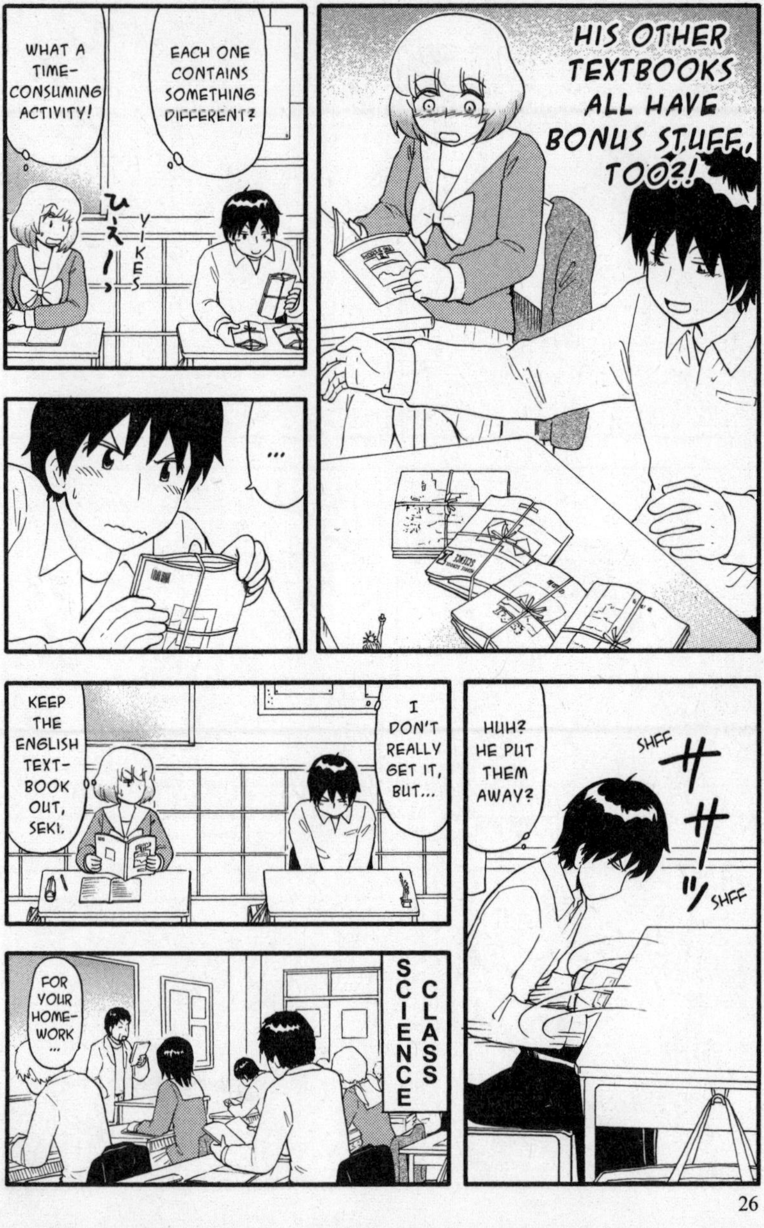
HIS OTHER TEXTBOOKS ALL HAVE BONUS STUFF, TOO?!
EACH ONE CONTAINS SOMETHING DIFFERENT?
WHAT A TIME-CONSUMING ACTIVITY!
ひえ～
YIKES
...
HUH? HE PUT THEM AWAY?
SHFF
ササッ
SHFF
I DON'T REALLY GET IT, BUT...
KEEP THE ENGLISH TEXT-BOOK OUT, SEKI.
SCIENCE CLASS
FOR YOUR HOME-WORK...

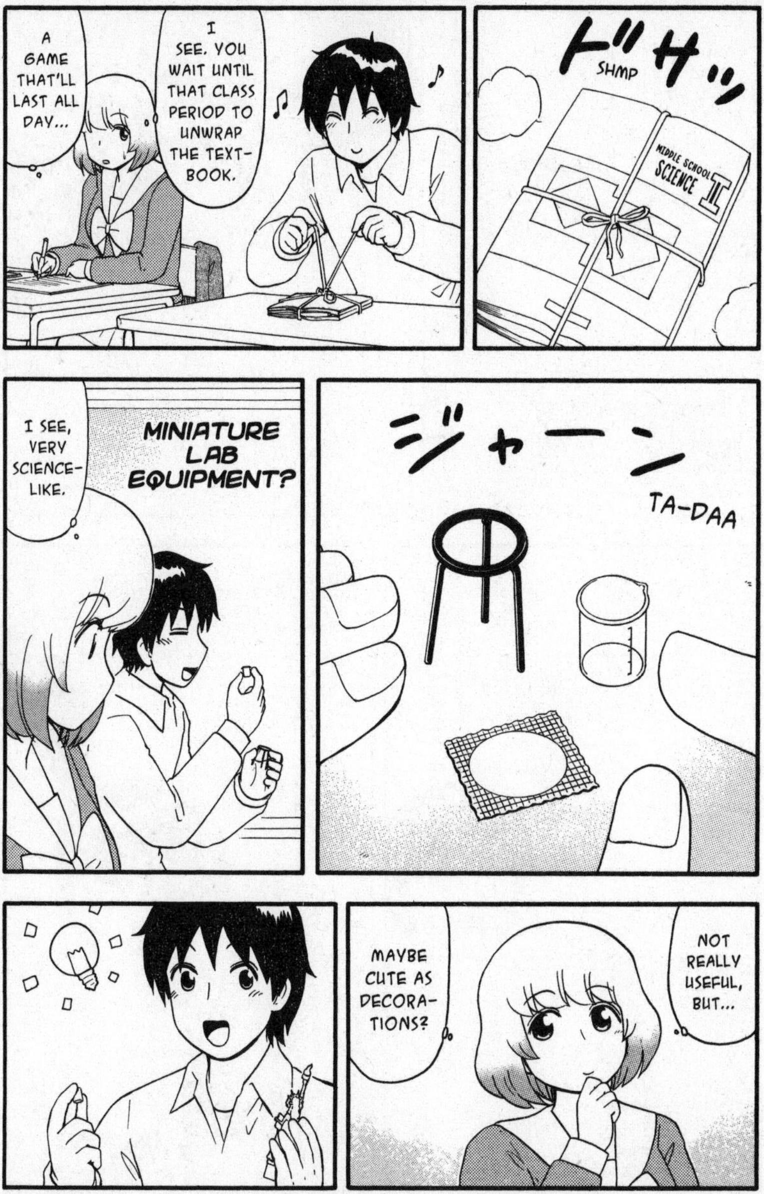
ドサッ
SHMP
MIDDLE SCHOOL SCIENCE II
I SEE. YOU WAIT UNTIL THAT CLASS PERIOD TO UNWRAP THE TEXT-BOOK.
A GAME THAT'LL LAST ALL DAY...
ジャーン
TA-DAA
MINIATURE LAB EQUIPMENT?
I SEE, VERY SCIENCE-LIKE.
NOT REALLY USEFUL, BUT...
MAYBE CUTE AS DECORA-TIONS?

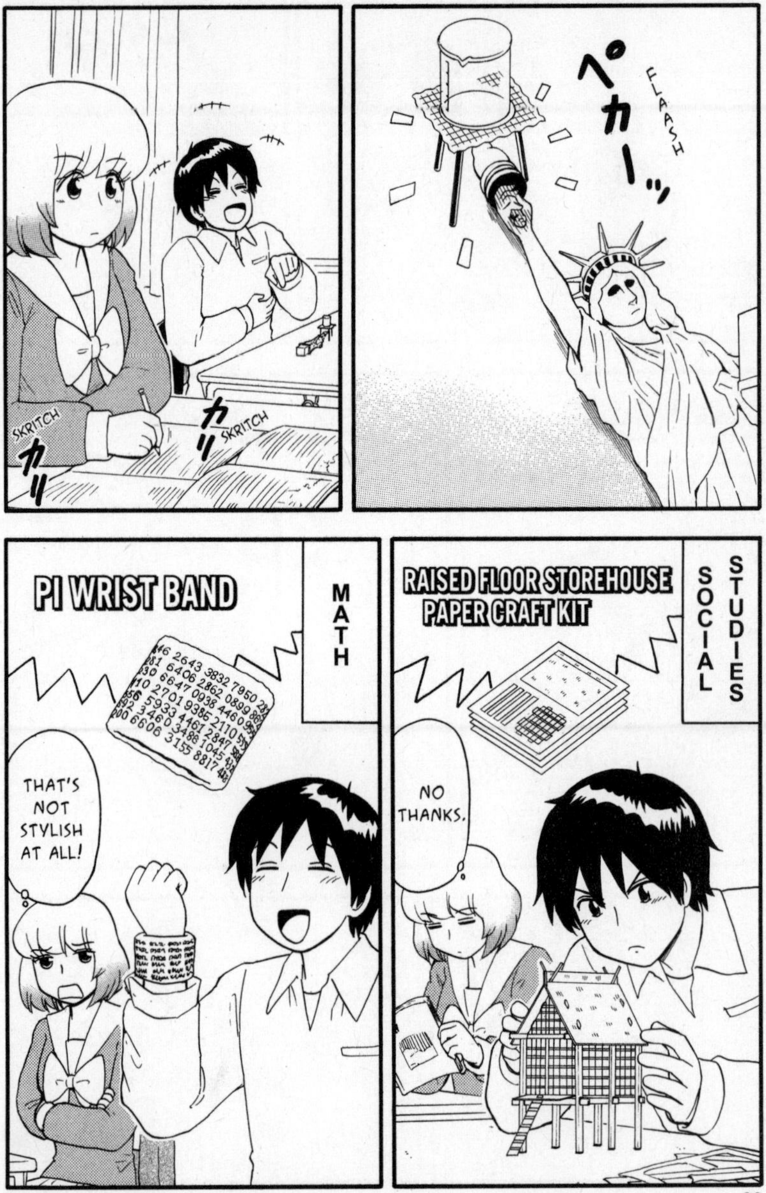
ペカーッ
FLASH
カリ
SKRITCH
カリ
SKRITCH
SOCIAL STUDIES
RAISED FLOOR STOREHOUSE PAPER CRAFT KIT
NO THANKS.
MATH
PI WRIST BAND
THAT'S NOT STYLISH AT ALL!

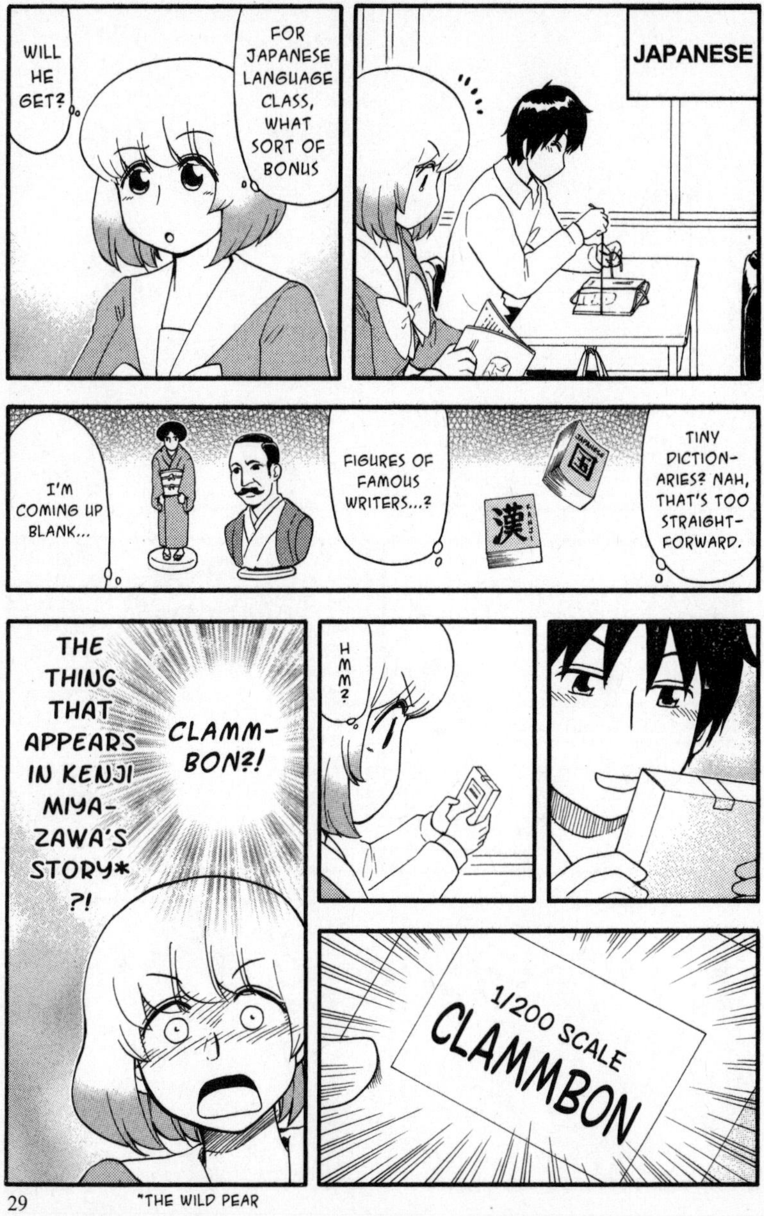
JAPANESE
FOR JAPANESE LANGUAGE CLASS, WHAT SORT OF BONUS
WILL HE GET?
TINY DICTIONARIES? NAH, THAT'S TOO STRAIGHTFORWARD.
JAPANESE
漢
FIGURES OF FAMOUS WRITERS...?
I'M COMING UP BLANK...
HMM?
1/200 SCALE CLAMMBON
CLAMMBON?!
THE THING THAT APPEARS IN KENJI MIYAZAWA'S STORY* ?!

*THE WILD PEAR

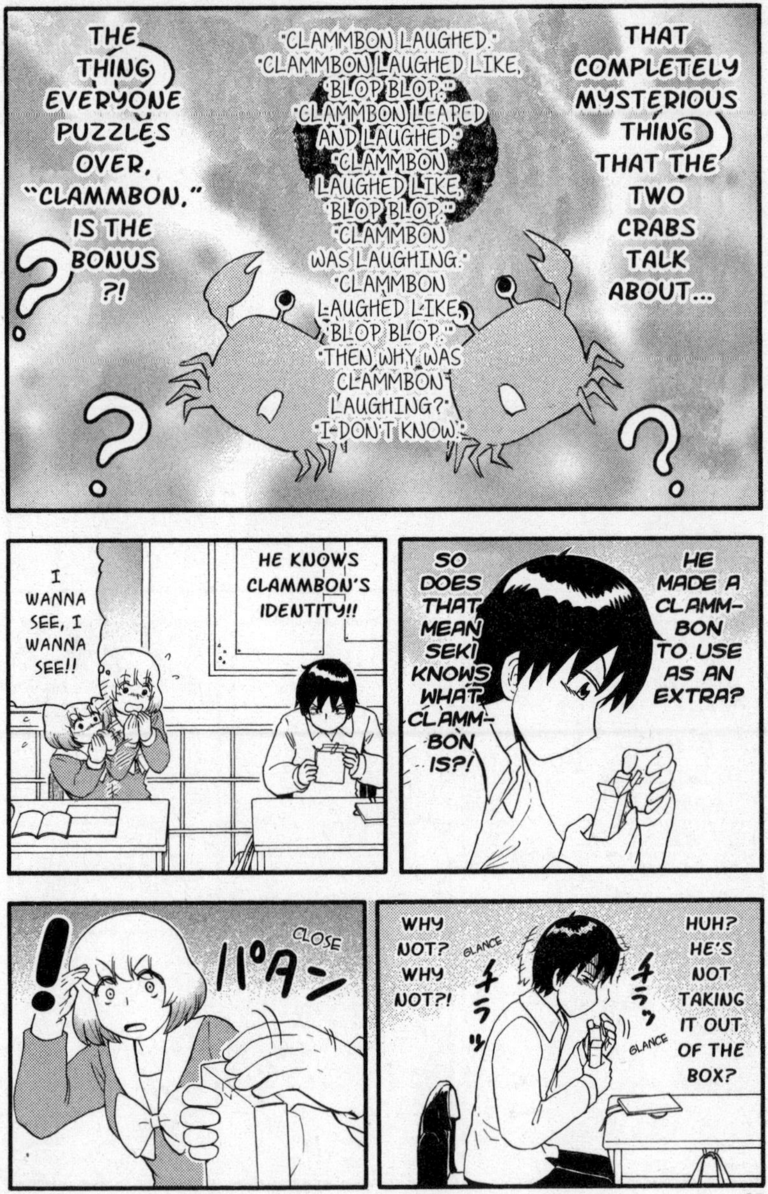

THAT COMPLETELY MYSTERIOUS THING THAT THE TWO CRABS TALK ABOUT...
"CLAMMBON LAUGHED." "CLAMMBON LAUGHED LIKE, 'BLOP BLOP.'" "CLAMMBON LEAPED AND LAUGHED." "CLAMMBON LAUGHED LIKE, 'BLOP BLOP.'" "CLAMMBON WAS LAUGHING." "CLAMMBON LAUGHED LIKE, 'BLOP BLOP.'" "THEN WHY WAS CLAMMBON LAUGHING?" "I DON'T KNOW."
THE THING EVERYONE PUZZLES OVER, "CLAMMBON," IS THE BONUS ?!
HE MADE A CLAMMBON TO USE AS AN EXTRA?
SO DOES THAT MEAN SEKI KNOWS WHAT CLAMMBON IS?!
HE KNOWS CLAMMBON'S IDENTITY!!
I WANNA SEE, I WANNA SEE!!
HUH? HE'S NOT TAKING IT OUT OF THE BOX?
チラッ
GLANCE
WHY NOT? WHY NOT?!
GLANCE
チラッ
CLOSE
パタン
!

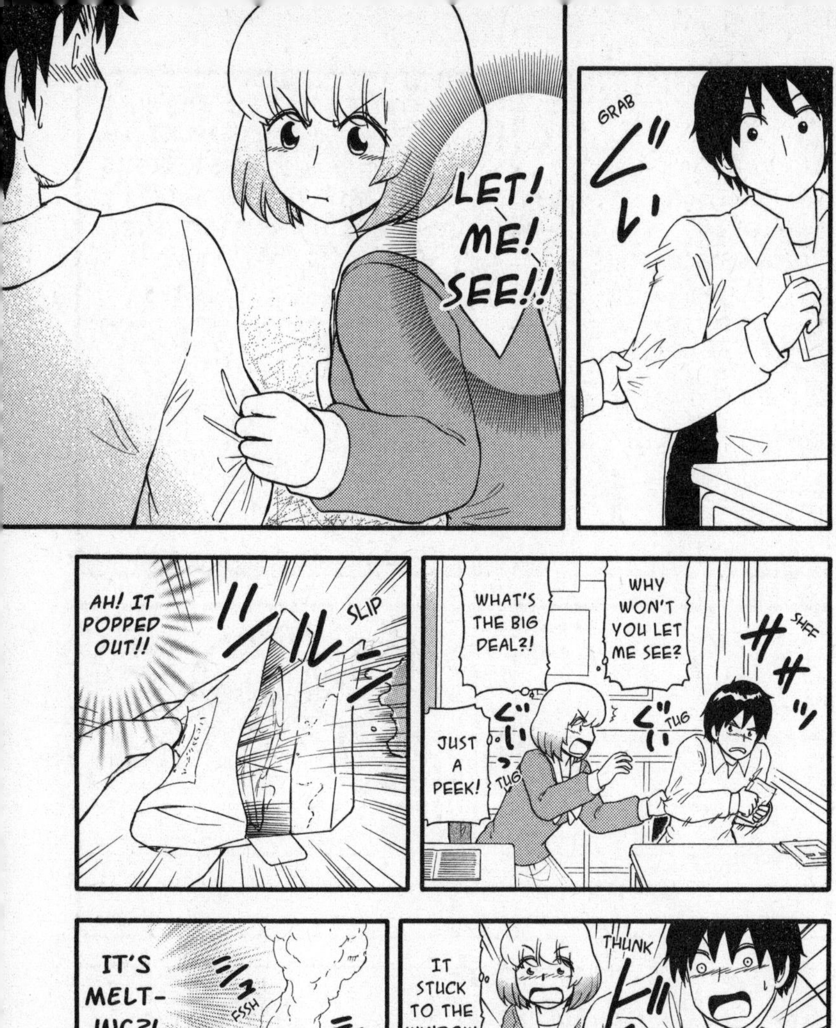

GRAB
LET! ME! SEE!!
SHFF
WHY WON'T YOU LET ME SEE?
WHAT'S THE BIG DEAL?!
TUG
JUST A PEEK!
TUG
SLIP
AH! IT POPPED OUT!!
THUNK
IT STUCK TO THE WINDOW?!
FSSH
FSSH
FSSH
FSSH
FSSH
IT'S MELT-ING?!

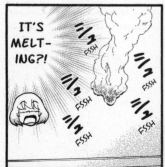

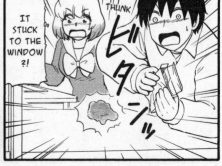

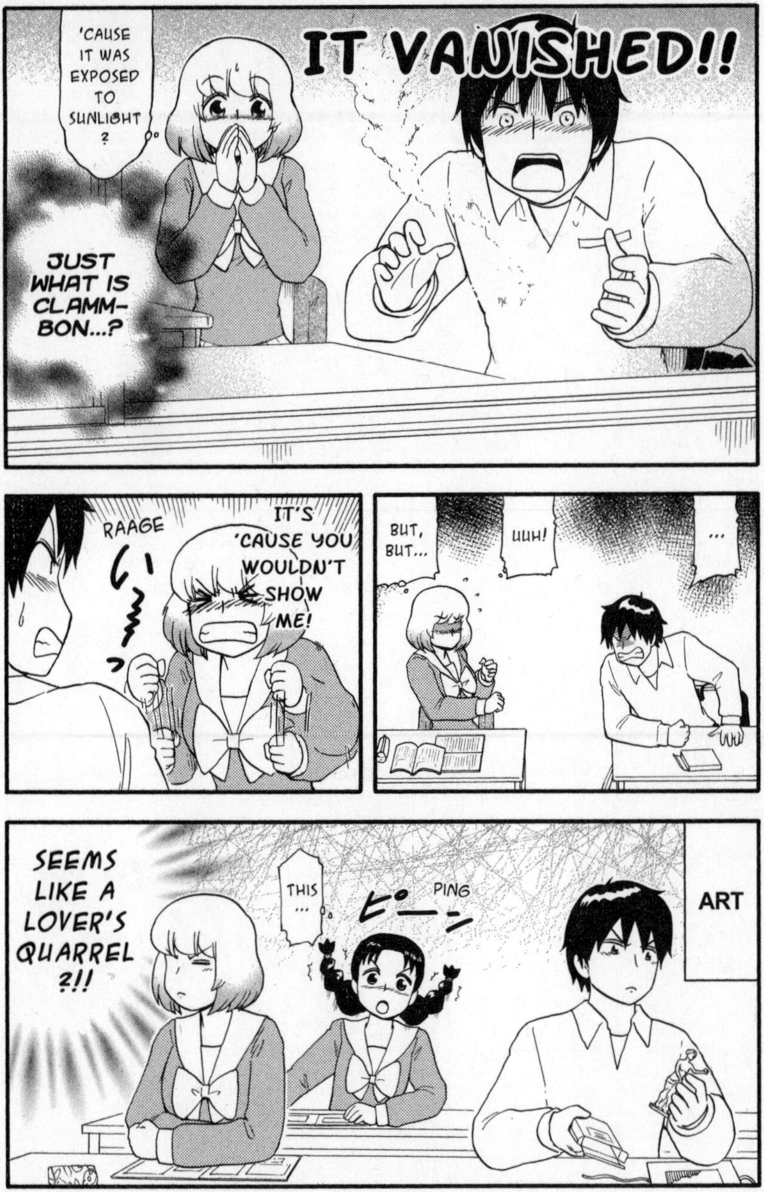
IT VANISHED!!
'CAUSE IT WAS EXPOSED TO SUNLIGHT ?
JUST WHAT IS CLAMM-BON...?
...
UUH!
BUT, BUT...
IT'S 'CAUSE YOU WOULDN'T SHOW ME!
RAAGE
ART
PING
THIS ...
SEEMS LIKE A LOVER'S QUARREL ?!!

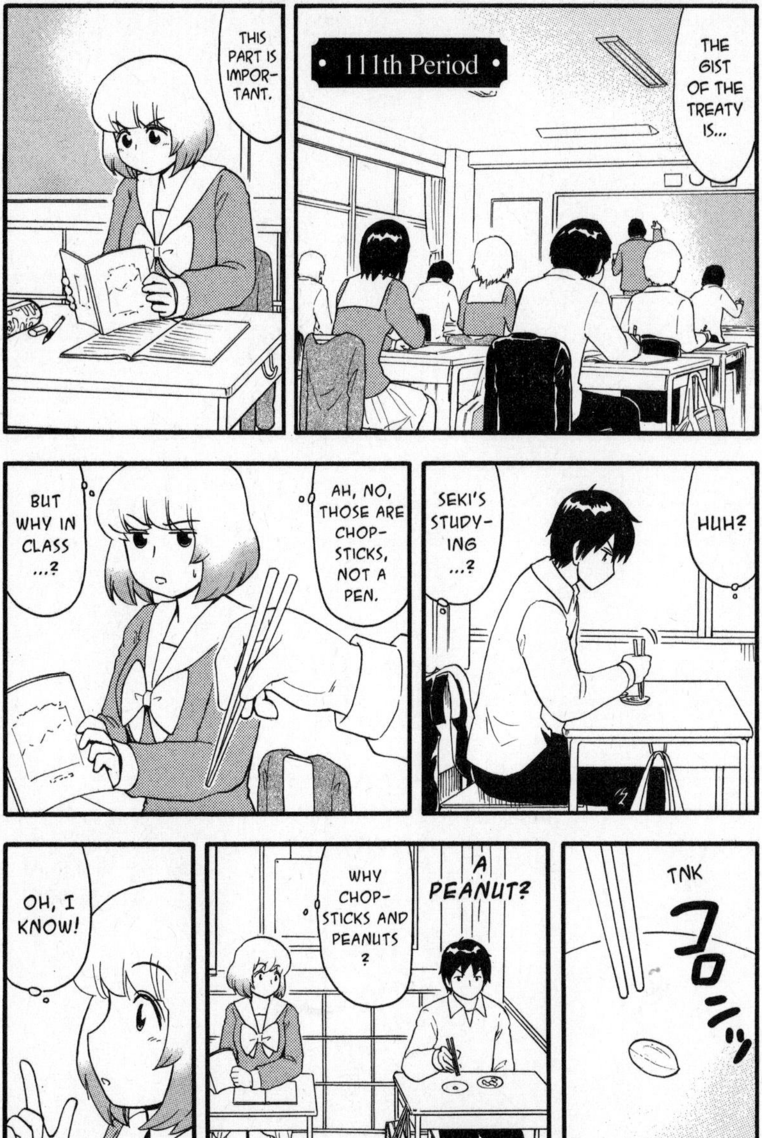

• 111th Period •
THE GIST OF THE TREATY IS...
THIS PART IS IMPORTANT.
HUH?
SEKI'S STUDYING ...?
AH, NO, THOSE ARE CHOPSTICKS, NOT A PEN.
BUT WHY IN CLASS ...?
TNK
コロンッ
A PEANUT?
WHY CHOPSTICKS AND PEANUTS ?
OH, I KNOW!

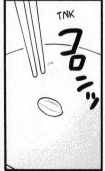

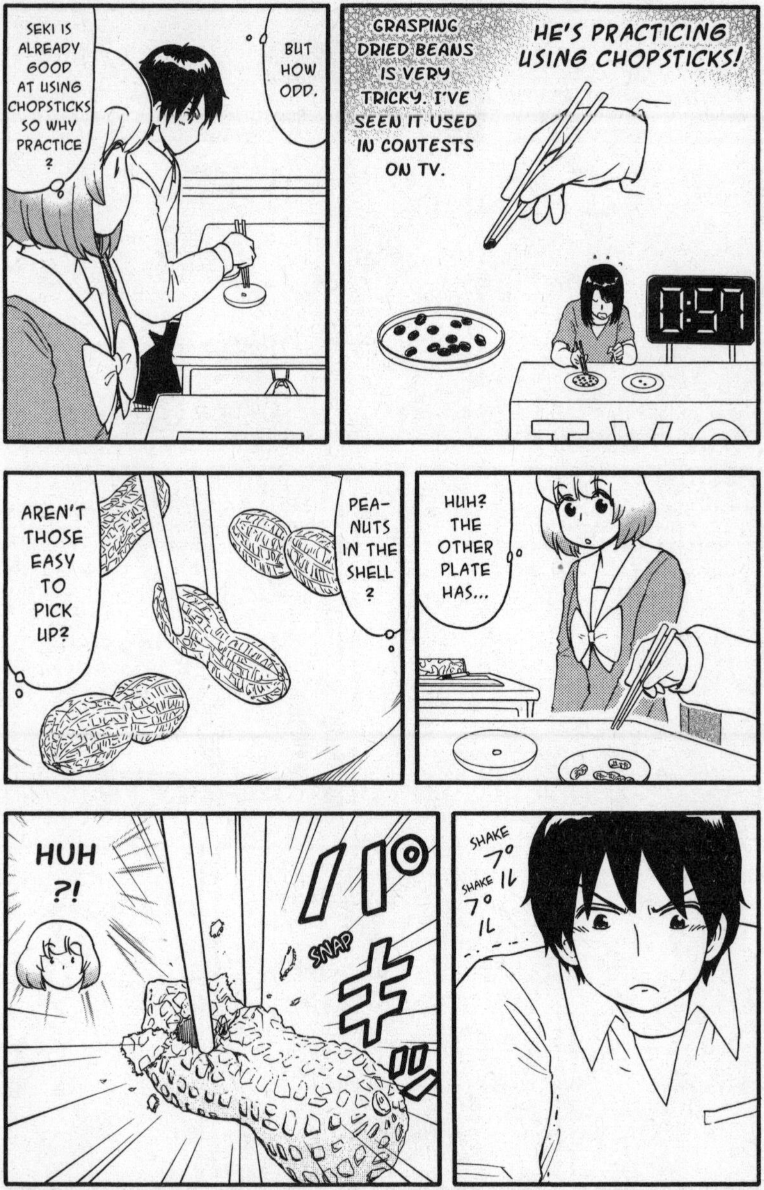
HE'S PRACTICING USING CHOPSTICKS!
GRASPING DRIED BEANS IS VERY TRICKY. I'VE SEEN IT USED IN CONTESTS ON TV.
BUT HOW ODD.
SEKI IS ALREADY GOOD AT USING CHOPSTICKS SO WHY PRACTICE?
HUH? THE OTHER PLATE HAS...
PEA-NUTS IN THE SHELL?
AREN'T THOSE EASY TO PICK UP?
SHAKE プル
SHAKE プル
...
パキッ
SNAP
HUH ?!

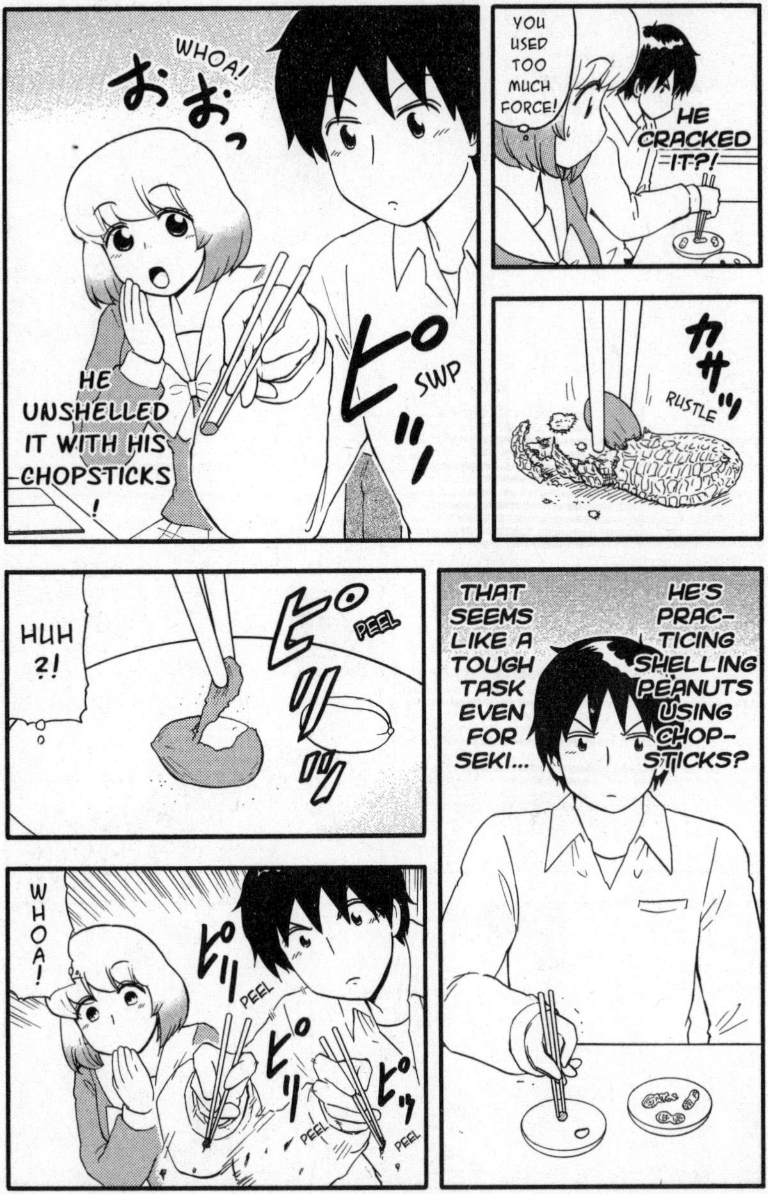
HE CRACKED IT?!
YOU USED TOO MUCH FORCE!
カサッ
RUSTLE
おおっ
WHOA!
ピッ
SWP
HE UNSHELLED IT WITH HIS CHOPSTICKS!
HE'S PRAC-TICING SHELLING PEANUTS USING CHOP-STICKS?
THAT SEEMS LIKE A TOUGH TASK EVEN FOR SEKI...
ピリッ
PEEL
HUH?!
ピリ
PEEL
WHOA!
ピリ
PEEL
ピッ
PEEL

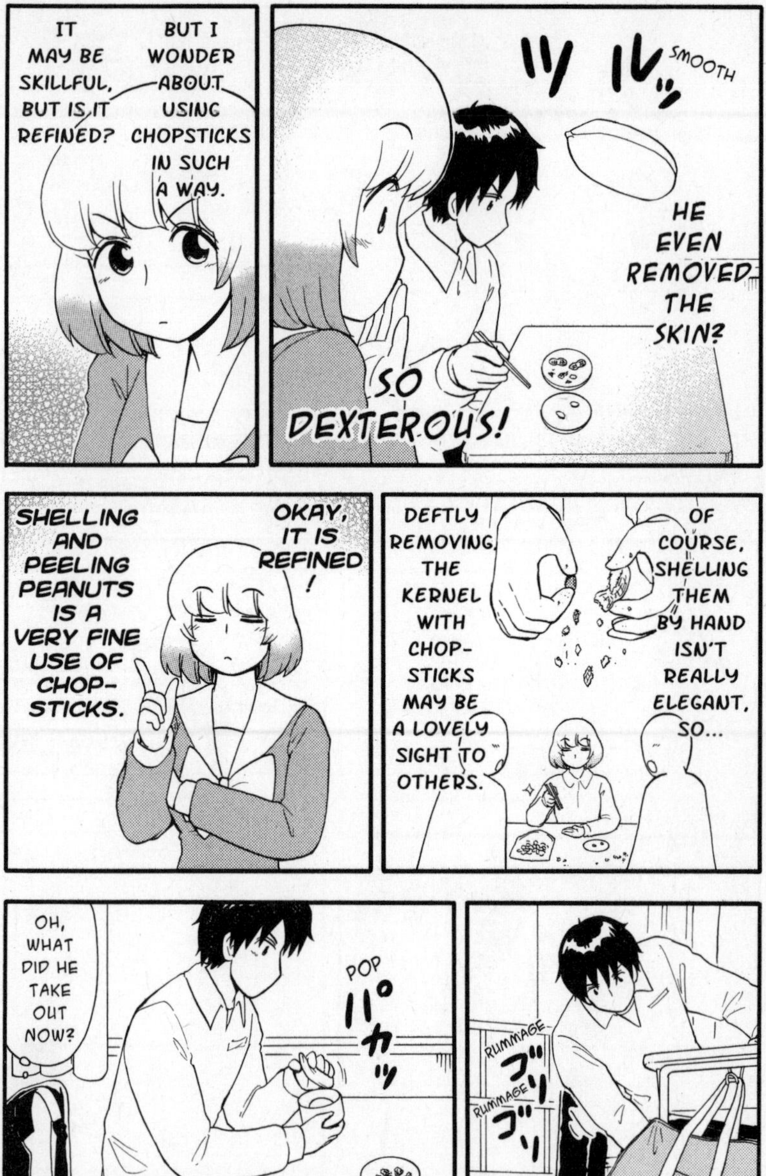
ツルッ
SMOOTH
HE EVEN REMOVED THE SKIN?
SO DEXTEROUS!
BUT I WONDER ABOUT USING CHOPSTICKS IN SUCH A WAY.
IT MAY BE SKILLFUL, BUT IS IT REFINED?
OF COURSE, SHELLING THEM BY HAND ISN'T REALLY ELEGANT, SO...
DEFTLY REMOVING THE KERNEL WITH CHOPSTICKS MAY BE A LOVELY SIGHT TO OTHERS.
OKAY, IT IS REFINED!
SHELLING AND PEELING PEANUTS IS A VERY FINE USE OF CHOPSTICKS.
RUMMAGE
ゴソ
RUMMAGE
ゴソ
POP
パカッ
OH, WHAT DID HE TAKE OUT NOW?

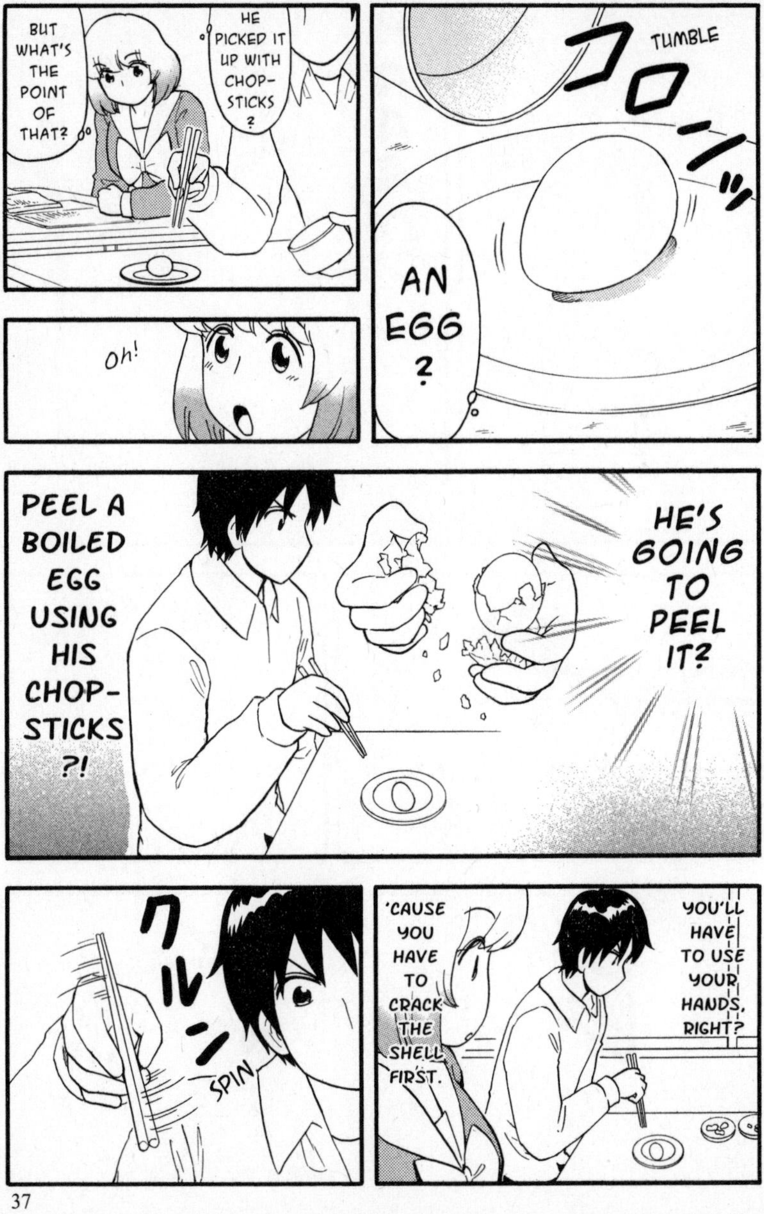
TUMBLE
AN EGG?
HE PICKED IT UP WITH CHOP-STICKS?
BUT WHAT'S THE POINT OF THAT?
Oh!
HE'S GOING TO PEEL IT?
PEEL A BOILED EGG USING HIS CHOP-STICKS?!
YOU'LL HAVE TO USE YOUR HANDS, RIGHT?
'CAUSE YOU HAVE TO CRACK THE SHELL FIRST.
SPIN

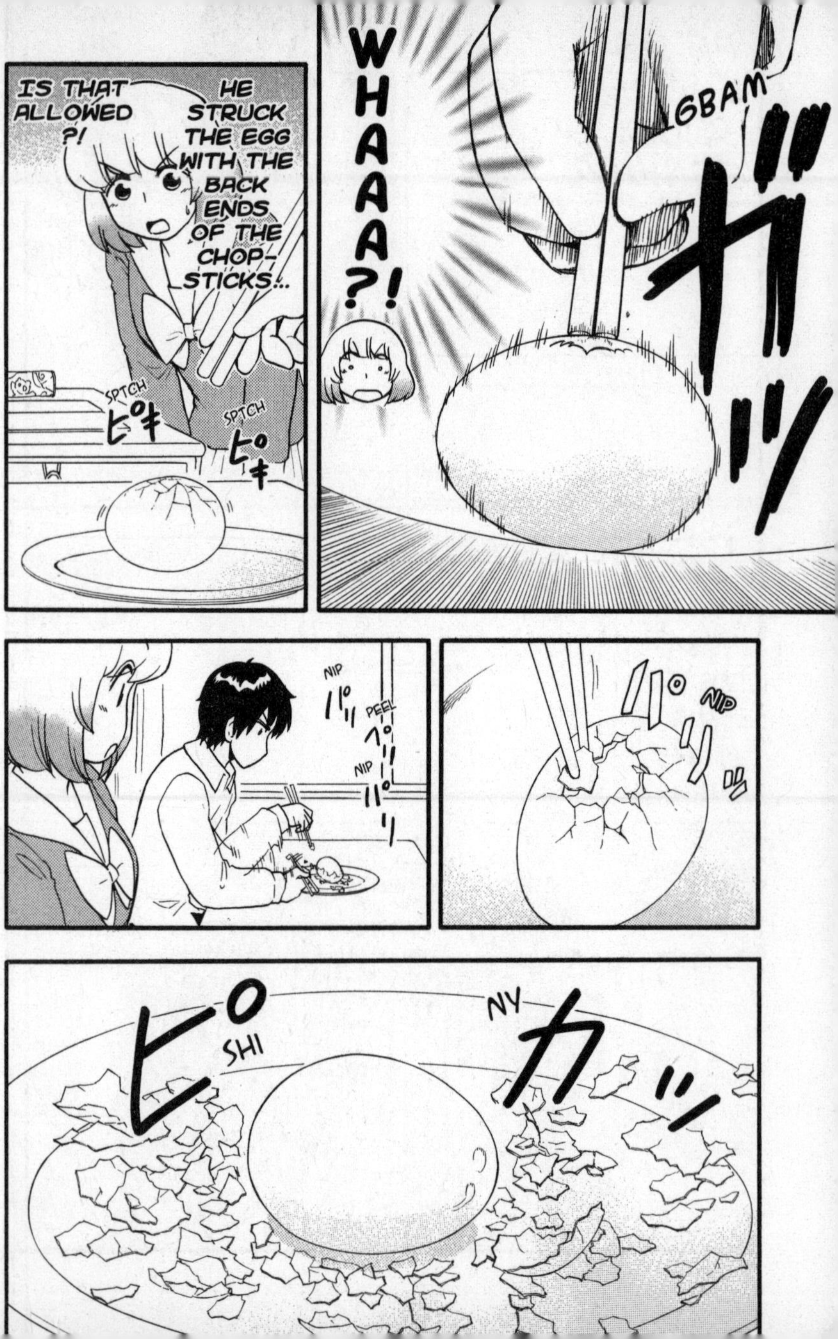
GBAM
ガッ
WHAAAA?!
HE STRUCK THE EGG WITH THE BACK ENDS OF THE CHOP-STICKS...
IS THAT ALLOWED ?!
SPTCH
ピキ
SPTCH
ピキ
NIP
パッ
NIP
パッ
PEEL
ペリ
NIP
パリ
SHI
ピ
NY
カッ

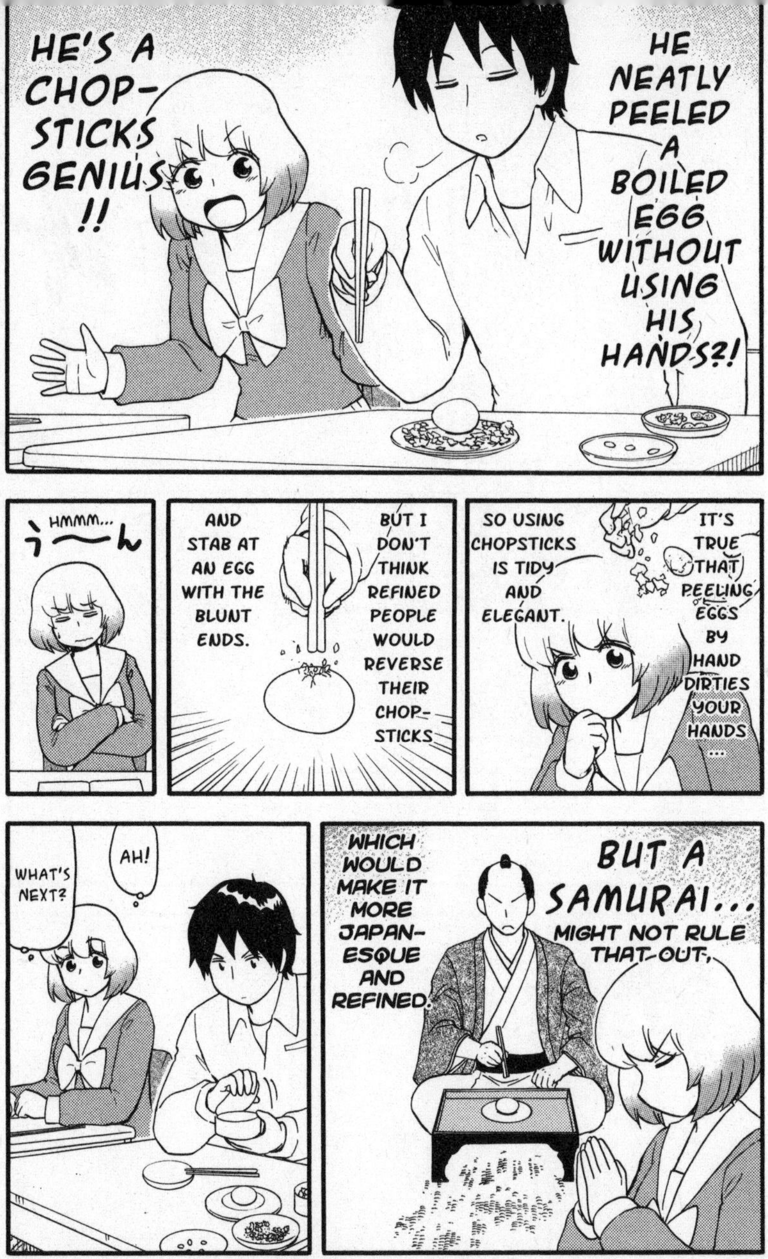
HE NEATLY PEELED A BOILED EGG WITHOUT USING HIS HANDS?!
HE'S A CHOP-STICKS GENIUS!!
IT'S TRUE THAT PEELING EGGS BY HAND DIRTIES YOUR HANDS...
SO USING CHOPSTICKS IS TIDY AND ELEGANT.
BUT I DON'T THINK REFINED PEOPLE WOULD REVERSE THEIR CHOP-STICKS
AND STAB AT AN EGG WITH THE BLUNT ENDS.
うーん
HMMM...
BUT A SAMURAI... MIGHT NOT RULE THAT OUT,
WHICH WOULD MAKE IT MORE JAPAN-ESQUE AND REFINED.
AH!
WHAT'S NEXT?

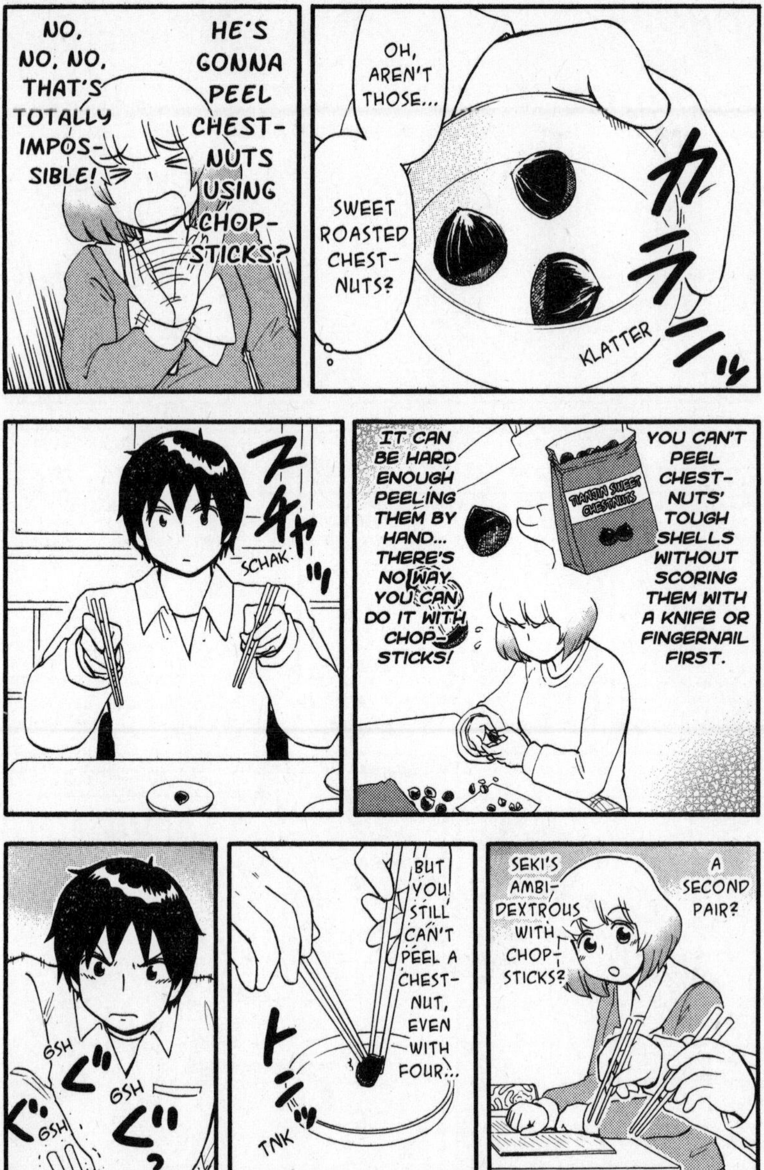

OH, AREN'T THOSE...
SWEET ROASTED CHEST-NUTS?
KLATTER
HE'S GONNA PEEL CHEST-NUTS USING CHOP-STICKS?
NO, NO, NO, THAT'S TOTALLY IMPOS-SIBLE!
YOU CAN'T PEEL CHEST-NUTS' TOUGH SHELLS WITHOUT SCORING THEM WITH A KNIFE OR FINGERNAIL FIRST.
TIANJIN SWEET CHESTNUTS
IT CAN BE HARD ENOUGH PEELING THEM BY HAND... THERE'S NO WAY YOU CAN DO IT WITH CHOP-STICKS!
SCHAK
A SECOND PAIR?
SEKI'S AMBI-DEXTROUS WITH CHOP-STICKS?
BUT YOU STILL CAN'T PEEL A CHEST-NUT, EVEN WITH FOUR...
TNK
GSH
GSH
GSH

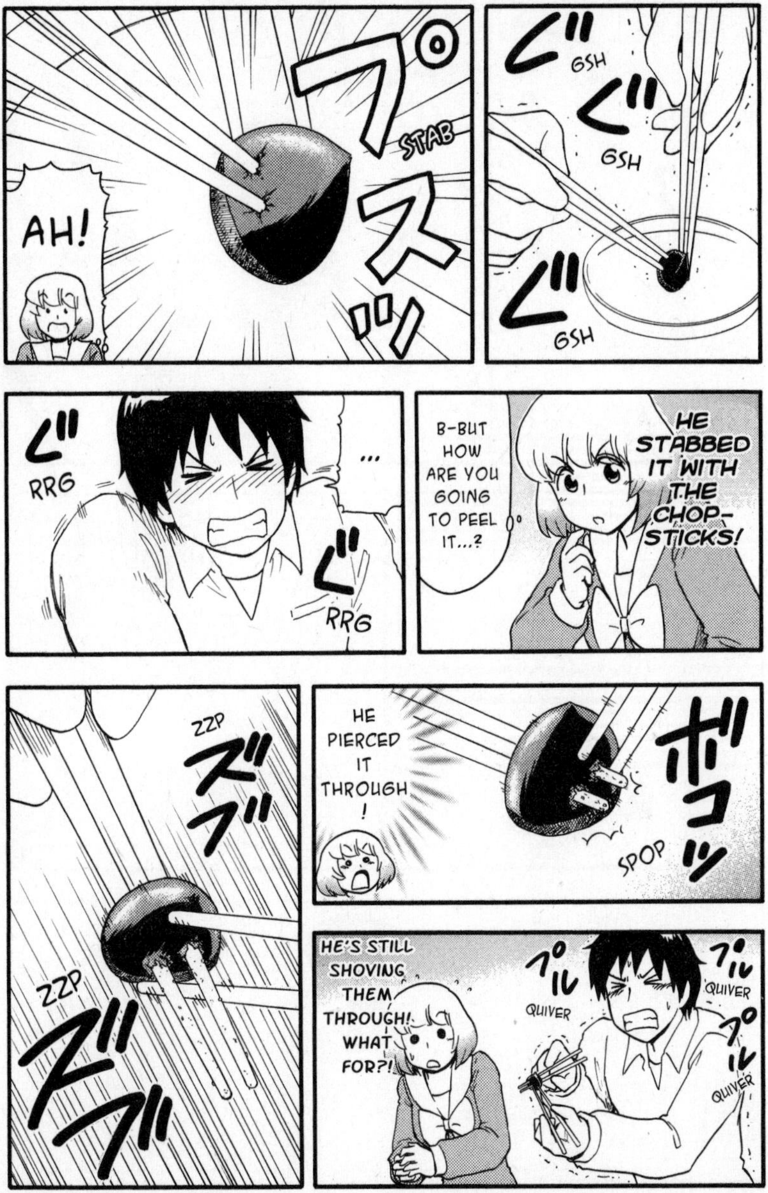

ぐ
GSH
ぐ
GSH
ぐ
GSH
プ
STAB
スッ
AH!
HE STABBED IT WITH THE CHOP-STICKS!
B-BUT HOW ARE YOU GOING TO PEEL IT...?
...
ぐ
RRG
ぐ
RRG
ボコッ
HE PIERCED IT THROUGH!
SPOP
プル
QUIVER
プル
QUIVER
プル
QUIVER
HE'S STILL SHOVING THEM THROUGH! WHAT FOR?!
ZZP
ズブ
ZZP
ズブ

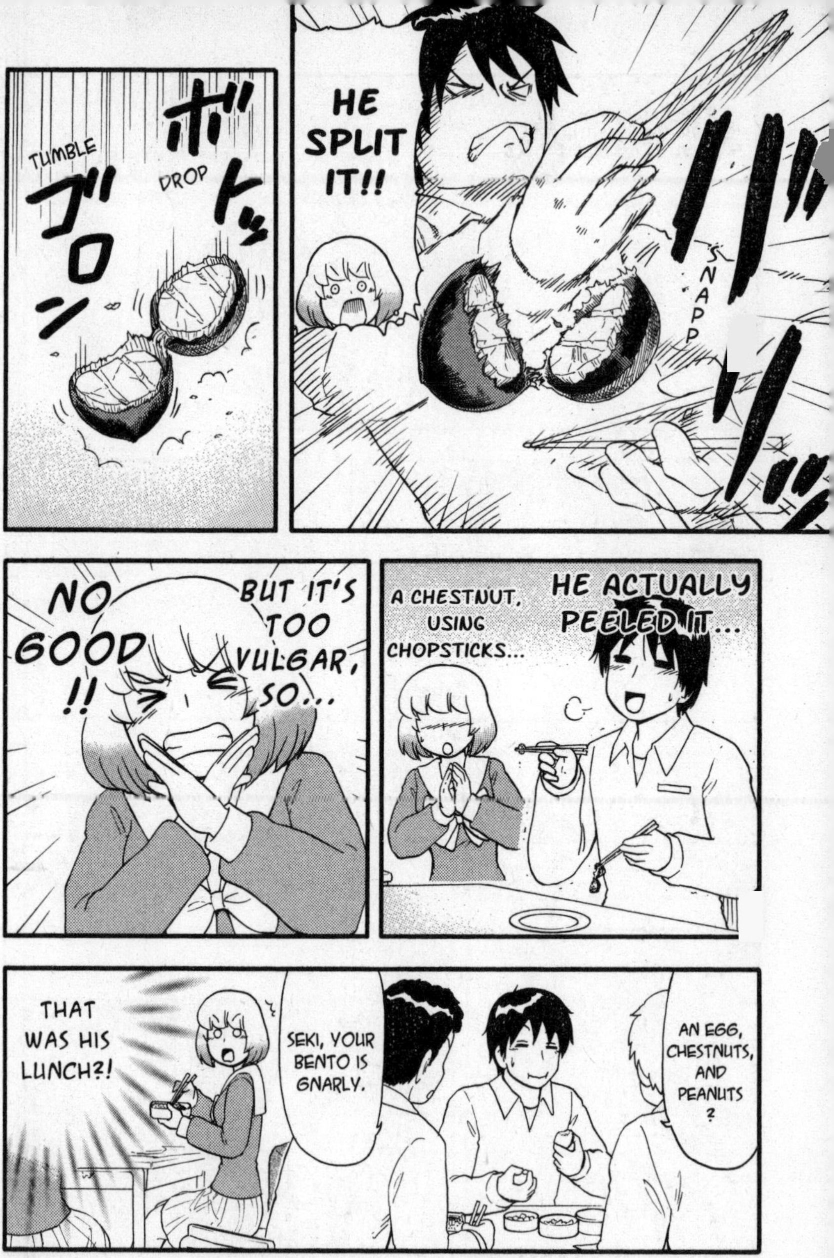
SNAPP
HE SPLIT IT!!
ボトッ
DROP
ゴロン
TUMBLE
HE ACTUALLY PEELED IT...
A CHESTNUT, USING CHOPSTICKS...
BUT IT'S TOO VULGAR, SO...
NO GOOD!!
AN EGG, CHESTNUTS, AND PEANUTS?
SEKI, YOUR BENTO IS GNARLY.
THAT WAS HIS LUNCH?!

• 112th Period •

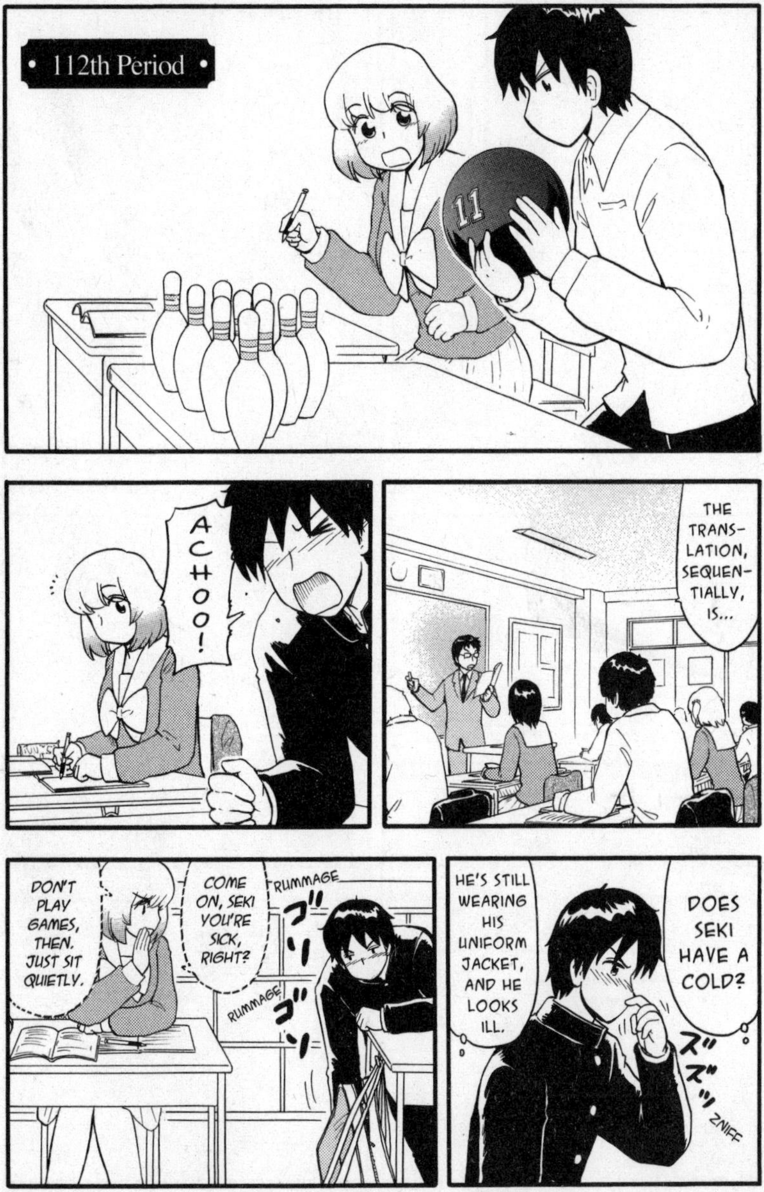
11
THE TRANSLATION, SEQUENTIALLY, IS...
ACHOO!
DOES SEKI HAVE A COLD?
HE'S STILL WEARING HIS UNIFORM JACKET, AND HE LOOKS ILL.
ZNIFF
RUMMAGE
COME ON, SEKI YOU'RE SICK, RIGHT?
DON'T PLAY GAMES, THEN. JUST SIT QUIETLY.
RUMMAGE

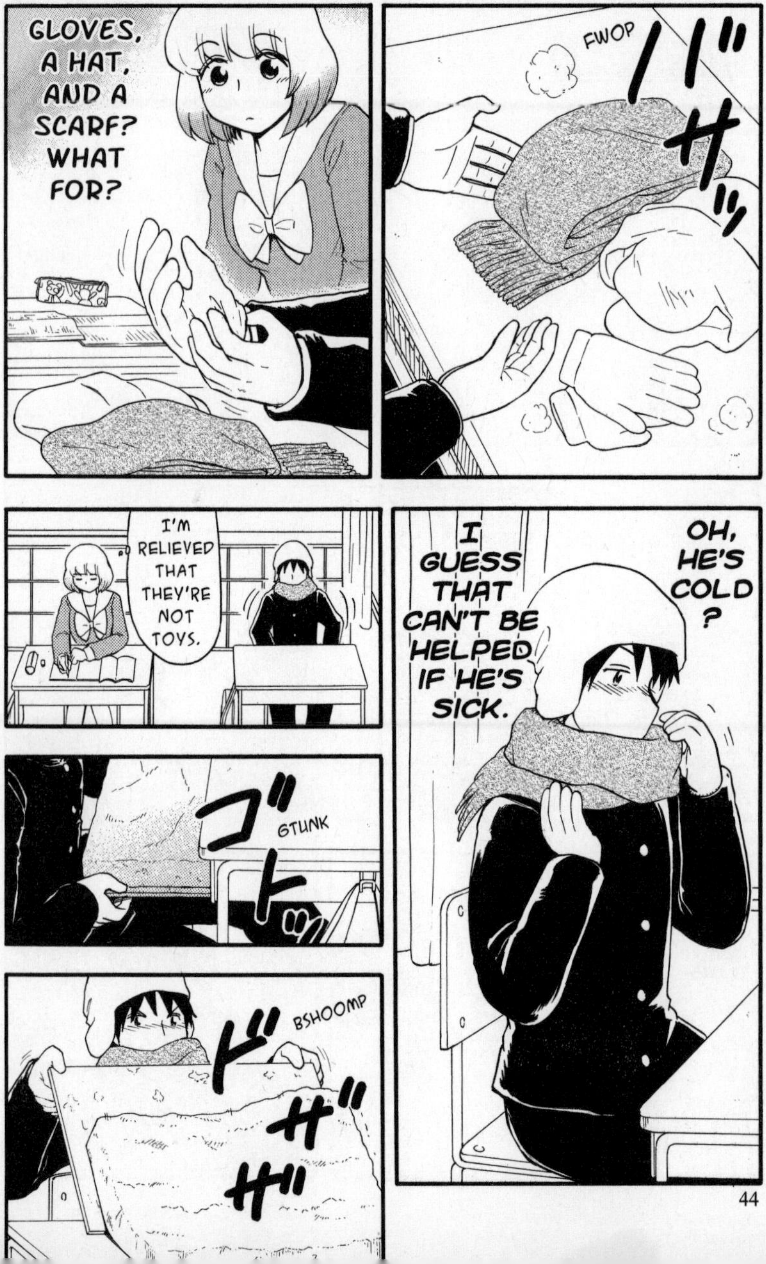
FWOP
バサッ
GLOVES, A HAT, AND A SCARF? WHAT FOR?
OH, HE'S COLD?
I GUESS THAT CAN'T BE HELPED IF HE'S SICK.
I'M RELIEVED THAT THEY'RE NOT TOYS.
ゴトッ
GTUNK
ドザザ
BSHOOMP

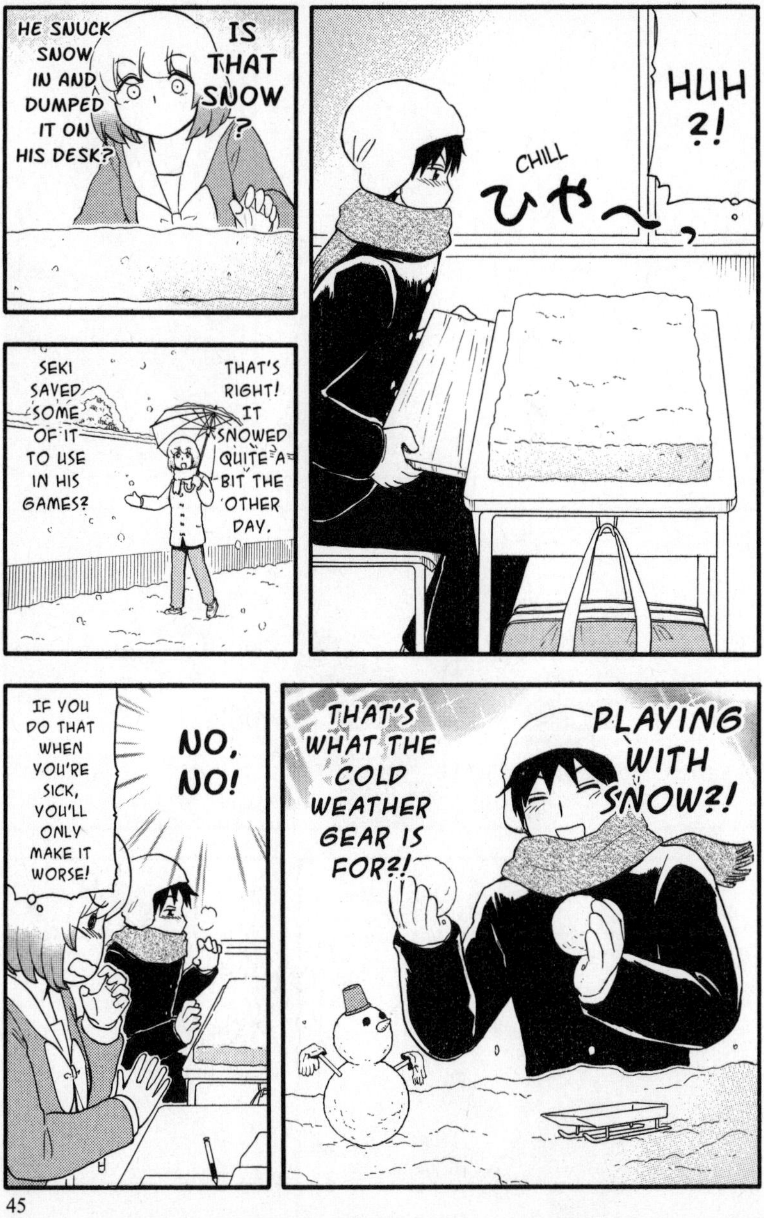
HUH ?!
CHILL
ひや〜
IS THAT SNOW?
HE SNUCK SNOW IN AND DUMPED IT ON HIS DESK?
THAT'S RIGHT! IT SNOWED QUITE A BIT THE OTHER DAY.
SEKI SAVED SOME OF IT TO USE IN HIS GAMES?
PLAYING WITH SNOW?!
THAT'S WHAT THE COLD WEATHER GEAR IS FOR?!
NO, NO!
IF YOU DO THAT WHEN YOU'RE SICK, YOU'LL ONLY MAKE IT WORSE!

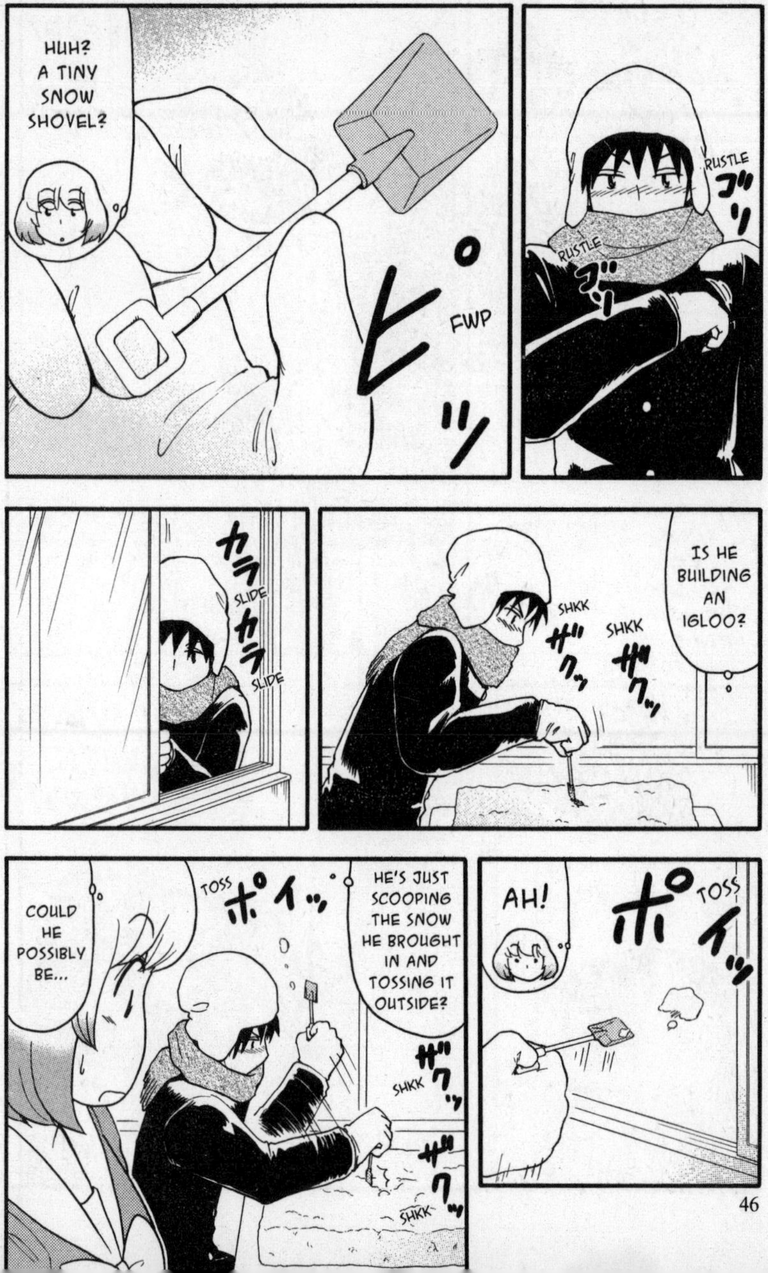
RUSTLE
ゴソ
RUSTLE
ゴソ
HUH? A TINY SNOW SHOVEL?
ピッ
FWP
IS HE BUILDING AN IGLOO?
SHKK
ザクッ
SHKK
ザクッ
カラ
SLIDE
カラ
SLIDE
AH!
ポイッ
TOSS
HE'S JUST SCOOPING THE SNOW HE BROUGHT IN AND TOSSING IT OUTSIDE?
TOSS
ポイッ
COULD HE POSSIBLY BE...
ザクッ
SHKK
ザクッ
SHKK

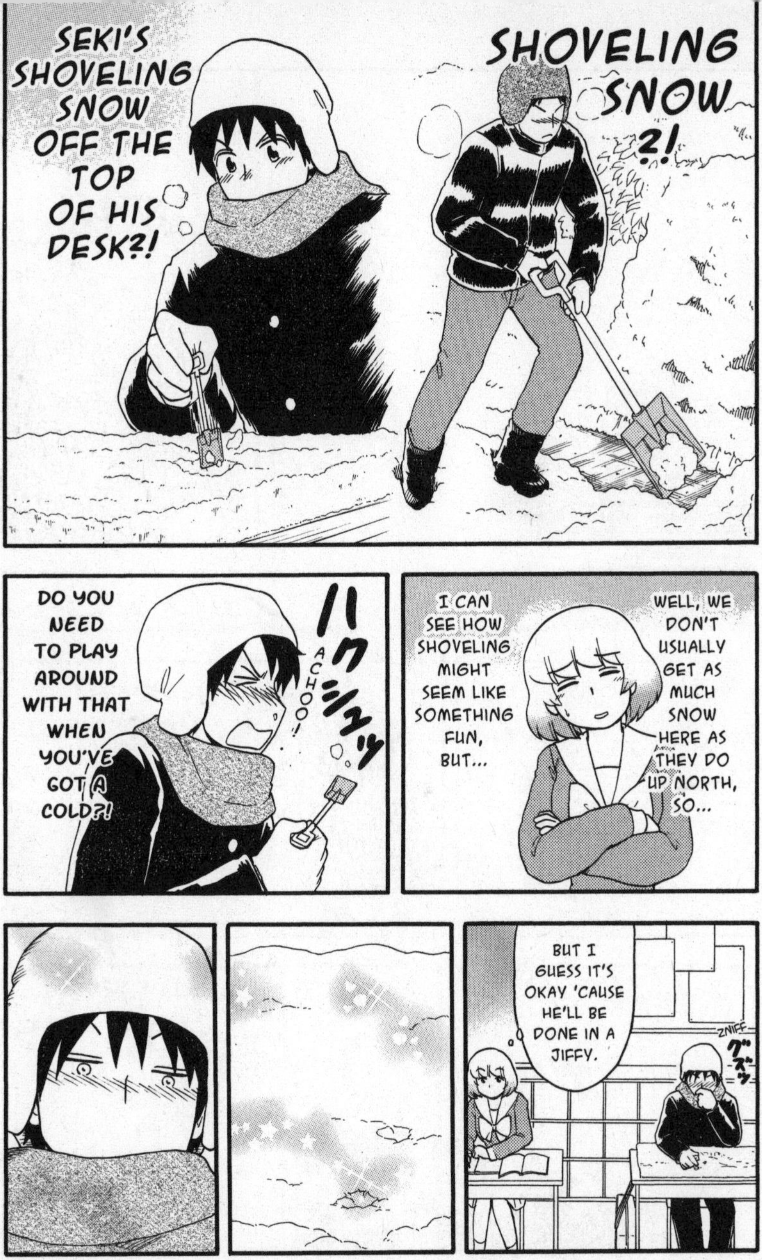
SHOVELING SNOW ?!
SEKI'S SHOVELING SNOW OFF THE TOP OF HIS DESK?!
WELL, WE DON'T USUALLY GET AS MUCH SNOW HERE AS THEY DO UP NORTH, SO...
I CAN SEE HOW SHOVELING MIGHT SEEM LIKE SOMETHING FUN, BUT...
ハクシュッ
ACHOO!
DO YOU NEED TO PLAY AROUND WITH THAT WHEN YOU'VE GOT A COLD?!
BUT I GUESS IT'S OKAY 'CAUSE HE'LL BE DONE IN A JIFFY.
ZNIFF
グズッ

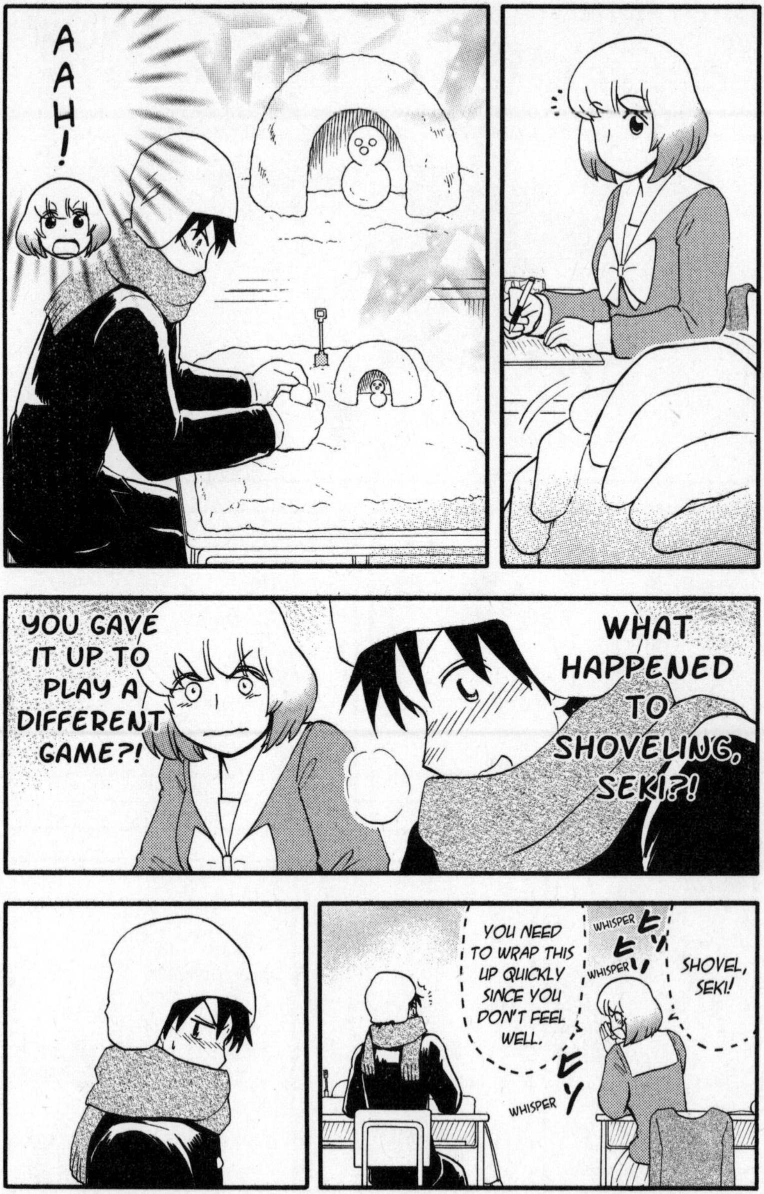
AAAH!
WHAT HAPPENED TO SHOVELING, SEKI?!
YOU GAVE IT UP TO PLAY A DIFFERENT GAME?!
SHOVEL, SEKI!
WHISPER
WHISPER
YOU NEED TO WRAP THIS UP QUICKLY SINCE YOU DON'T FEEL WELL.
WHISPER

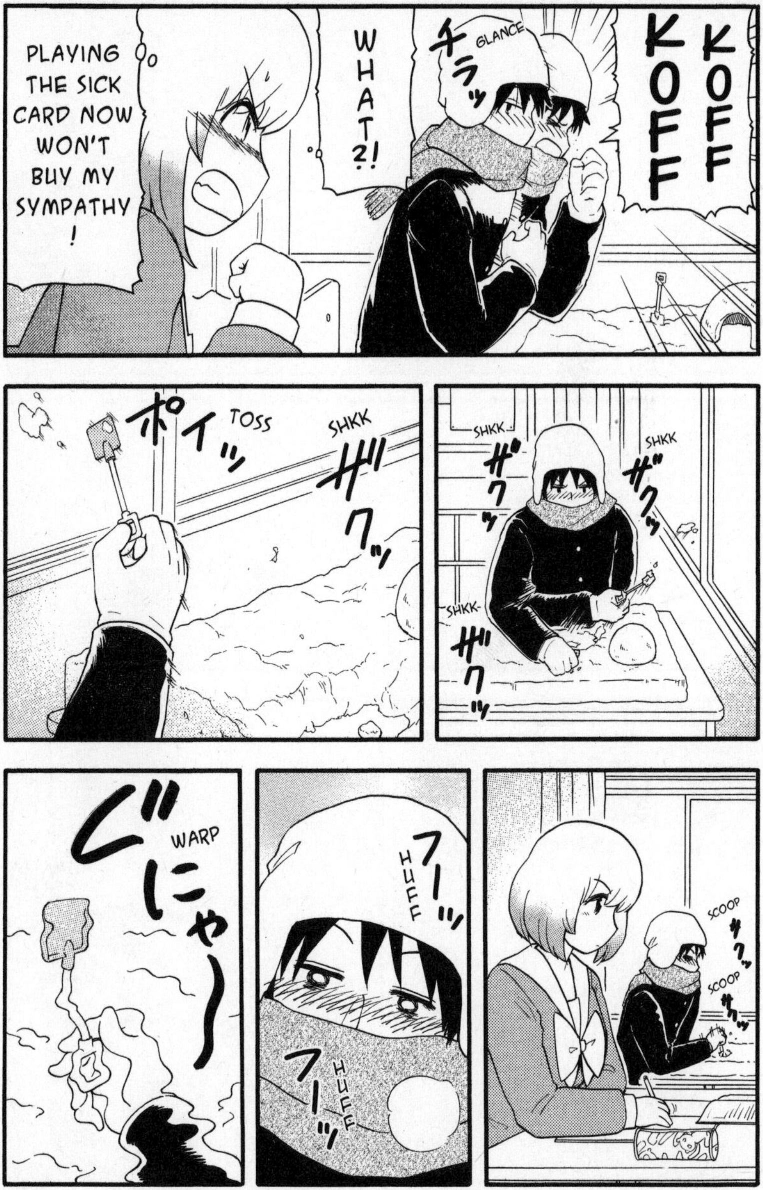
KOFF KOFF
チラッ
GLANCE
WHAT?!
PLAYING THE SICK CARD NOW WON'T BUY MY SYMPATHY!
SHKK
ザクッ
SHKK
ザクッ
SHKK
ザクッ
ポイッ
TOSS
SHKK
ザクッ
SCOOP
サクッ
SCOOP
サクッ
フーッ
HUFF
フーッ
HUFF
ぐにゃー
WARP

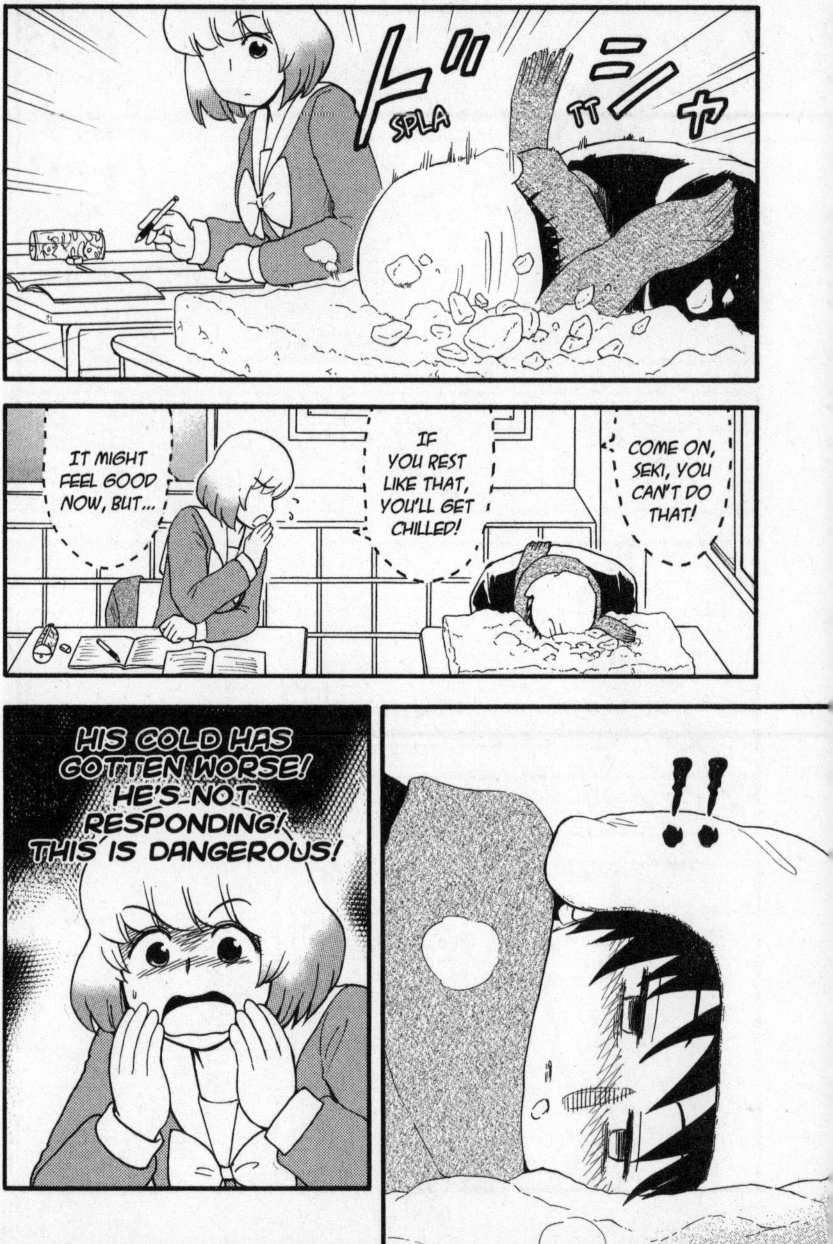
SPLA
TT
COME ON, SEKI, YOU CAN'T DO THAT!
IF YOU REST LIKE THAT, YOU'LL GET CHILLED!
IT MIGHT FEEL GOOD NOW, BUT...
!!
HIS COLD HAS GOTTEN WORSE! HE'S NOT RESPONDING! THIS IS DANGEROUS!

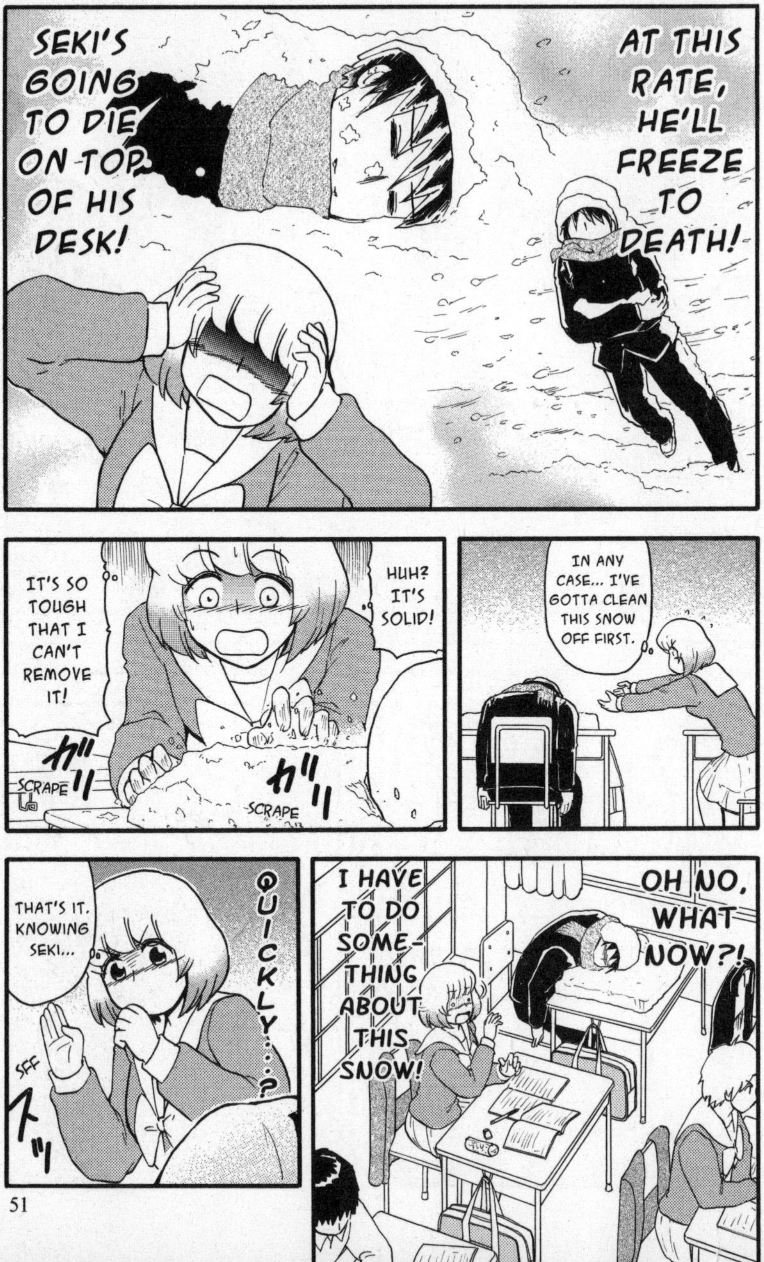
AT THIS RATE, HE'LL FREEZE TO DEATH!
SEKI'S GOING TO DIE ON TOP OF HIS DESK!
IN ANY CASE... I'VE GOTTA CLEAN THIS SNOW OFF FIRST.
HUH? IT'S SOLID!
IT'S SO TOUGH THAT I CAN'T REMOVE IT!
ガリ
SCRAPE
ガリ
SCRAPE
OH NO, WHAT NOW?!
I HAVE TO DO SOME-THING ABOUT THIS SNOW!
QUICKLY...?
THAT'S IT. KNOWING SEKI...
SFF
スッ

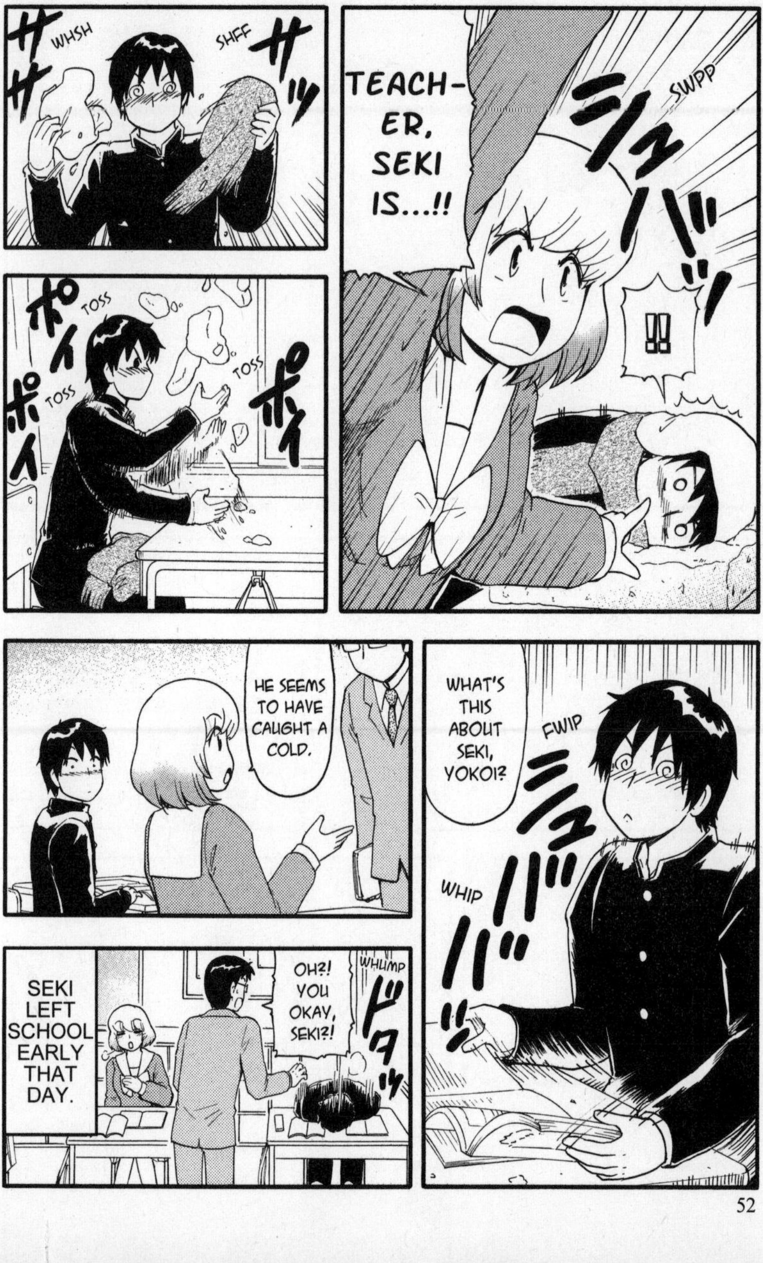
SWPP
TEACHER-ER, SEKI IS...!!
!!
SHFF
WHSH
TOSS
TOSS
TOSS
WHAT'S THIS ABOUT SEKI, YOKOI!?
FWIP
WHIP
HE SEEMS TO HAVE CAUGHT A COLD.
WHUMP
OH?! YOU OKAY, SEKI?!
SEKI LEFT SCHOOL EARLY THAT DAY.

My Neighbor Seki

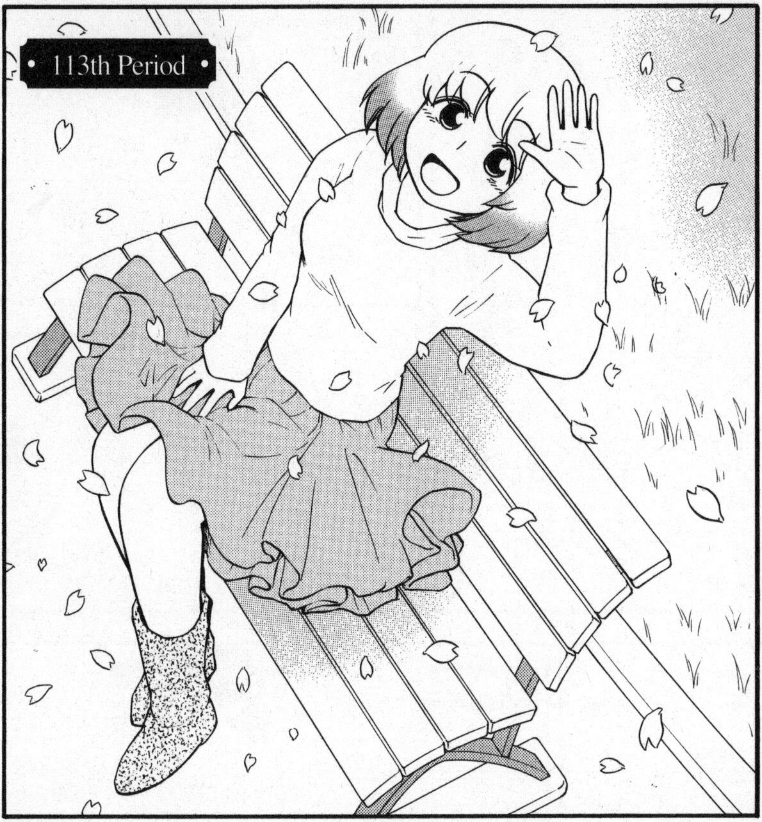
113th Period

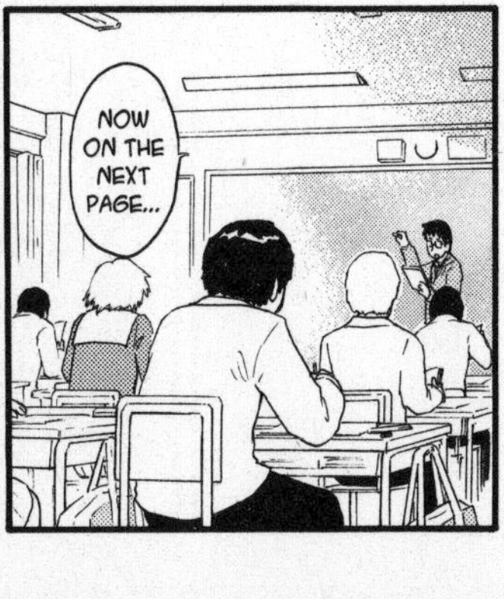
NOW ON THE NEXT PAGE...

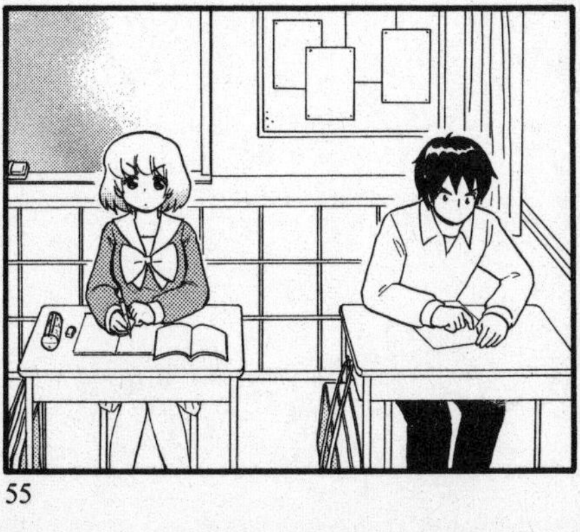

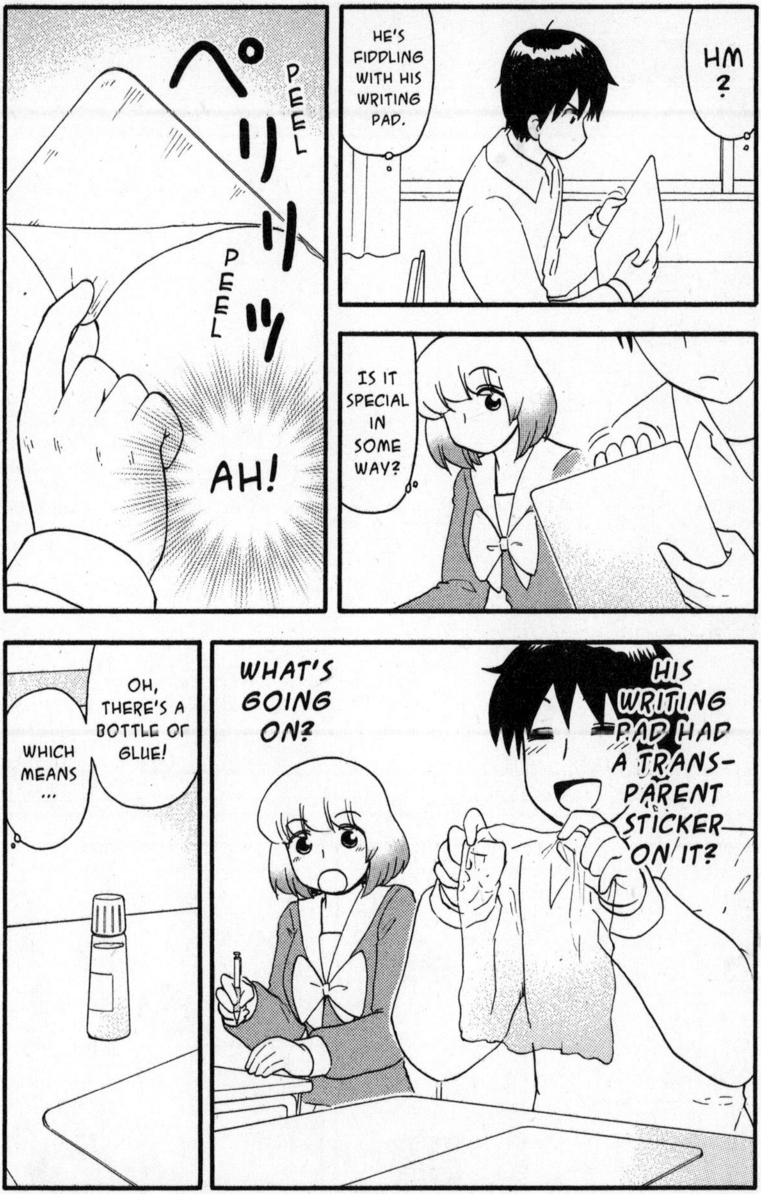
HM ?
HE'S FIDDLING WITH HIS WRITING PAD.
IS IT SPECIAL IN SOME WAY?
ペリリッ
PEEL PEEL
AH!
HIS WRITING PAD HAD A TRANS-PARENT STICKER ON IT?
WHAT'S GOING ON?
OH, THERE'S A BOTTLE OF GLUE!
WHICH MEANS ...

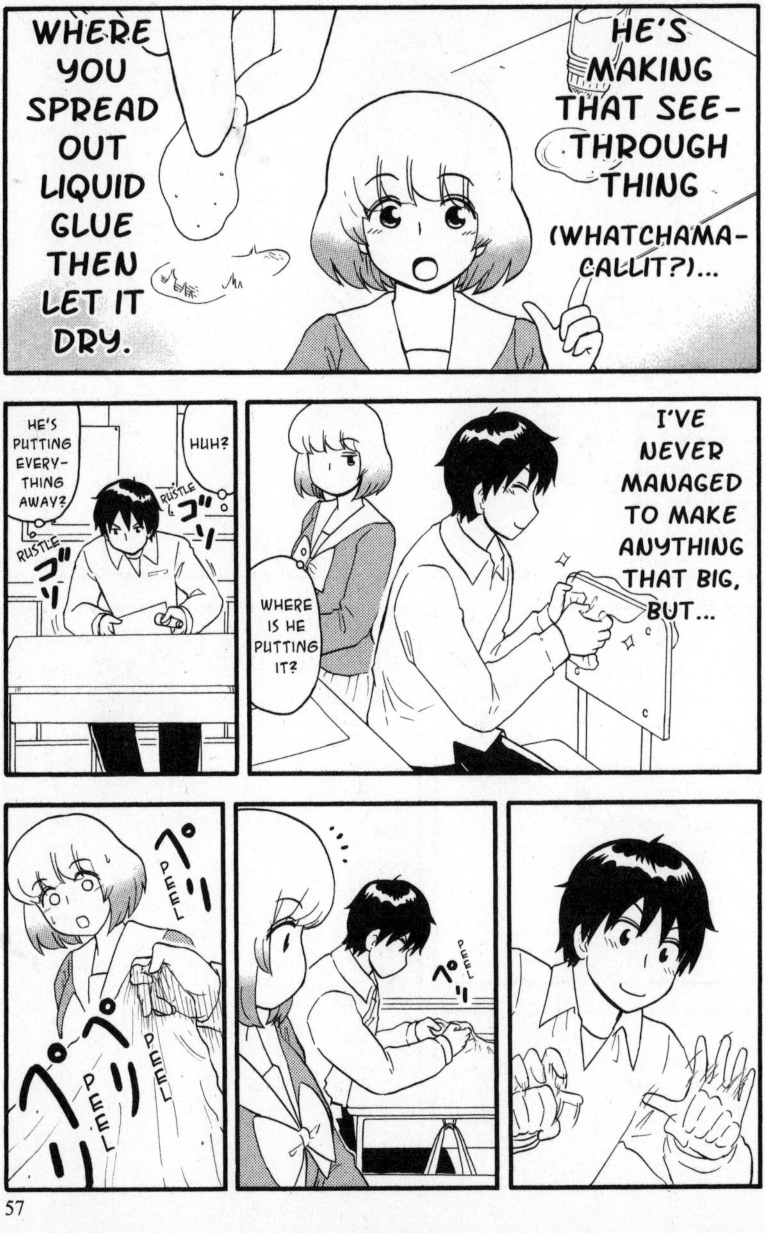

HE'S MAKING THAT SEE-THROUGH THING
(WHATCHAMA-CALLIT?)...
WHERE YOU SPREAD OUT LIQUID GLUE THEN LET IT DRY.
I'VE NEVER MANAGED TO MAKE ANYTHING THAT BIG, BUT...
WHERE IS HE PUTTING IT?
HUH?
HE'S PUTTING EVERY-THING AWAY?
RUSTLE
ゴソ
RUSTLE
ゴソ
...
ペリ
PEEL
ペリ
PEEL
ペリ
PEEL
ペリ
PEEL

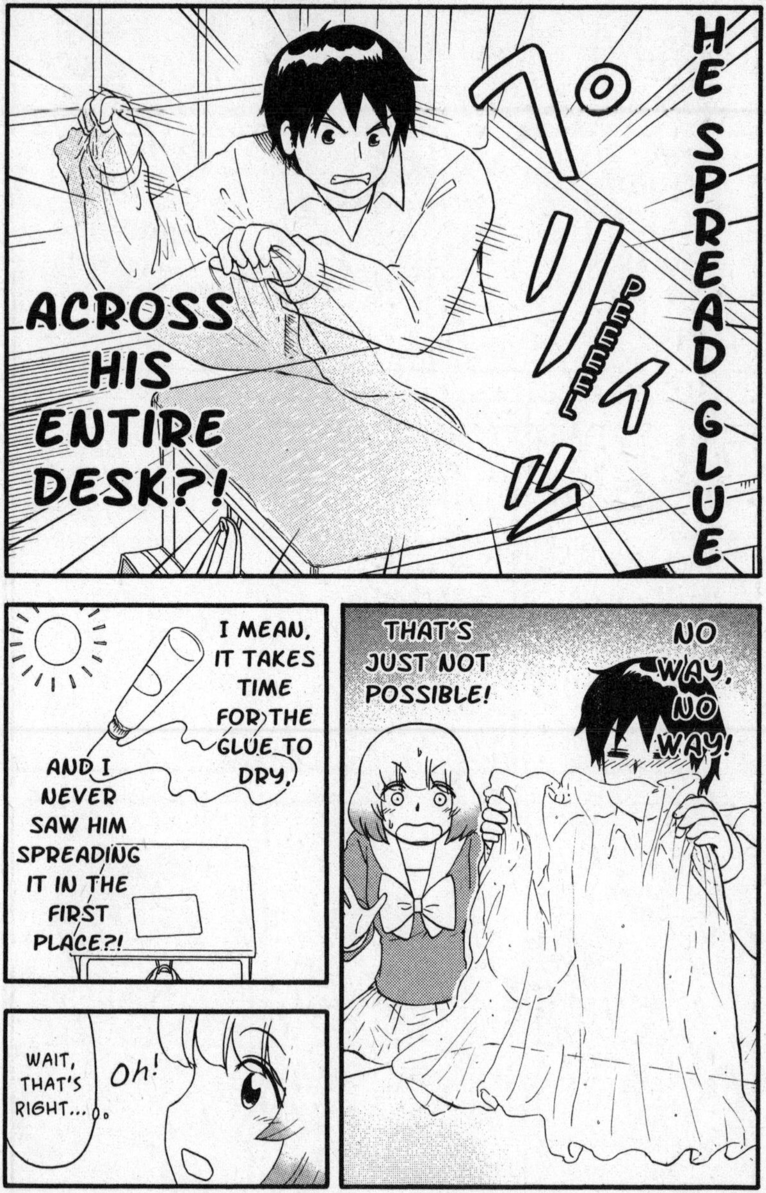
HE SPREAD GLUE
PEEEEL
ACROSS HIS ENTIRE DESK?!
NO WAY, NO WAY, NO WAY!
THAT'S JUST NOT POSSIBLE!
I MEAN, IT TAKES TIME FOR THE GLUE TO DRY,
AND I NEVER SAW HIM SPREADING IT IN THE FIRST PLACE?!
Oh!
WAIT, THAT'S RIGHT...

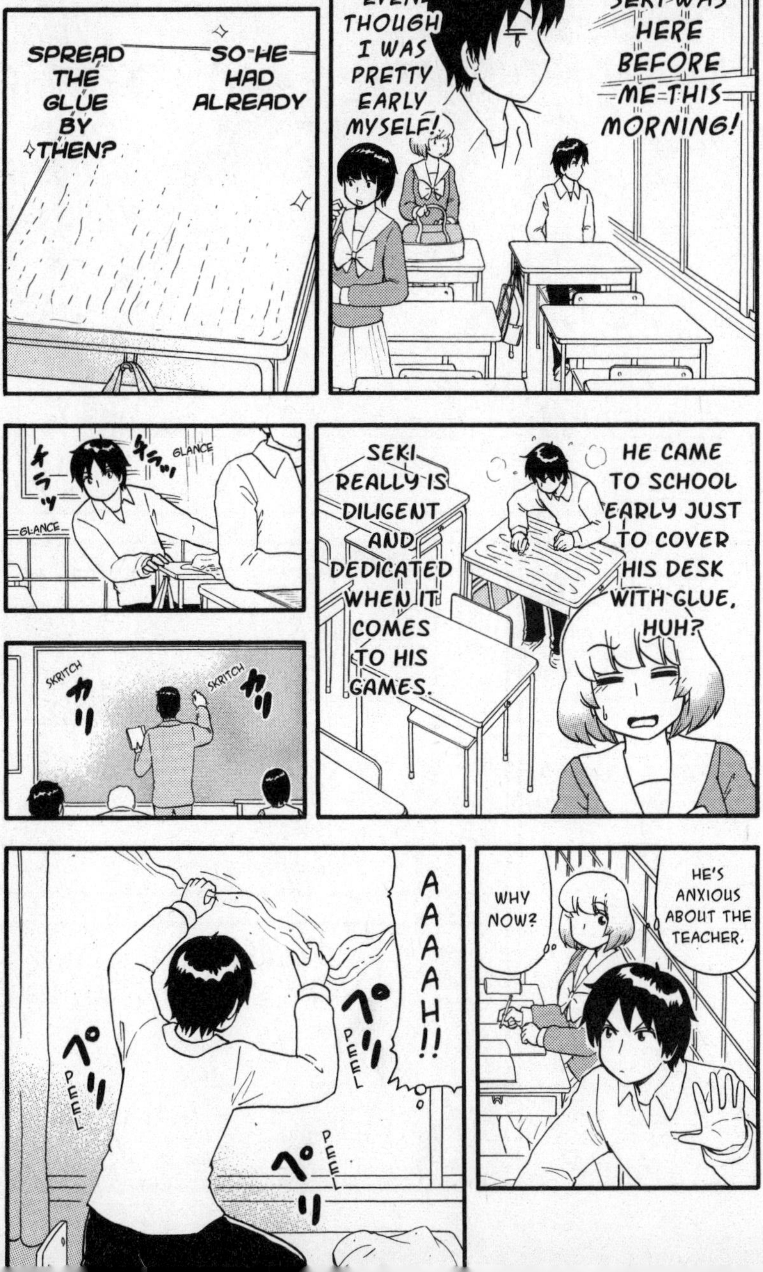
SEKI WAS HERE BEFORE ME THIS MORNING!
EVEN THOUGH I WAS PRETTY EARLY MYSELF!
SO HE HAD ALREADY
SPREAD THE GLUE BY THEN?
HE CAME TO SCHOOL EARLY JUST TO COVER HIS DESK WITH GLUE, HUH?
SEKI REALLY IS DILIGENT AND DEDICATED WHEN IT COMES TO HIS GAMES.
チラッ
GLANCE
チラッ
GLANCE
カリ
SKRITCH
カリ
SKRITCH
HE'S ANXIOUS ABOUT THE TEACHER.
WHY NOW?
AAAAAH!!
ペリ
PEEL
ペリ
PEEL
ペリ
PEEL

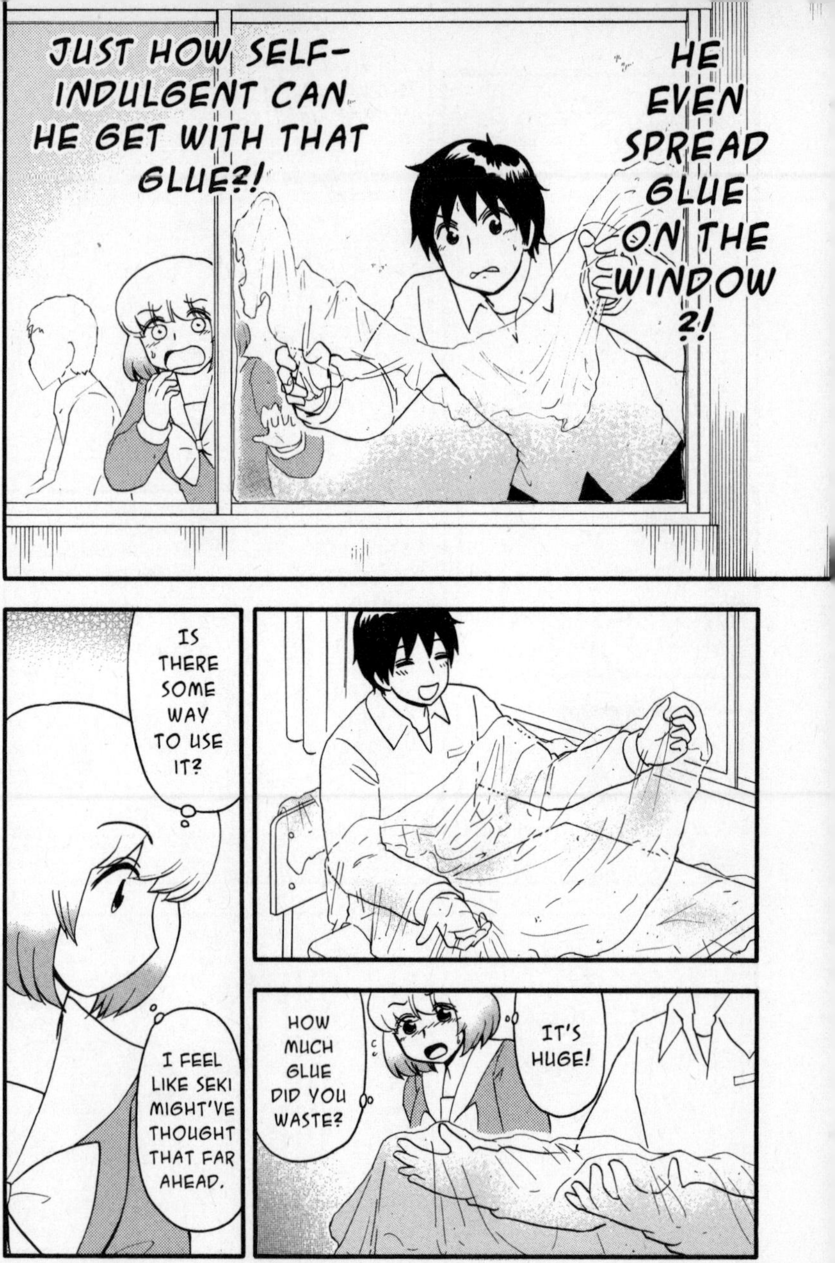
HE EVEN SPREAD GLUE ON THE WINDOW ?!
JUST HOW SELF-INDULGENT CAN HE GET WITH THAT GLUE?!
IT'S HUGE!
HOW MUCH GLUE DID YOU WASTE?
IS THERE SOME WAY TO USE IT?
I FEEL LIKE SEKI MIGHT'VE THOUGHT THAT FAR AHEAD.

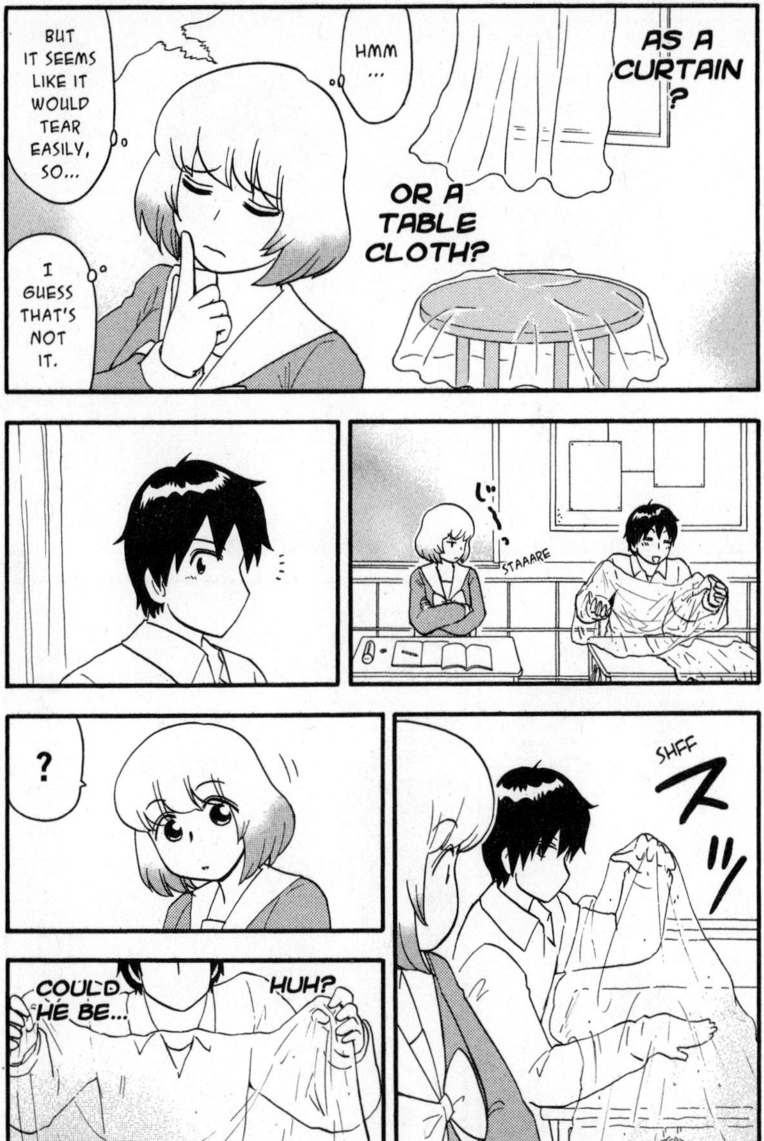
AS A CURTAIN?
OR A TABLE CLOTH?
HMM ...
BUT IT SEEMS LIKE IT WOULD TEAR EASILY, SO...
I GUESS THAT'S NOT IT.
じ〜っ
STAAARE
SHFF
スッ
?
HUH?
COULD HE BE...

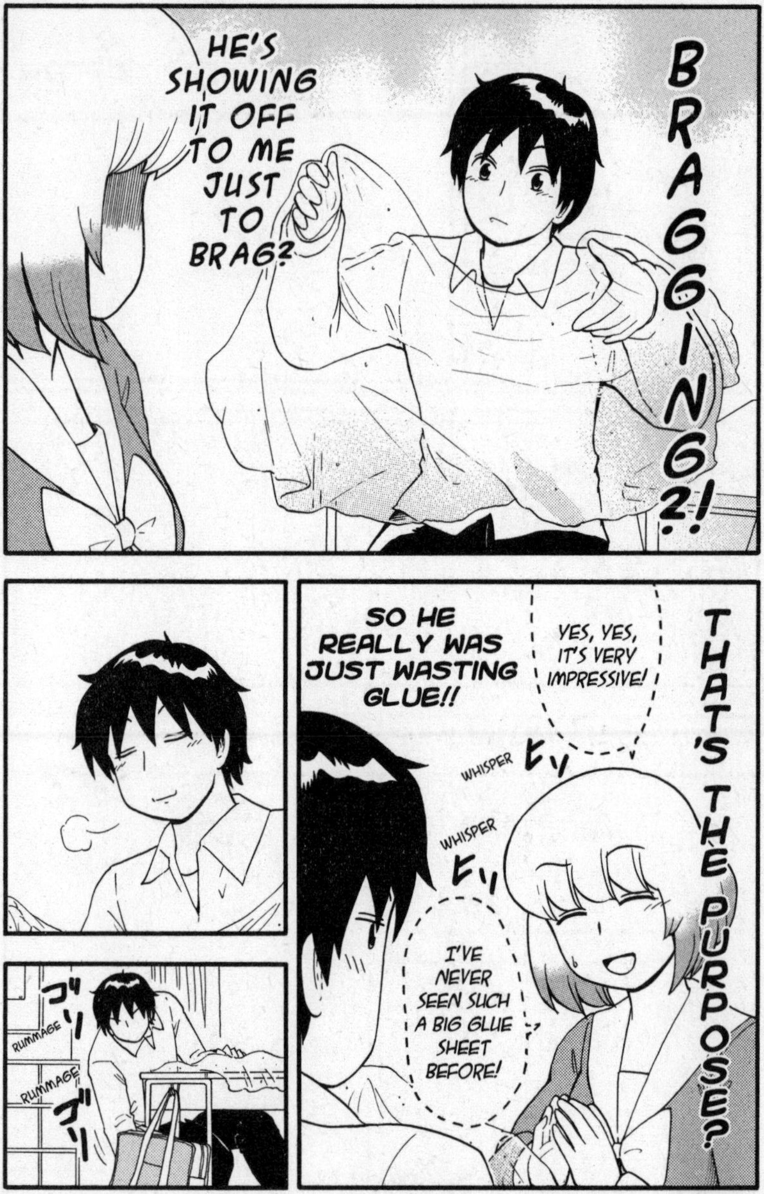
BRAGGING?!
HE'S SHOWING IT OFF TO ME JUST TO BRAG?
THAT'S THE PURPOSE?
YES, YES, IT'S VERY IMPRESSIVE!
SO HE REALLY WAS JUST WASTING GLUE!!
WHISPER
WHISPER
I'VE NEVER SEEN SUCH A BIG GLUE SHEET BEFORE!
RUMMAGE
RUMMAGE

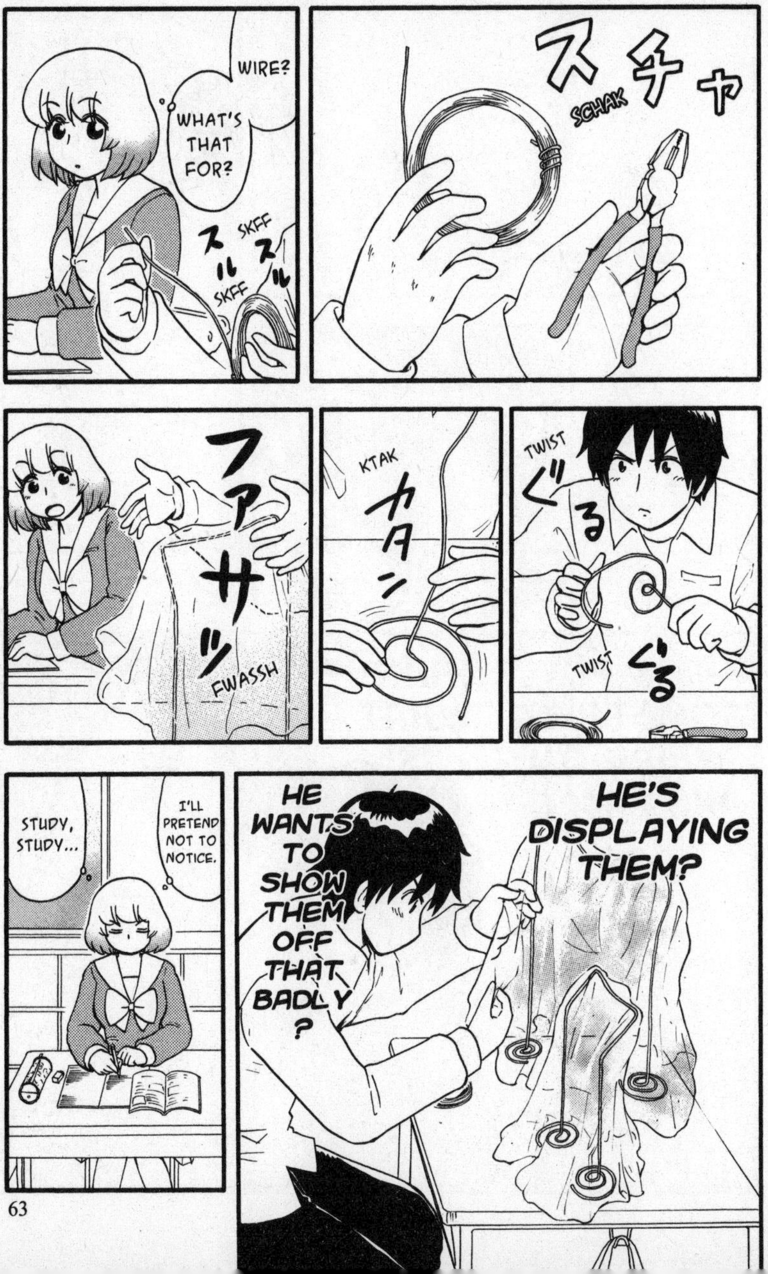
スチャ
SCHAK
WIRE?
WHAT'S THAT FOR?
スルスル
SKFF SKFF
ぐるぐる
TWIST TWIST
カタン
KTAK
ファサッ
FWASSH
HE'S DISPLAYING THEM?
HE WANTS TO SHOW THEM OFF THAT BADLY?
I'LL PRETEND NOT TO NOTICE.
STUDY, STUDY...

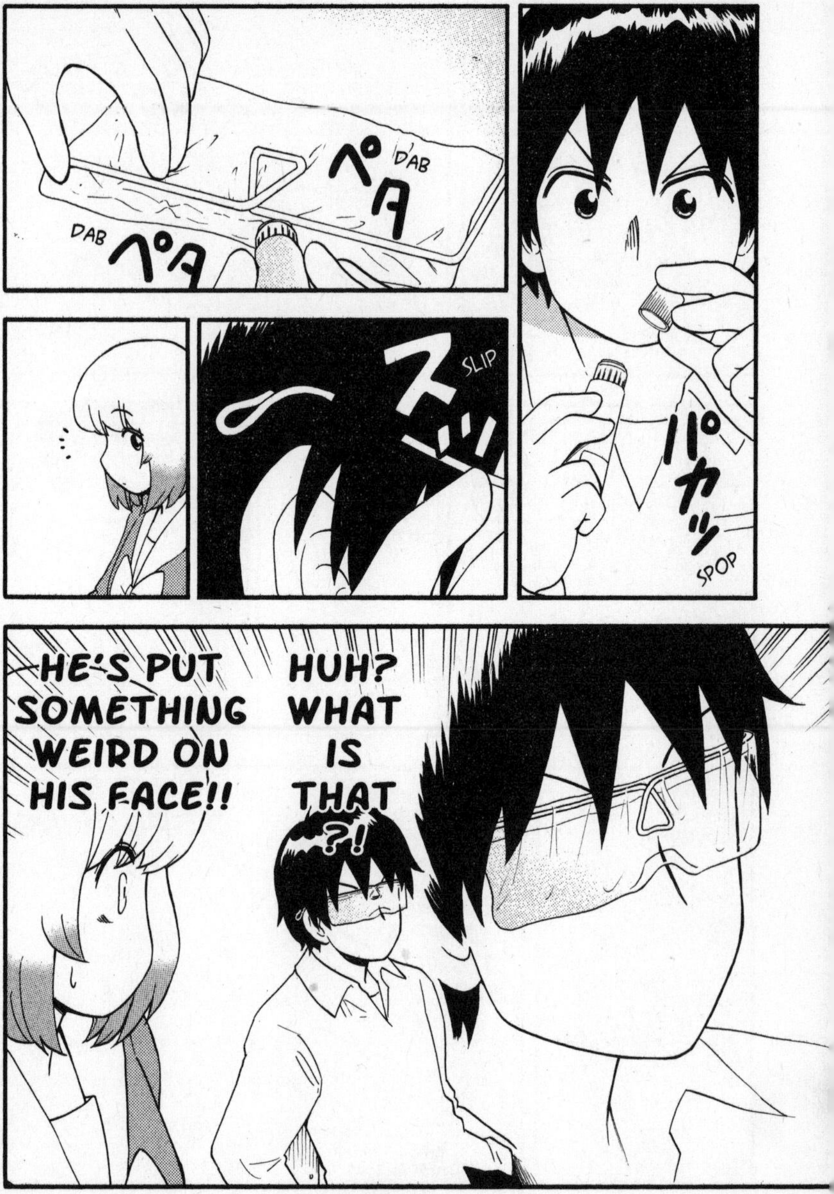
パカッ
SPOP
ペタ
DAB
ペタ
DAB
スッ
SLIP
HUH? WHAT IS THAT ?!
HE'S PUT SOMETHING WEIRD ON HIS FACE!!

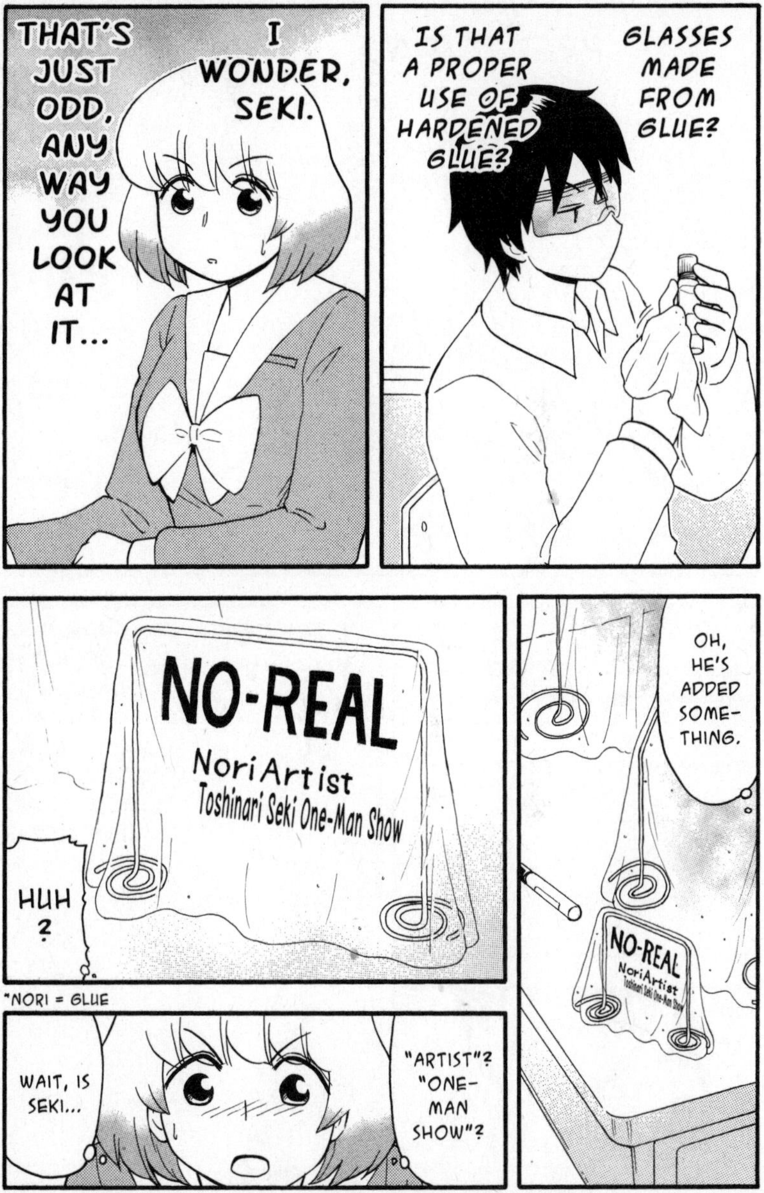
GLASSES MADE FROM GLUE?
IS THAT A PROPER USE OF HARDENED GLUE?
I WONDER, SEKI.
THAT'S JUST ODD, ANY WAY YOU LOOK AT IT...
OH, HE'S ADDED SOME-THING.
NO-REAL
NoriArtist
Toshinari Seki One-Man Show
NO-REAL
NoriArtist
Toshinari Seki One-Man Show
HUH?
*NORI = GLUE
"ARTIST"? "ONE-MAN SHOW"?
WAIT, IS SEKI...

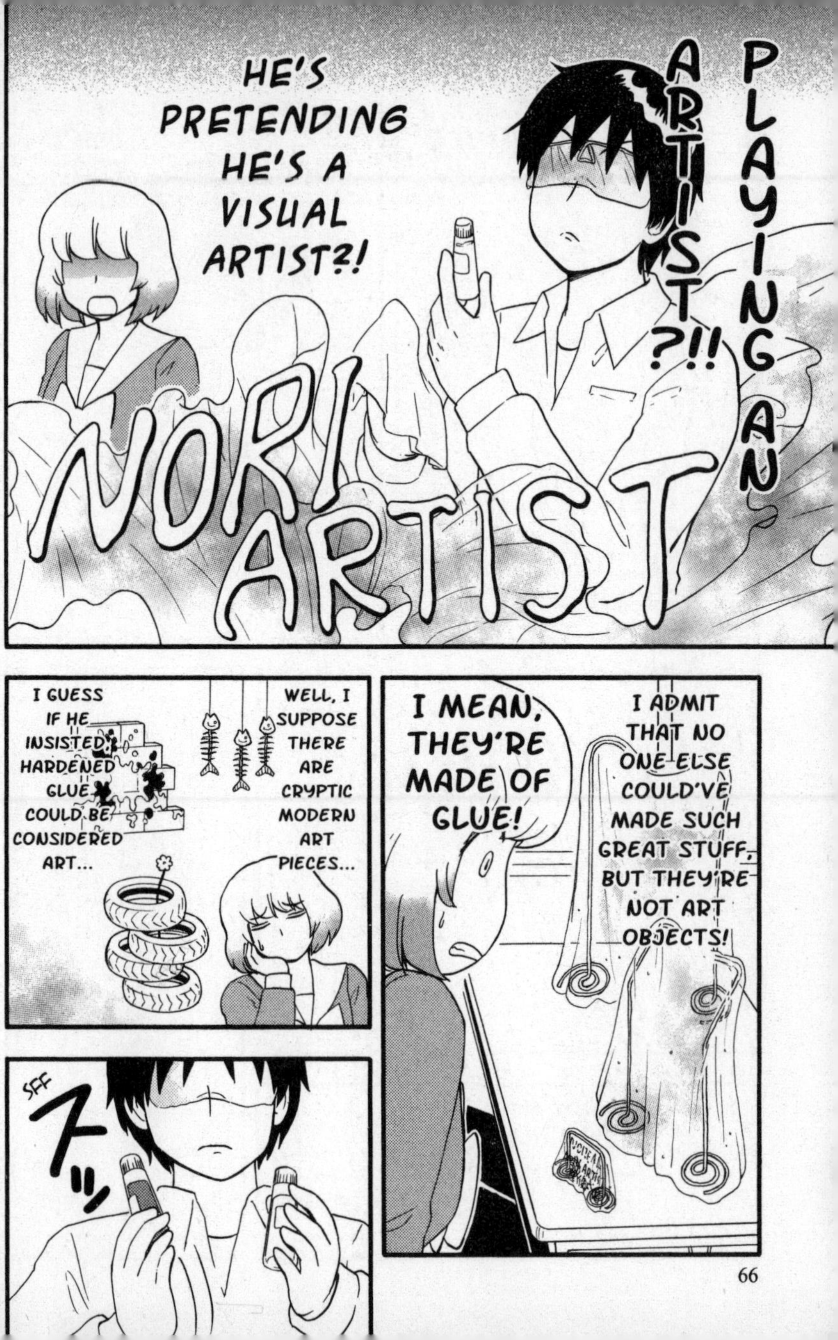
PLAYING AN ARTIST?!!
NORI ARTIST
HE'S PRETENDING HE'S A VISUAL ARTIST?!
I ADMIT THAT NO ONE ELSE COULD'VE MADE SUCH GREAT STUFF, BUT THEY'RE NOT ART OBJECTS!
I MEAN, THEY'RE MADE OF GLUE!
WELL, I SUPPOSE THERE ARE CRYPTIC MODERN ART PIECES...
I GUESS IF HE INSISTED HARDENED GLUE COULD BE CONSIDERED ART...
SFF

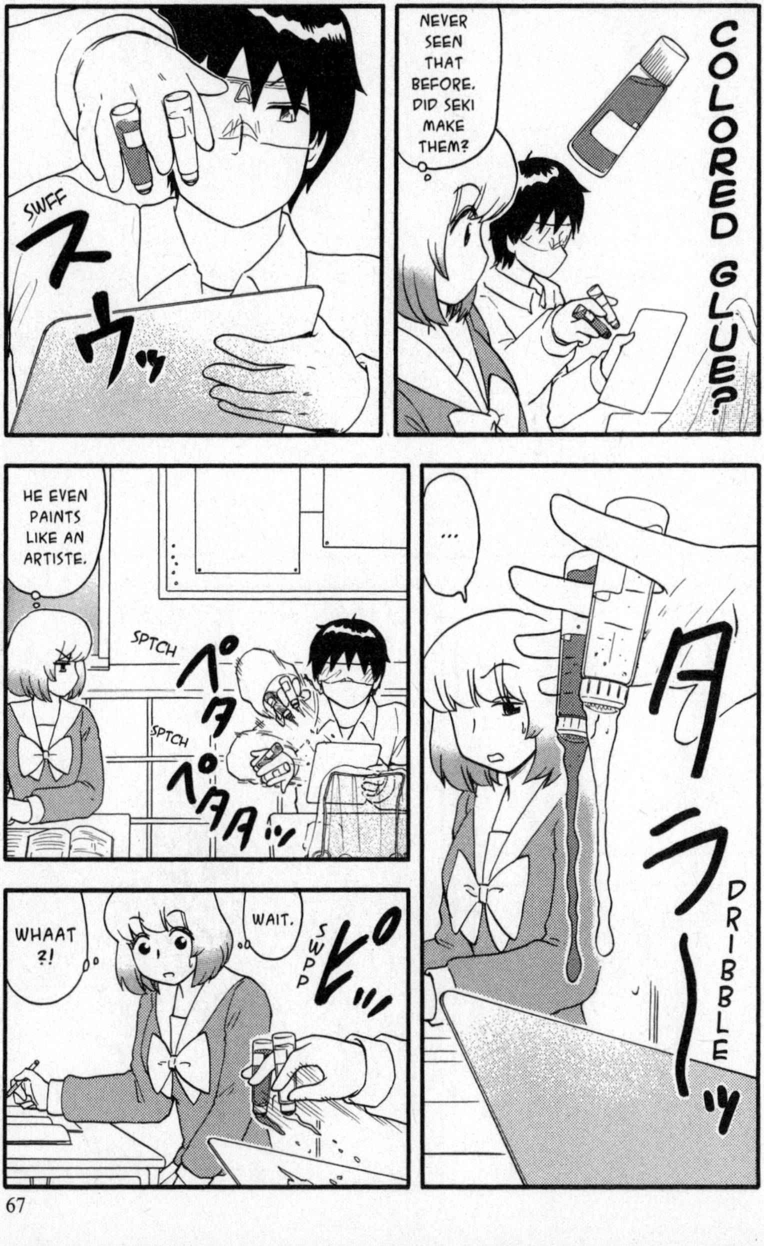
NEVER SEEN THAT BEFORE. DID SEKI MAKE THEM?
COLORED GLUE?
SWFF
スウッ
...
タラーッ
DRIBBLE
HE EVEN PAINTS LIKE AN ARTISTE.
SPTCH
ペタ
SPTCH
ペタタッ
WAIT.
SWPP
ピッ
WHAAT?!

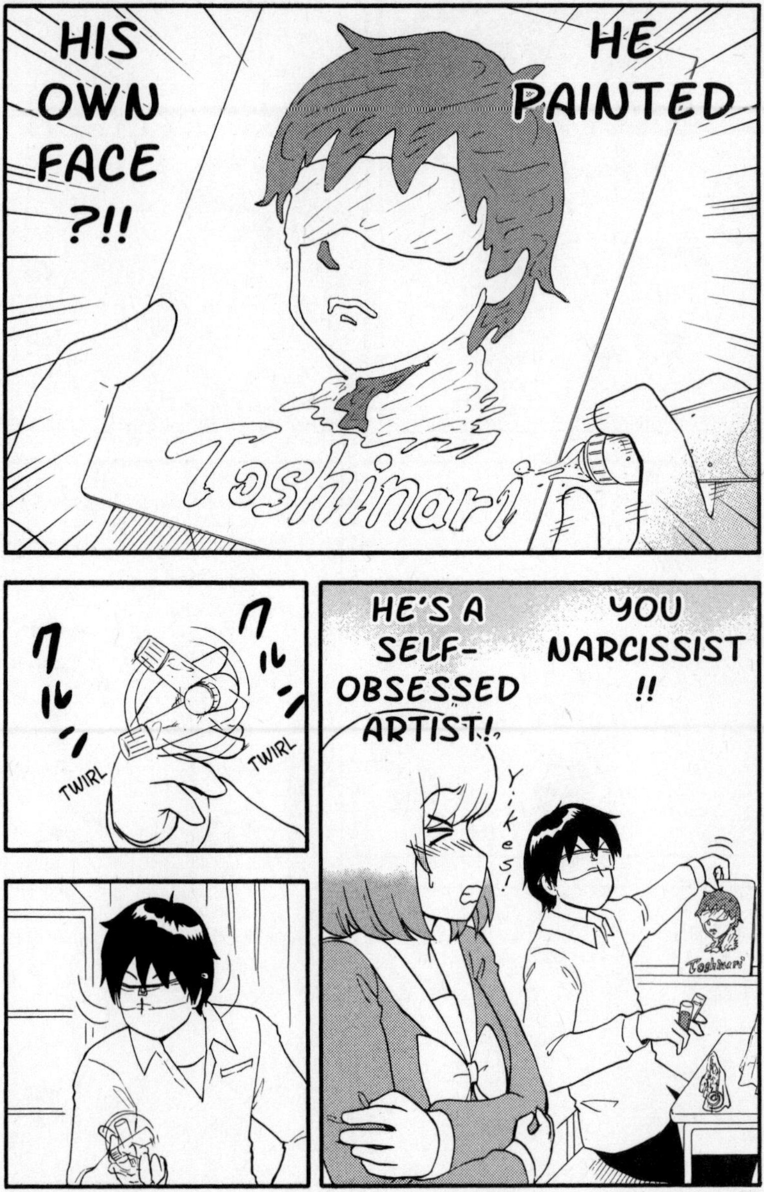
HE PAINTED
HIS OWN FACE ?!!
Toshinari
YOU NARCISSIST !!
HE'S A SELF-OBSESSED ARTIST!
Yikes!
Toshinari
クル
TWIRL
クル
TWIRL

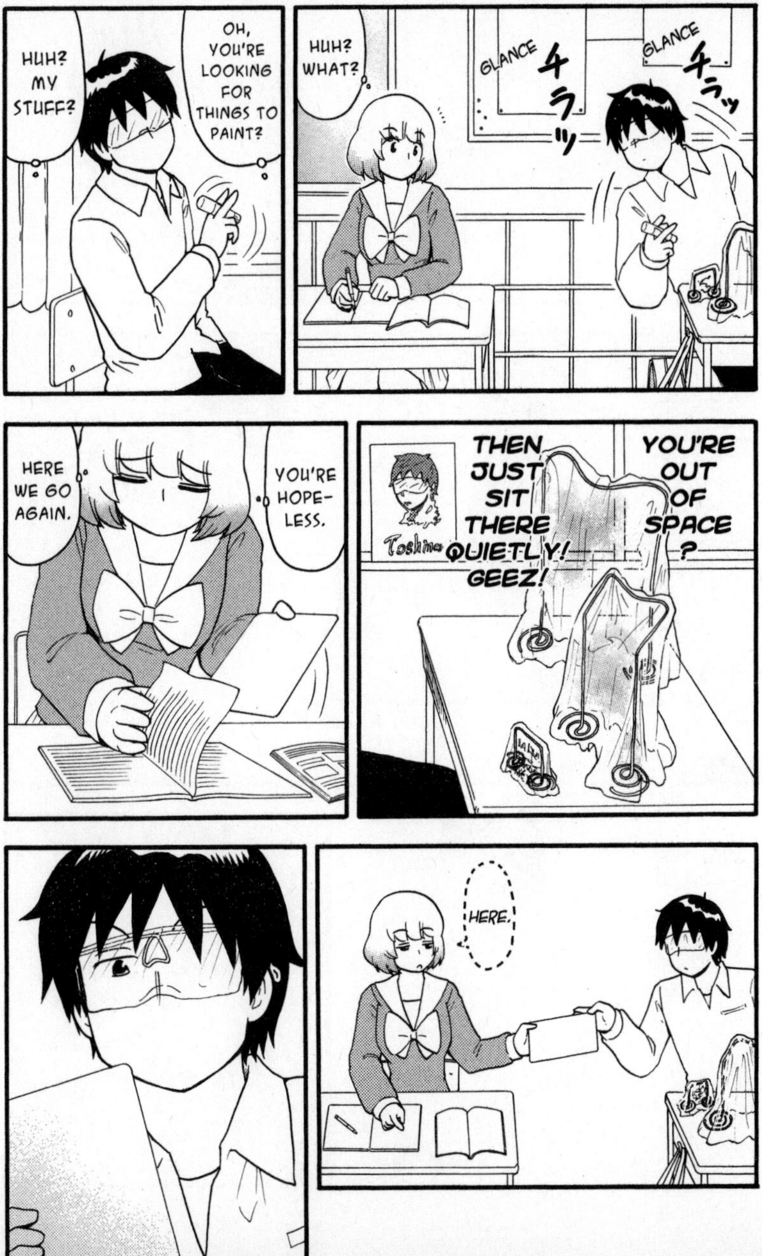
GLANCE
チラッ
GLANCE
チラッ
HUH? WHAT?
OH, YOU'RE LOOKING FOR THINGS TO PAINT?
HUH? MY STUFF?
YOU'RE OUT OF SPACE?
THEN JUST SIT THERE QUIETLY! GEEZ!
YOU'RE HOPELESS.
HERE WE GO AGAIN.
HERE.

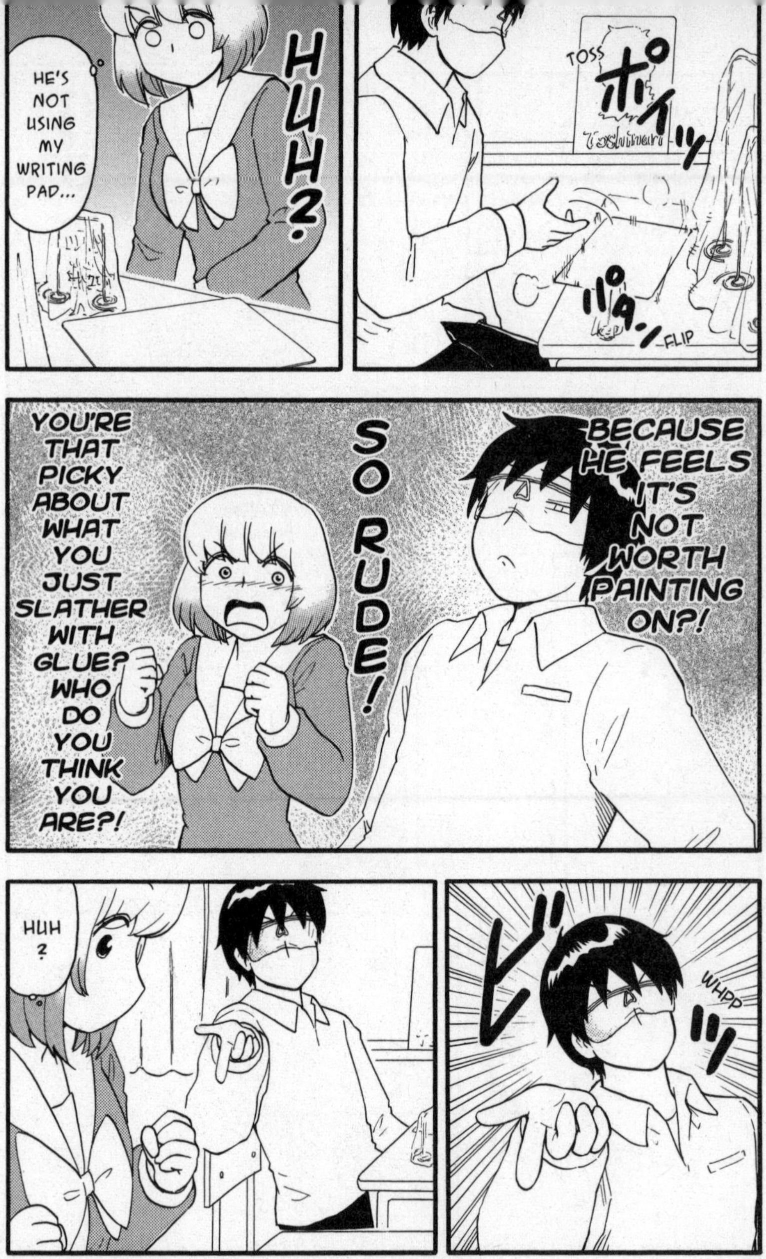

TOSS
ポイッ
FLIP
HE'S NOT USING MY WRITING PAD...
HUH?
BECAUSE HE FEELS IT'S NOT WORTH PAINTING ON?!
SO RUDE!
YOU'RE THAT PICKY ABOUT WHAT YOU JUST SLATHER WITH GLUE? WHO DO YOU THINK YOU ARE?!
ビッ
WHPP
HUH?

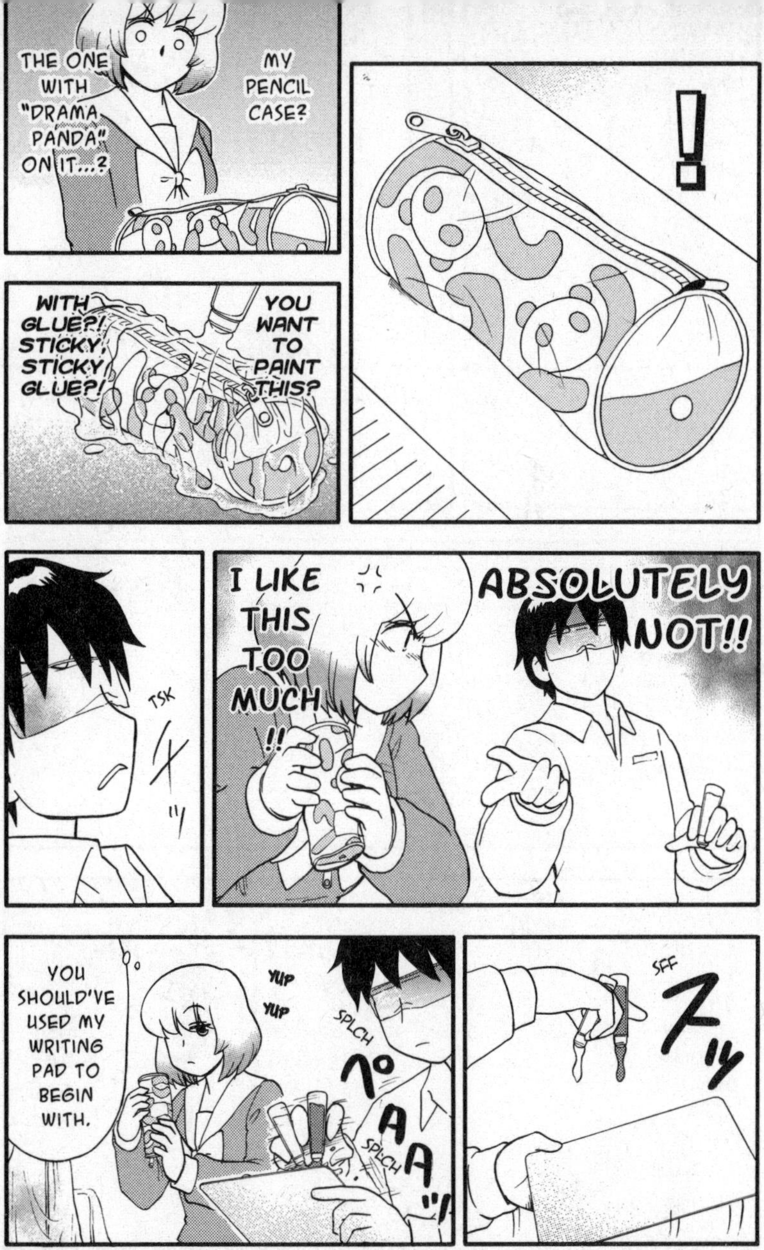
!
MY PENCIL CASE?
THE ONE WITH "DRAMA PANDA" ON IT...?
YOU WANT TO PAINT THIS?
WITH GLUE?! STICKY, STICKY GLUE?!
ABSOLUTELY NOT!!
I LIKE THIS TOO MUCH!!
TSK
SFF
YUP
YUP
SPLCH
SPLCH
YOU SHOULD'VE USED MY WRITING PAD TO BEGIN WITH.

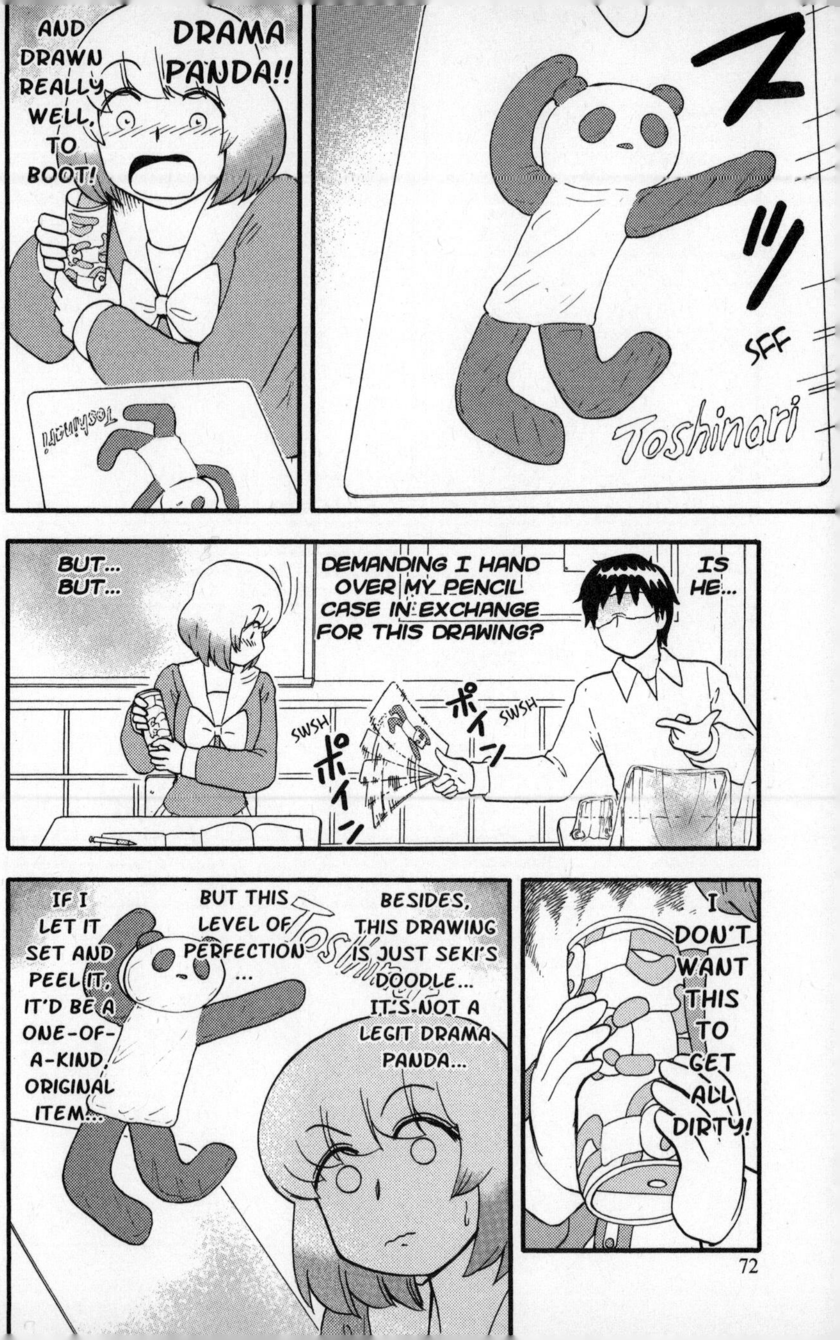
SFF
Toshinari
DRAMA PANDA!!
AND DRAWN REALLY WELL, TO BOOT!
Toshinari
IS HE...
DEMANDING I HAND OVER MY PENCIL CASE IN EXCHANGE FOR THIS DRAWING?
BUT... BUT...
SWSH
SWSH
I DON'T WANT THIS TO GET ALL DIRTY!
BESIDES, THIS DRAWING IS JUST SEKI'S DOODLE... IT'S NOT A LEGIT DRAMA PANDA...
BUT THIS LEVEL OF PERFECTION...
IF I LET IT SET AND PEEL IT, IT'D BE A ONE-OF-A-KIND, ORIGINAL ITEM...

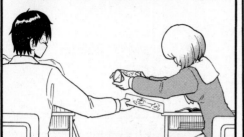

PLEASE TAKE GOOD CARE OF IT

SWISH ズッ

トロッ

DRIB...

ギュウウッ

SQUEEEEZE

73

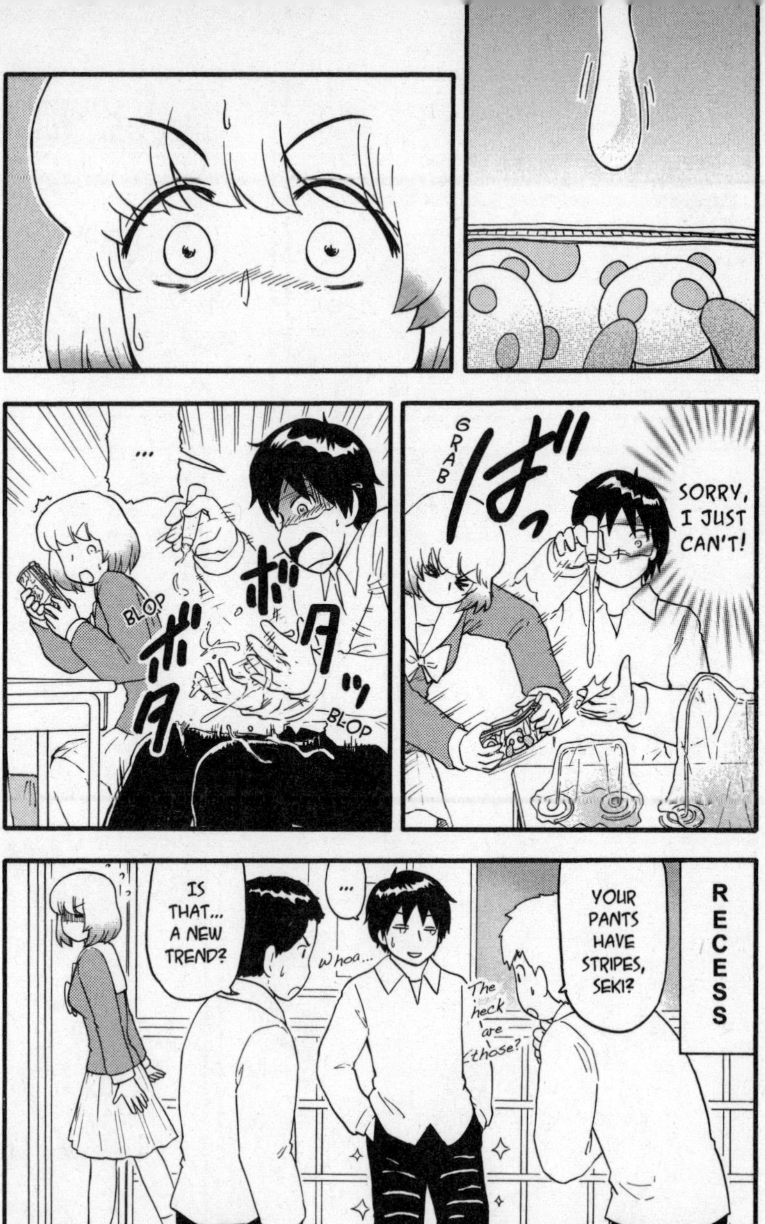
GRAB
ばっ
SORRY, I JUST CAN'T!
...
BLOP
ボタ
ボタッ
BLOP
RECESS
YOUR PANTS HAVE STRIPES, SEKI?
The heck are those?
...
whoa...
IS THAT... A NEW TREND?

114th Period

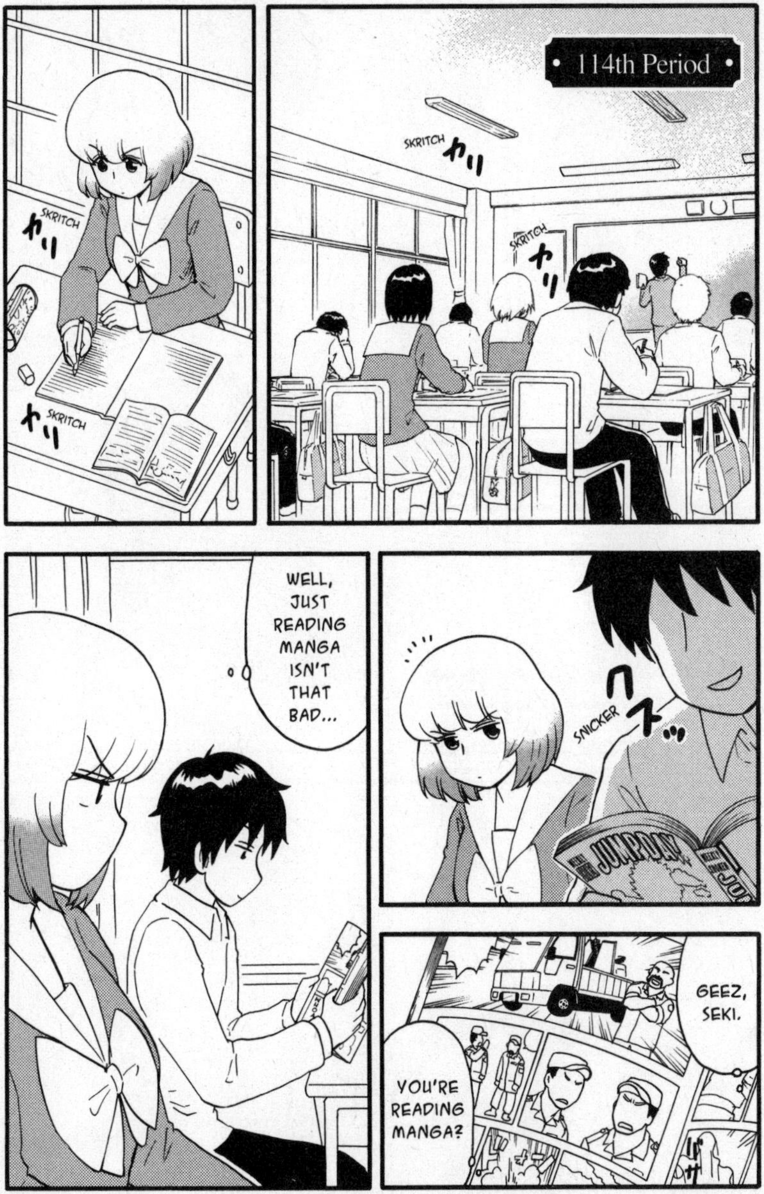

SKRITCH ヤリ
SKRITCH ヤリ
SKRITCH ヤリ
SKRITCH ヤリ
SNICKER
GEEZ, SEKI.
YOU'RE READING MANGA?
WELL, JUST READING MANGA ISN'T THAT BAD...

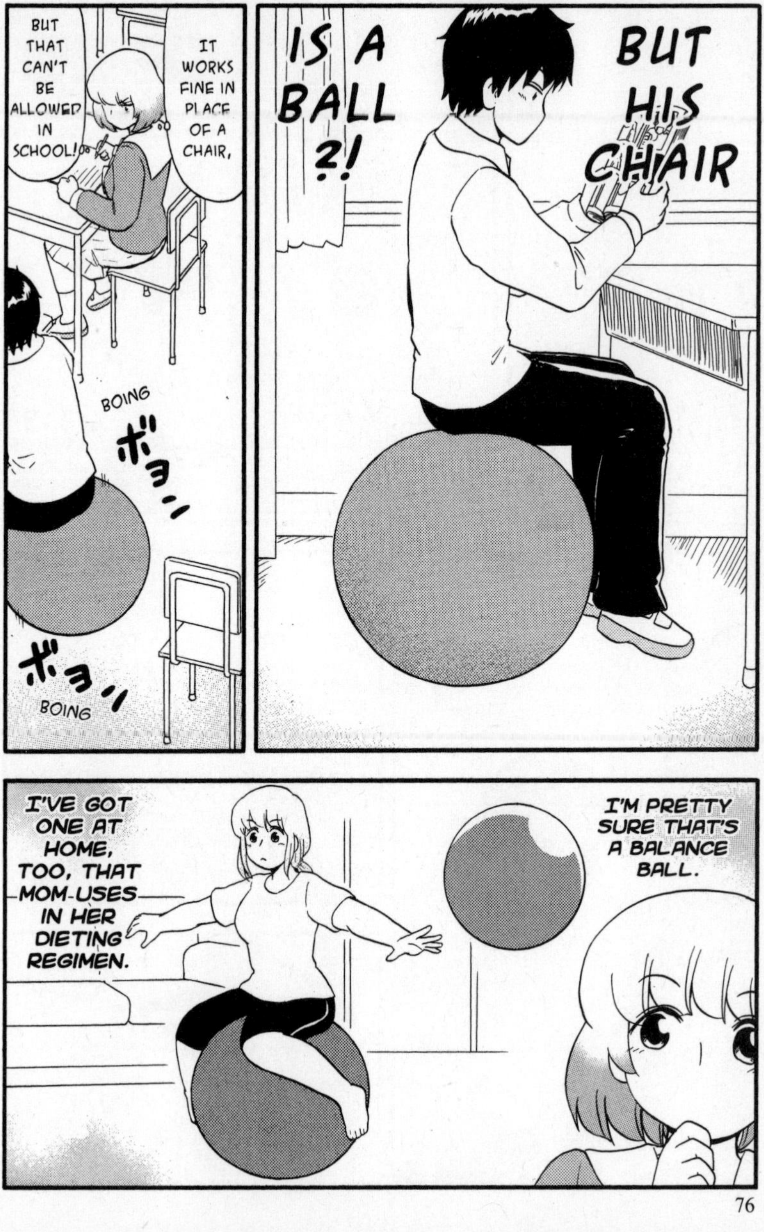
BUT HIS CHAIR
IS A BALL ?!
IT WORKS FINE IN PLACE OF A CHAIR,
BUT THAT CAN'T BE ALLOWED IN SCHOOL!
ボヨン
BOING
ボヨン
BOING
I'M PRETTY SURE THAT'S A BALANCE BALL.
I'VE GOT ONE AT HOME, TOO, THAT MOM USES IN HER DIETING REGIMEN.

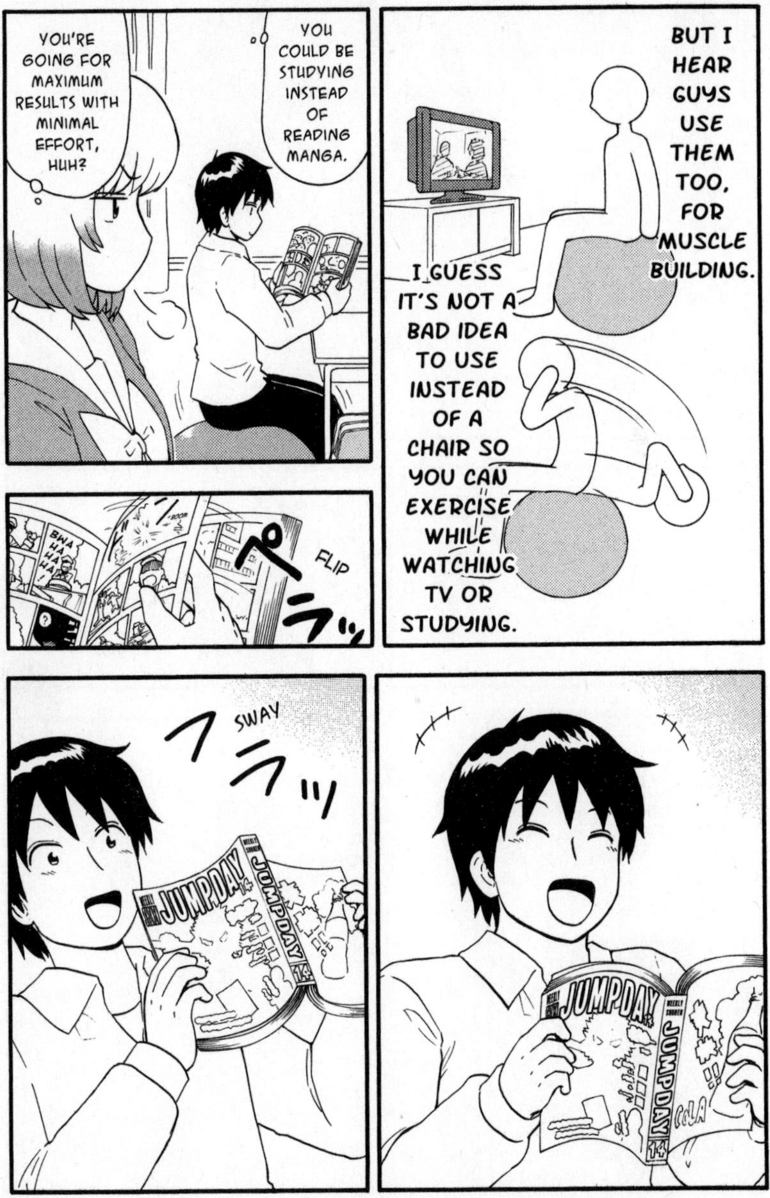
BUT I HEAR GUYS USE THEM TOO, FOR MUSCLE BUILDING.
I GUESS IT'S NOT A BAD IDEA TO USE INSTEAD OF A CHAIR SO YOU CAN EXERCISE WHILE WATCHING TV OR STUDYING.
YOU COULD BE STUDYING INSTEAD OF READING MANGA.
YOU'RE GOING FOR MAXIMUM RESULTS WITH MINIMAL EFFORT, HUH?
BWA HA HA HA!
FLIP
JUMPDAY
SWAY
JUMPDAY

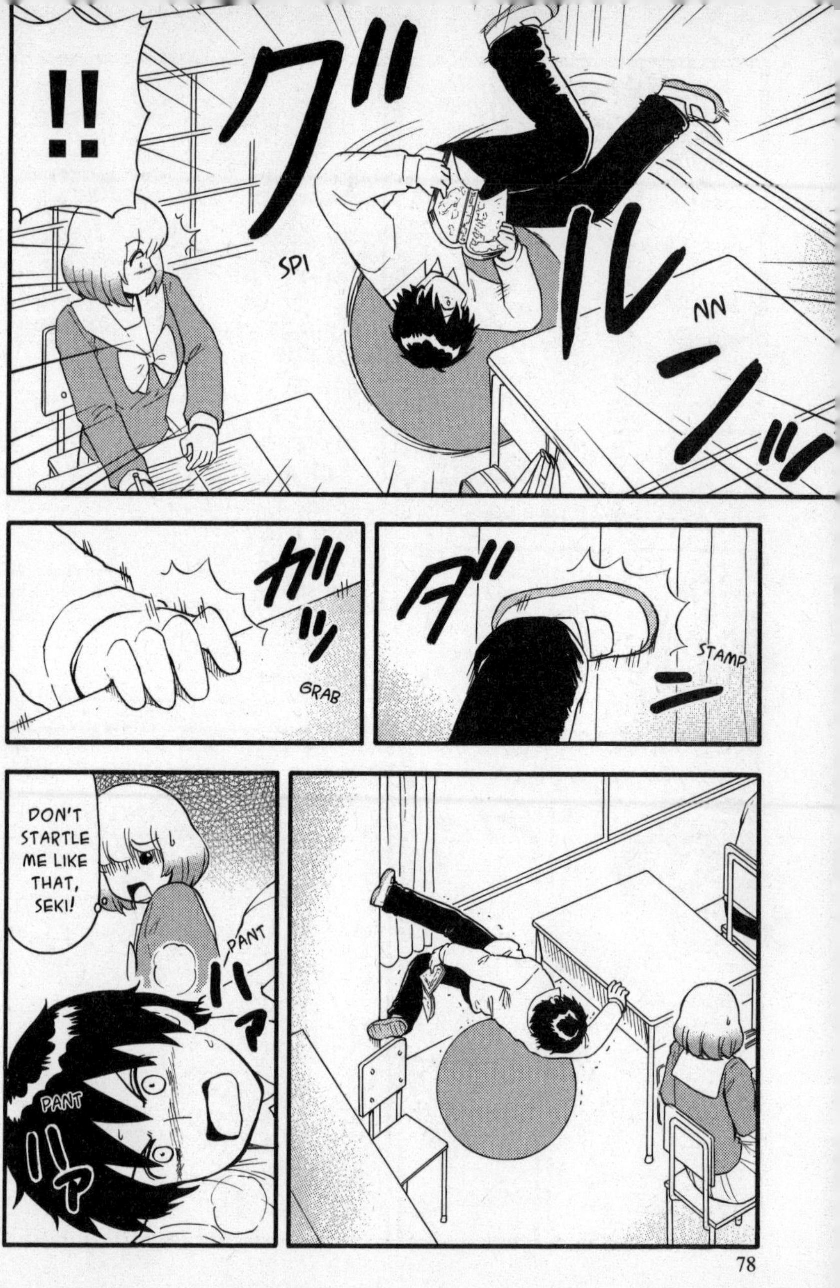

グルンッ
SPI
NN
!!
ダン
STAMP
ガッ
GRAB
DON'T STARTLE ME LIKE THAT, SEKI!
ハァ
PANT
ハァ
PANT

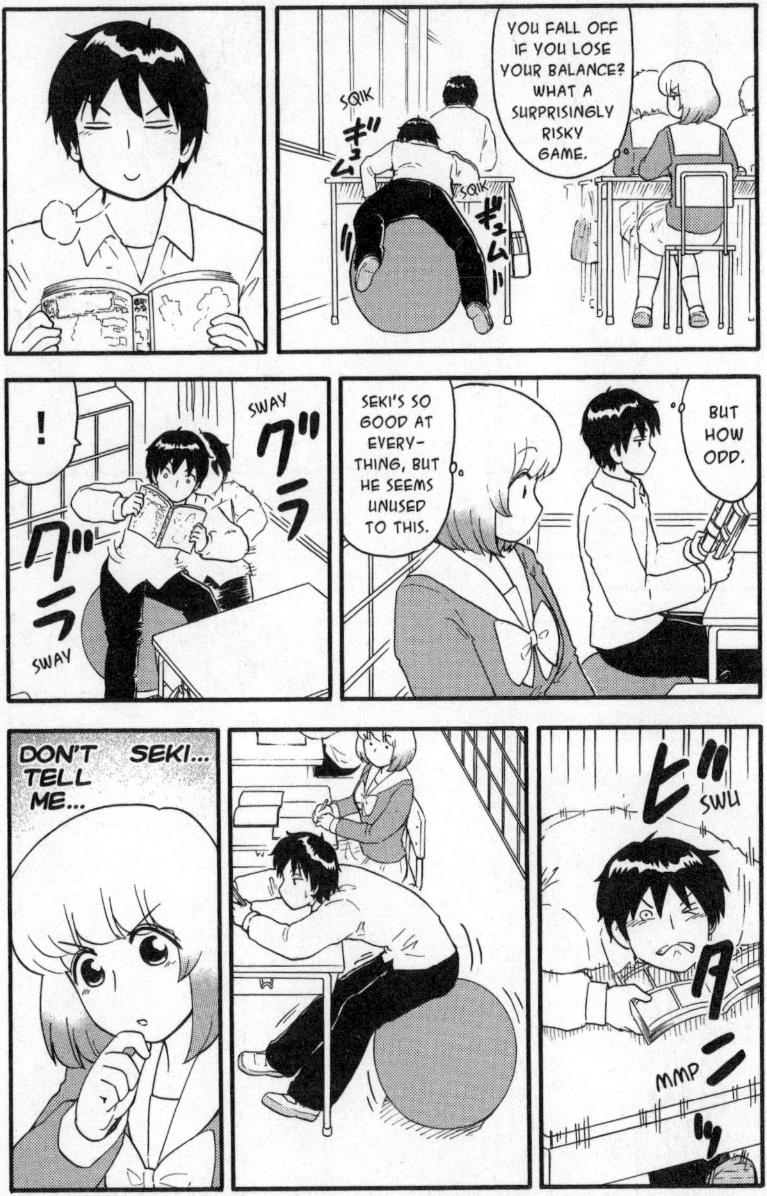
SQIK
SQIK
YOU FALL OFF IF YOU LOSE YOUR BALANCE? WHAT A SURPRISINGLY RISKY GAME.
BUT HOW ODD.
SEKI'S SO GOOD AT EVERY-THING, BUT HE SEEMS UNUSED TO THIS.
SWAY
!
SWAY
SWU
MMP
SEKI...
DON'T TELL ME...

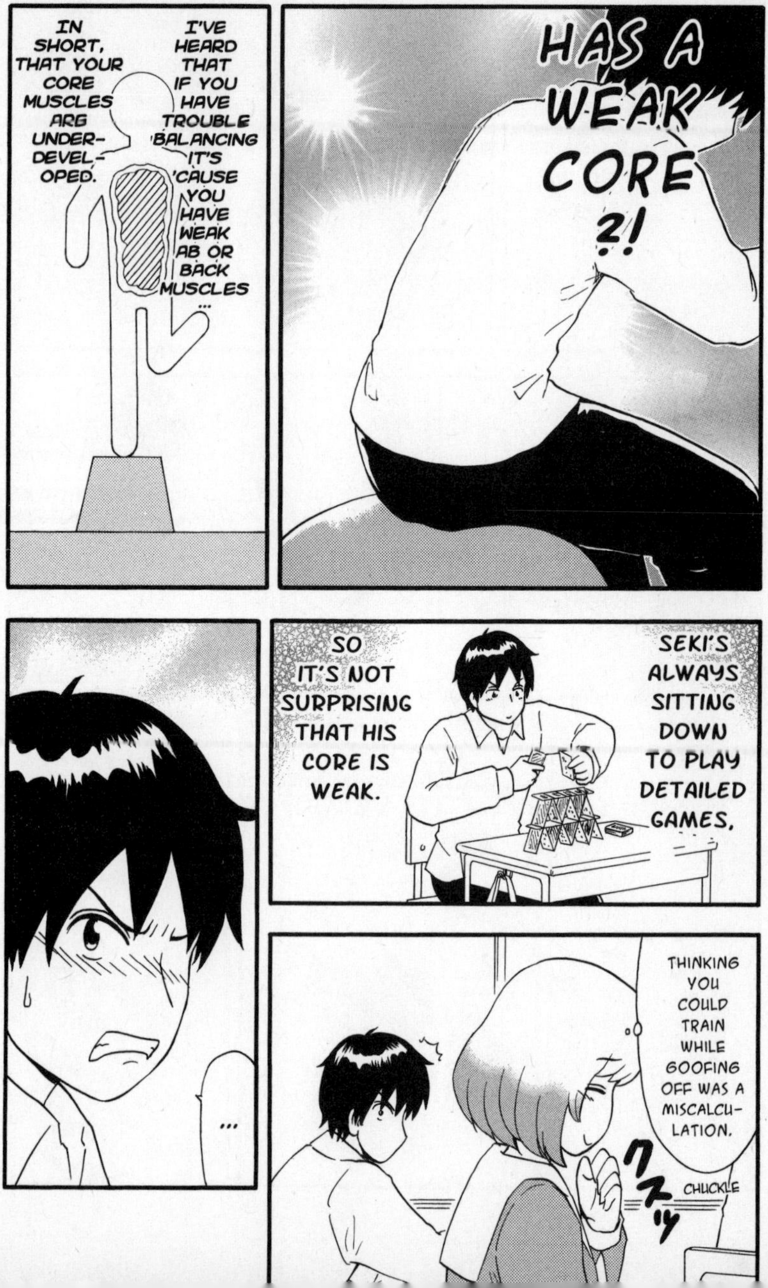
HAS A WEAK CORE ?!
I'VE HEARD THAT IF YOU HAVE TROUBLE BALANCING IT'S 'CAUSE YOU HAVE WEAK AB OR BACK MUSCLES ...
IN SHORT, THAT YOUR CORE MUSCLES ARE UNDER-DEVEL-OPED.
SEKI'S ALWAYS SITTING DOWN TO PLAY DETAILED GAMES,
SO IT'S NOT SURPRISING THAT HIS CORE IS WEAK.
THINKING YOU COULD TRAIN WHILE GOOFING OFF WAS A MISCALCU-LATION.
CHUCKLE
...

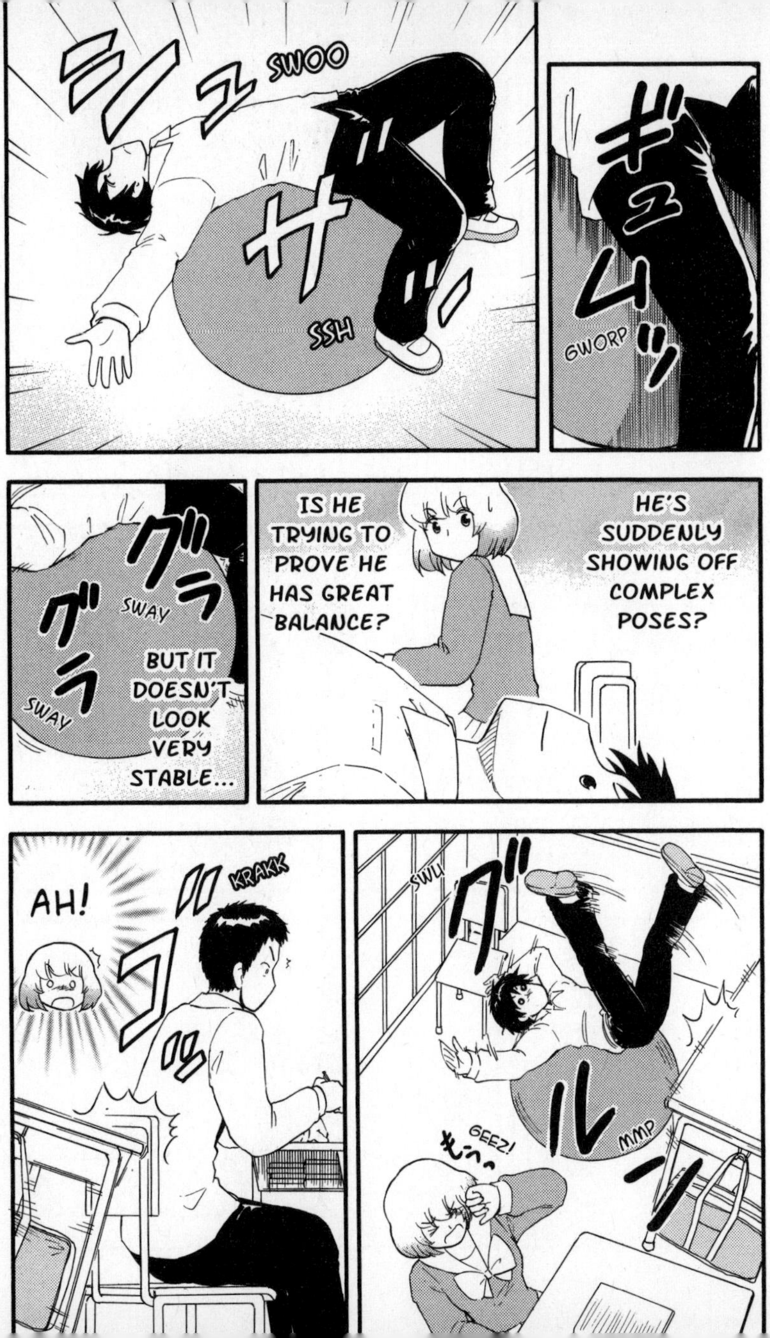
GWORP
SWOO
SSH
HE'S SUDDENLY SHOWING OFF COMPLEX POSES?
IS HE TRYING TO PROVE HE HAS GREAT BALANCE?
SWAY
SWAY
BUT IT DOESN'T LOOK VERY STABLE...
SWLI
MMP
GEEZ!
KRAKK
AH!

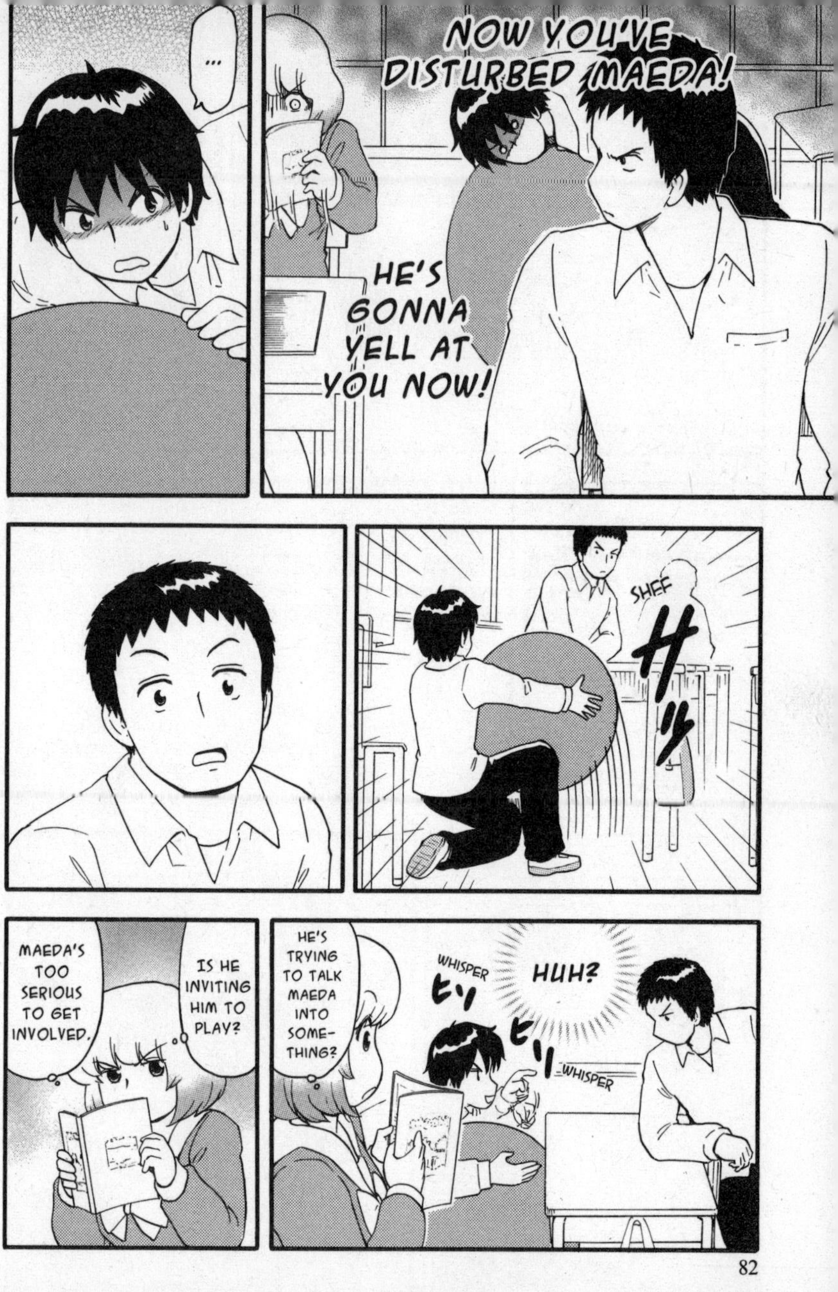
NOW YOU'VE DISTURBED MAEDA!
HE'S GONNA YELL AT YOU NOW!
...
SHFF
サッ
HUH?
WHISPER
ヒソ
HE'S TRYING TO TALK MAEDA INTO SOME-THING?
ヒソ
WHISPER
IS HE INVITING HIM TO PLAY?
MAEDA'S TOO SERIOUS TO GET INVOLVED.

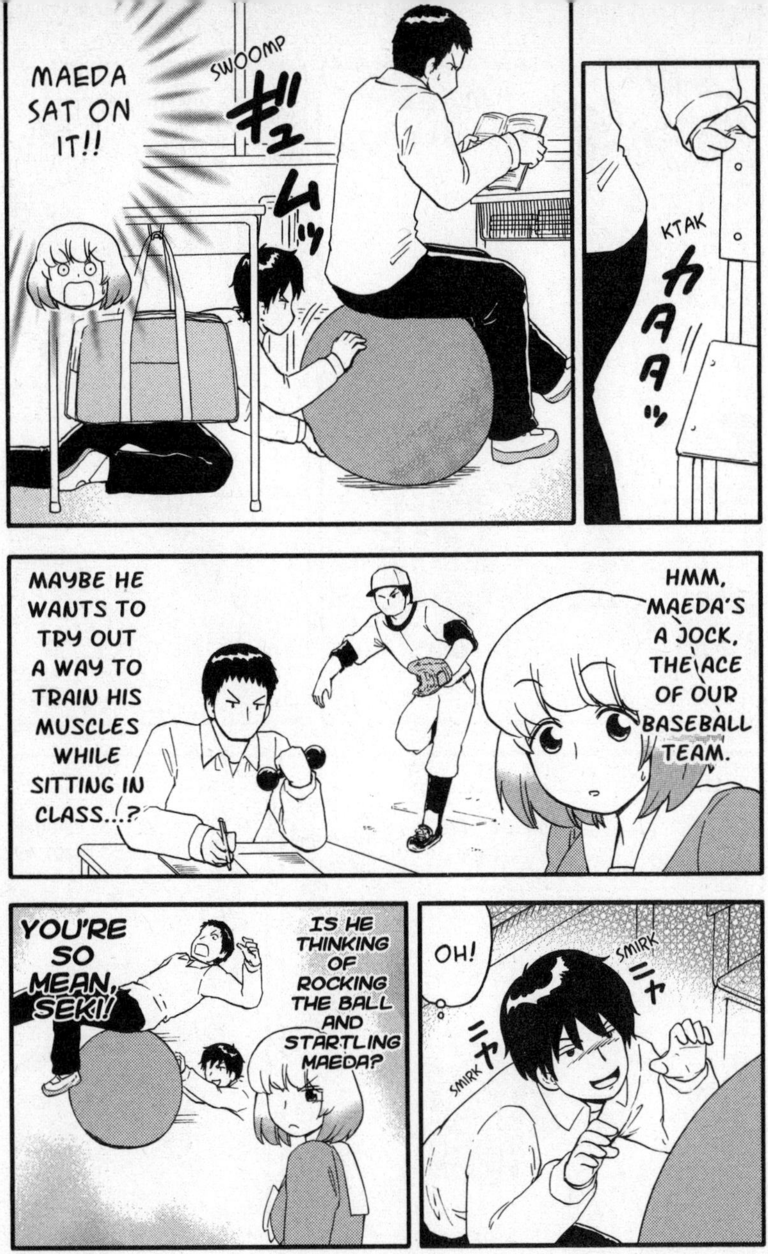
KTAK
カタタッ
MAEDA SAT ON IT!!
SWOOMP
ギュムッ
HMM, MAEDA'S A JOCK, THE ACE OF OUR BASEBALL TEAM.
MAYBE HE WANTS TO TRY OUT A WAY TO TRAIN HIS MUSCLES WHILE SITTING IN CLASS...?
OH!
SMIRK
ニヤ
ニヤ
SMIRK
IS HE THINKING OF ROCKING THE BALL AND STARTLING MAEDA?
YOU'RE SO MEAN, SEKI!

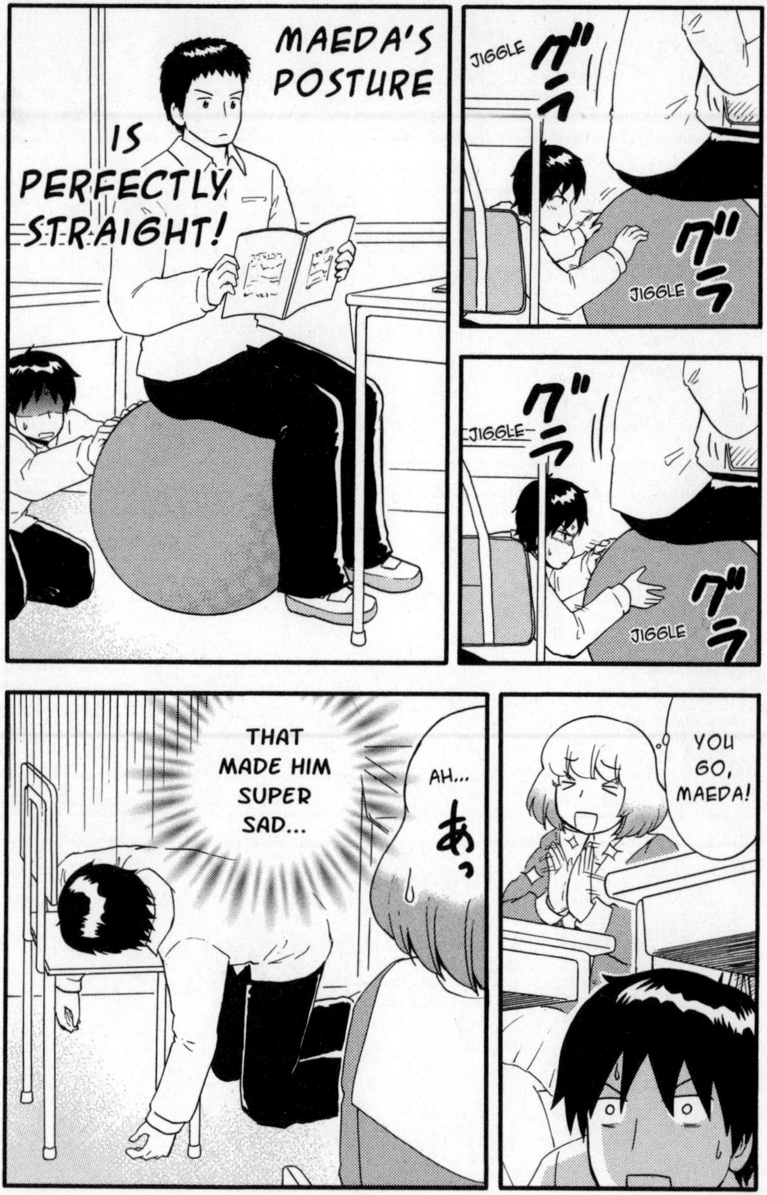

JIGGLE
グラ
JIGGLE
グラ
JIGGLE
グラ
JIGGLE
グラ
MAEDA'S POSTURE
IS PERFECTLY STRAIGHT!
YOU GO, MAEDA!
AH...
あっ
THAT MADE HIM SUPER SAD...

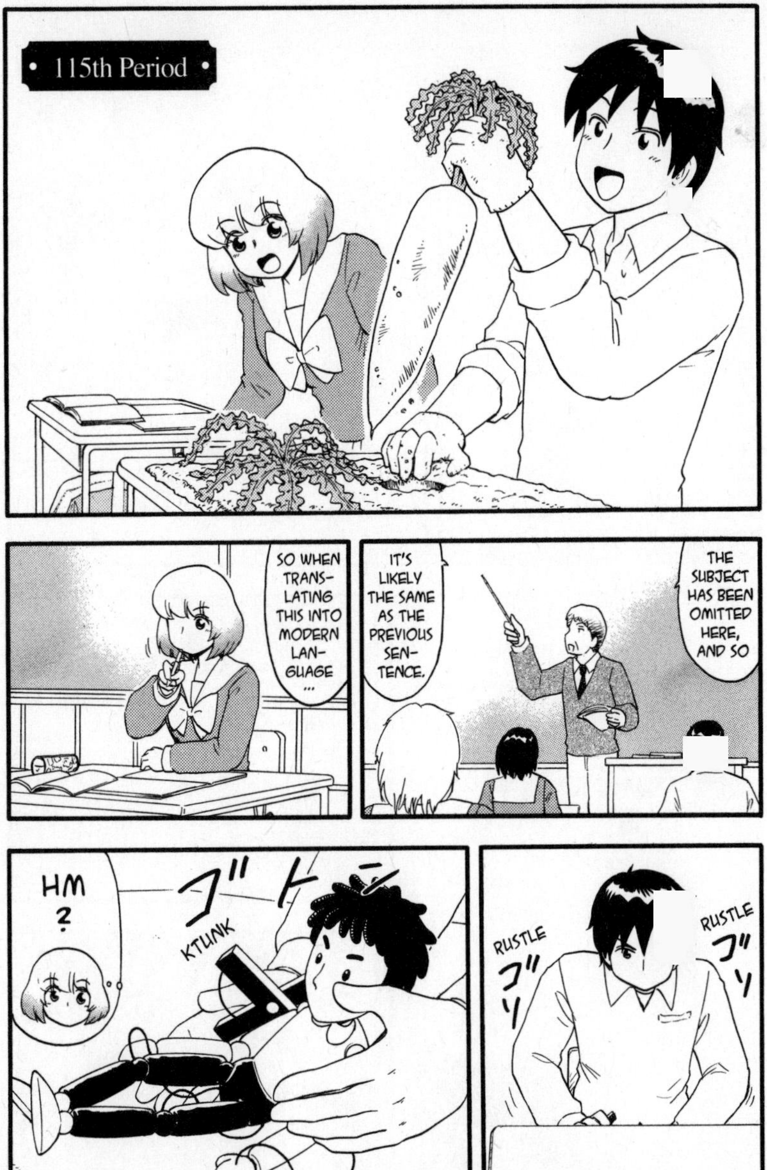
• 115th Period •
THE SUBJECT HAS BEEN OMITTED HERE, AND SO
IT'S LIKELY THE SAME AS THE PREVIOUS SENTENCE.
SO WHEN TRANSLATING THIS INTO MODERN LANGUAGE ...
RUSTLE ゴソ
RUSTLE ゴソ
HM ?
ゴトン
KTUNK

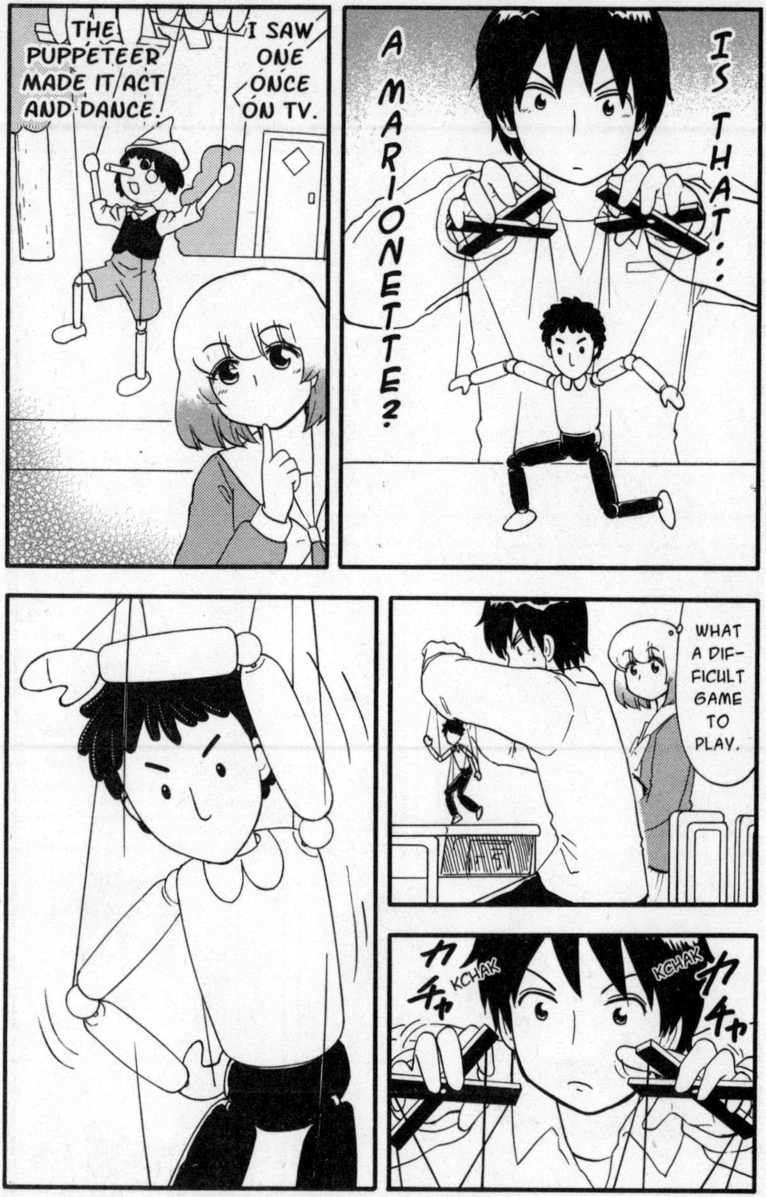
IS THAT...
A MARIONETTE?
I SAW ONE ONCE ON TV.
THE PUPPETEER MADE IT ACT AND DANCE.
WHAT A DIFFICULT GAME TO PLAY.
カチャ
KCHAK
カチャ
KCHAK

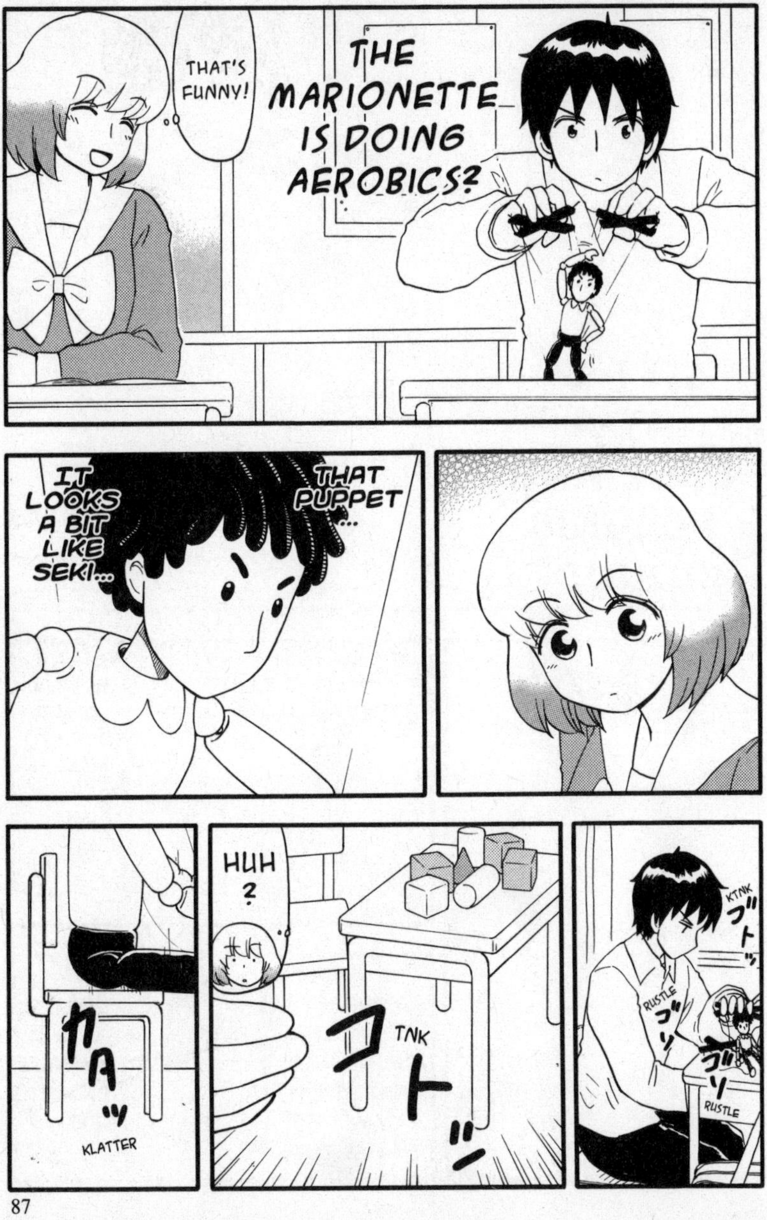

THE MARIONETTE IS DOING AEROBICS?
THAT'S FUNNY!
THAT PUPPET...
IT LOOKS A BIT LIKE SEKI...
KTNK
RUSTLE
RUSTLE
HUH?
TNK
KLATTER

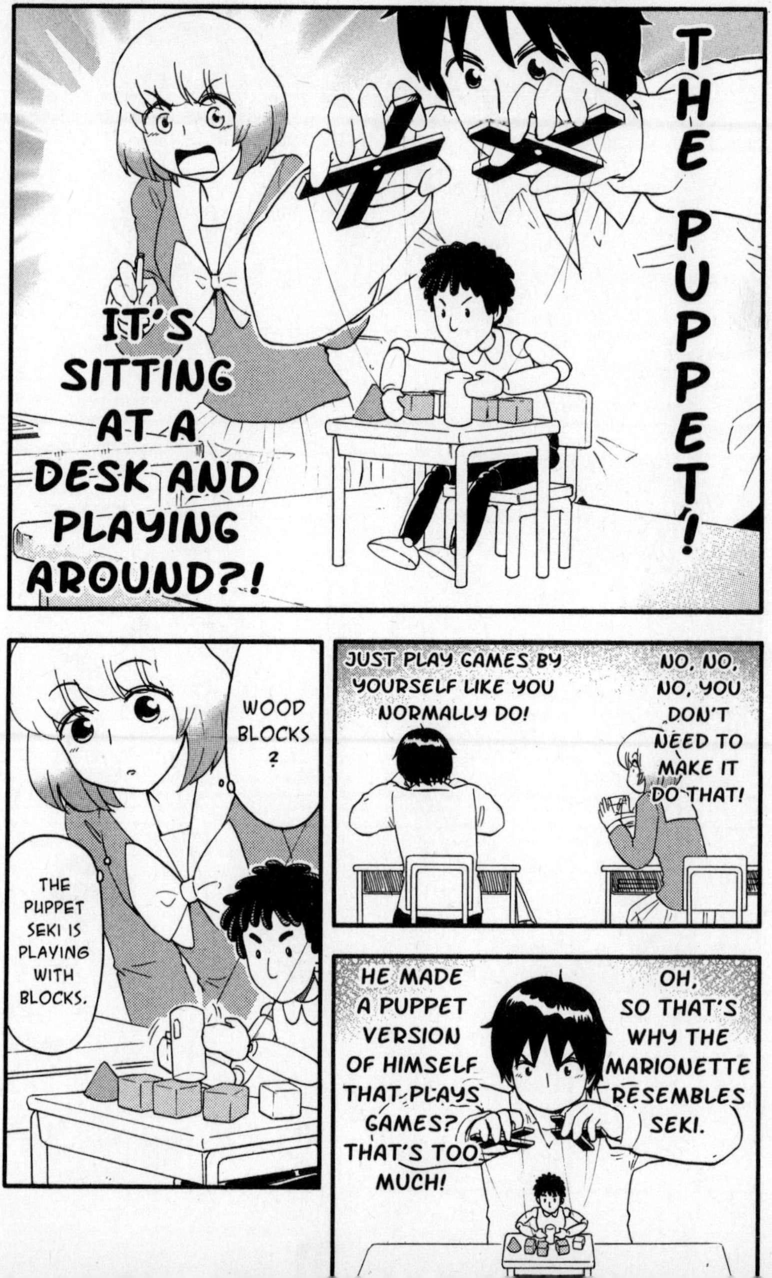
THE PUPPET!
IT'S SITTING AT A DESK AND PLAYING AROUND?!
NO, NO, NO, YOU DON'T NEED TO MAKE IT DO THAT!
JUST PLAY GAMES BY YOURSELF LIKE YOU NORMALLY DO!
OH, SO THAT'S WHY THE MARIONETTE RESEMBLES SEKI.
HE MADE A PUPPET VERSION OF HIMSELF THAT PLAYS GAMES? THAT'S TOO MUCH!
WOOD BLOCKS?
THE PUPPET SEKI IS PLAYING WITH BLOCKS.

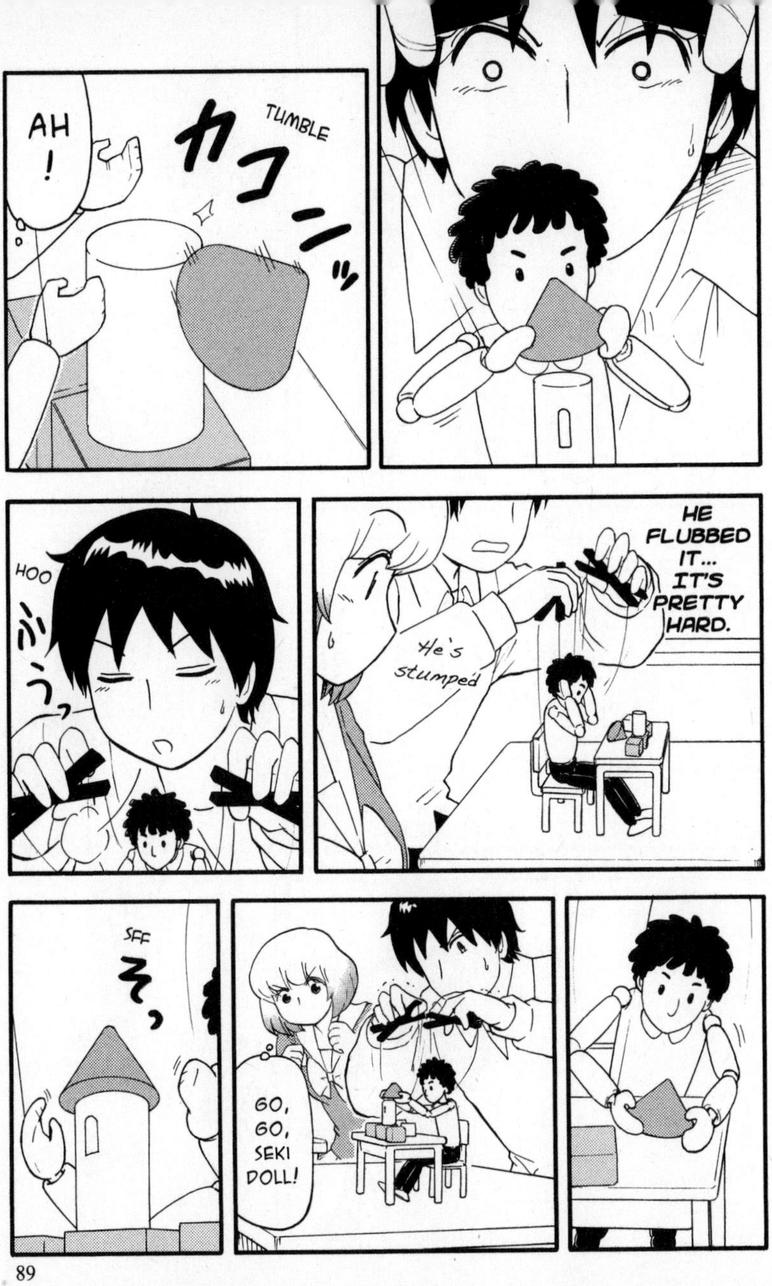
AH!
TUMBLE
カコンッ
HE FLUBBED IT... IT'S PRETTY HARD.
He's stumped
HOO
ふうっ
GO, GO, SEKI DOLL!
SFF
そっ

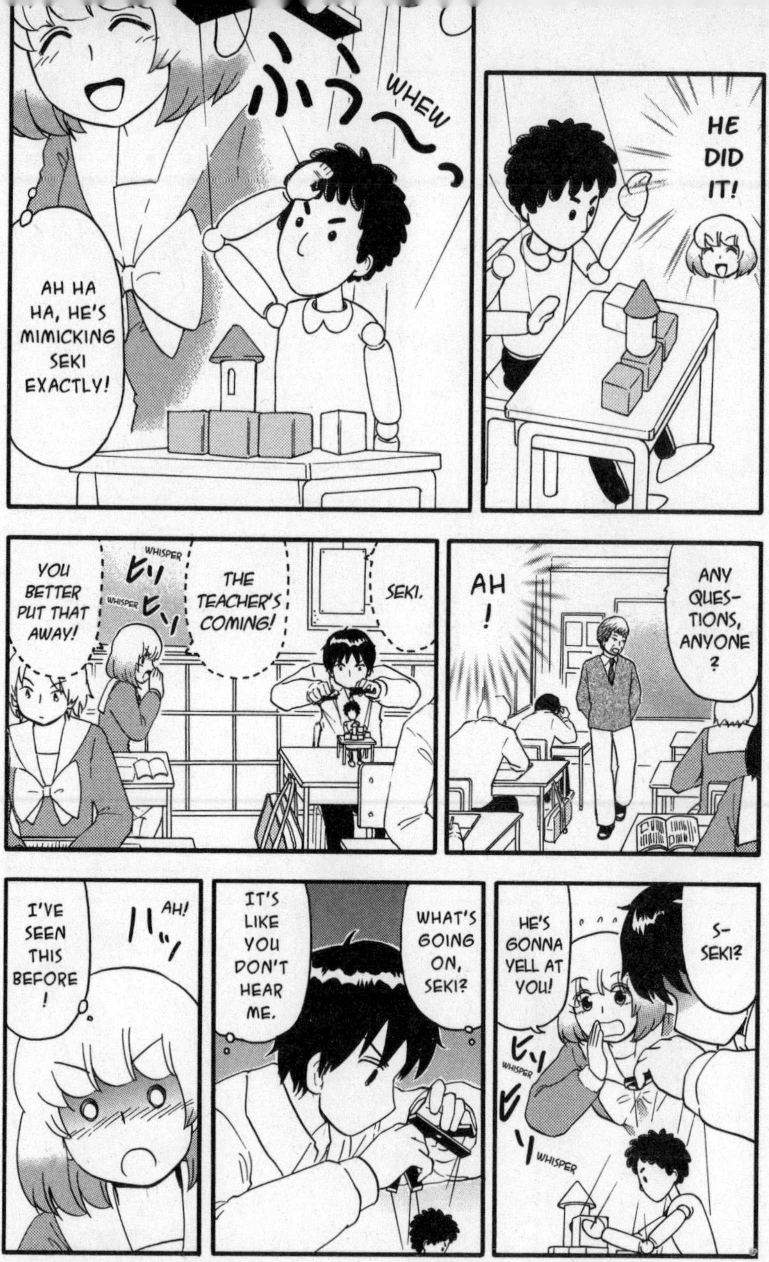
HE DID IT!
WHEW
AH HA HA, HE'S MIMICKING SEKI EXACTLY!
AH!
ANY QUESTIONS, ANYONE?
SEKI.
THE TEACHER'S COMING!
WHISPER
WHISPER
YOU BETTER PUT THAT AWAY!
S-SEKI?
HE'S GONNA YELL AT YOU!
WHISPER
WHISPER
WHAT'S GOING ON, SEKI?
IT'S LIKE YOU DON'T HEAR ME.
AH!
I'VE SEEN THIS BEFORE!

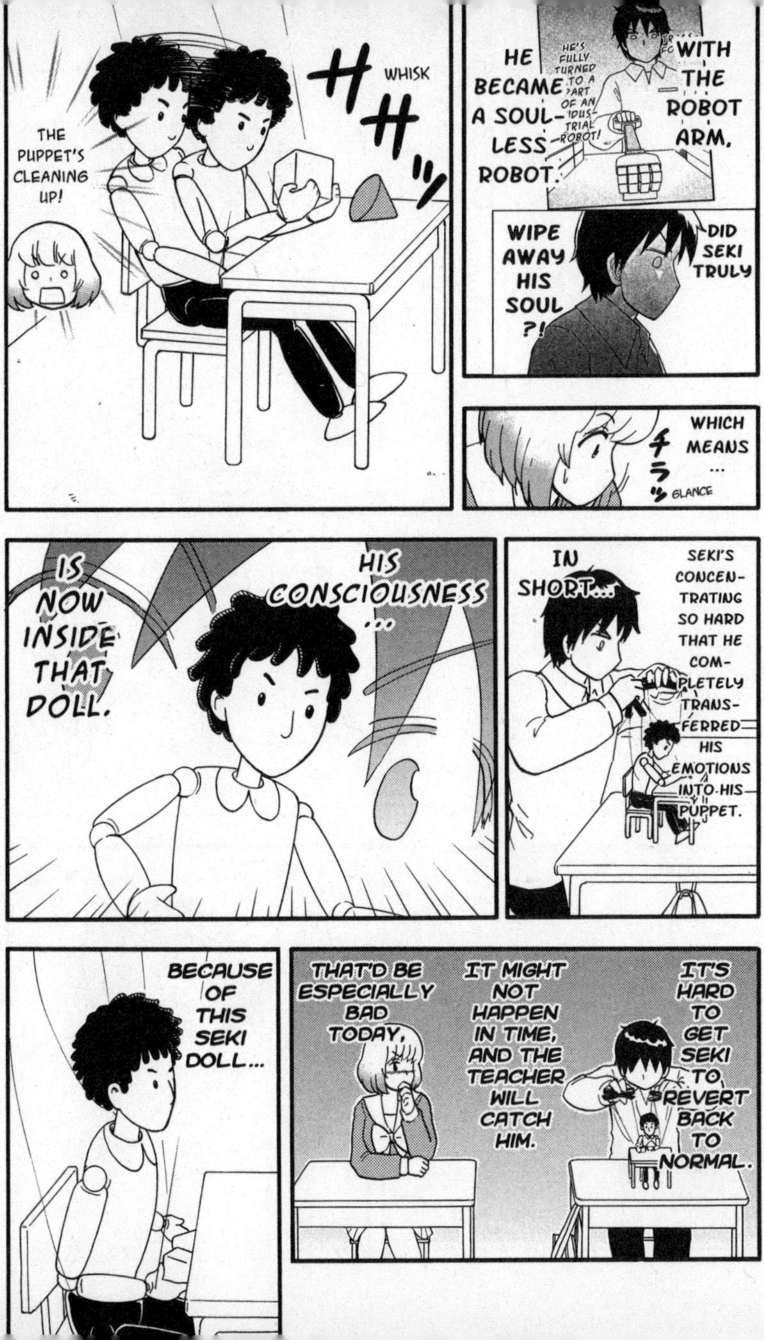
WITH THE ROBOT ARM,
HE BECAME A SOUL-LESS ROBOT.
HE'S FULLY TURNED TO A PART OF AN INDUS-TRIAL ROBOT!
DID SEKI TRULY
WIPE AWAY HIS SOUL?!
WHICH MEANS...
GLANCE
WHISK
THE PUPPET'S CLEANING UP!
IN SHORT...
SEKI'S CONCEN-TRATING SO HARD THAT HE COM-PLETELY TRANS-FERRED HIS EMOTIONS INTO HIS PUPPET.
HIS CONSCIOUSNESS...
IS NOW INSIDE THAT DOLL.
IT'S HARD TO GET SEKI TO REVERT BACK TO NORMAL.
IT MIGHT NOT HAPPEN IN TIME, AND THE TEACHER WILL CATCH HIM.
THAT'D BE ESPECIALLY BAD TODAY,
BECAUSE OF THIS SEKI DOLL...

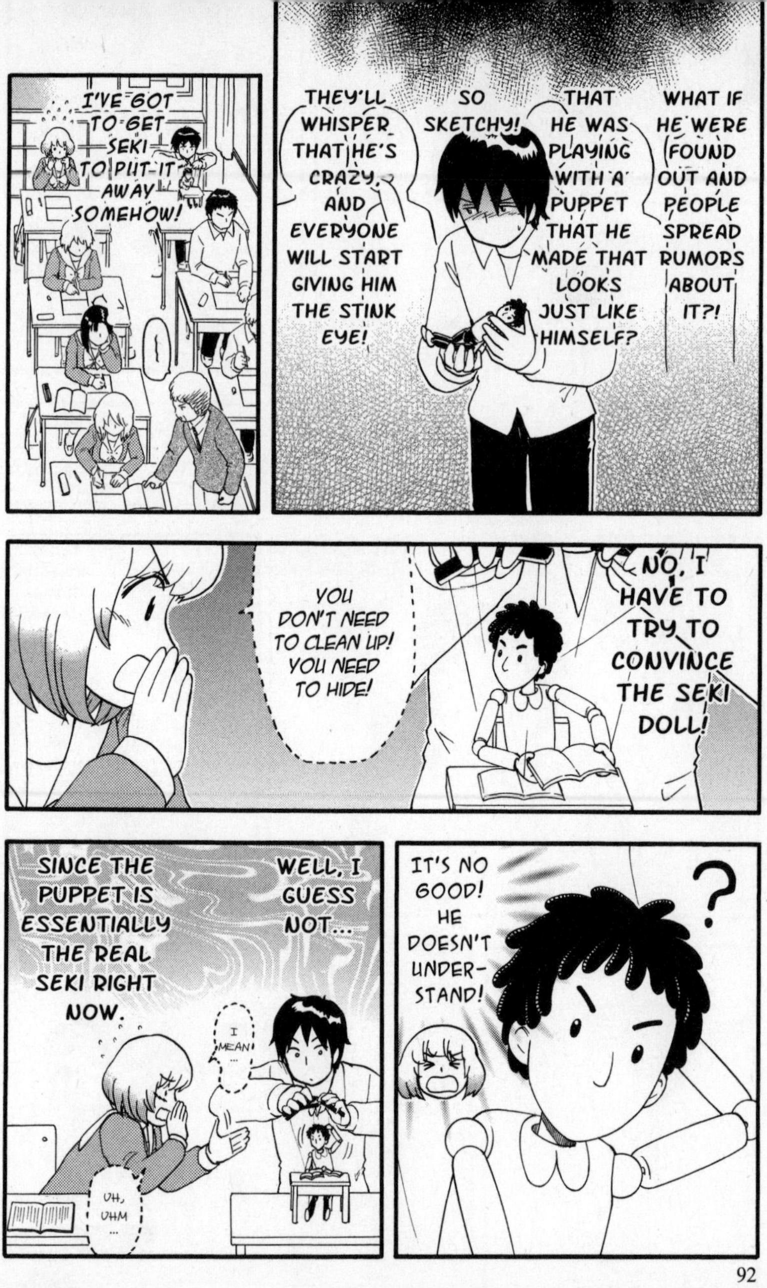
WHAT IF HE WERE FOUND OUT AND PEOPLE SPREAD RUMORS ABOUT IT?!
THAT HE WAS PLAYING WITH A PUPPET THAT HE MADE THAT LOOKS JUST LIKE HIMSELF?
SO SKETCHY!
THEY'LL WHISPER THAT HE'S CRAZY, AND EVERYONE WILL START GIVING HIM THE STINK EYE!
I'VE GOT TO GET SEKI TO PUT IT AWAY SOMEHOW!
NO, I HAVE TO TRY TO CONVINCE THE SEKI DOLL!
YOU DON'T NEED TO CLEAN UP! YOU NEED TO HIDE!
IT'S NO GOOD! HE DOESN'T UNDER-STAND!
WELL, I GUESS NOT...
SINCE THE PUPPET IS ESSENTIALLY THE REAL SEKI RIGHT NOW.
I MEAN ...
UH, UHM ...

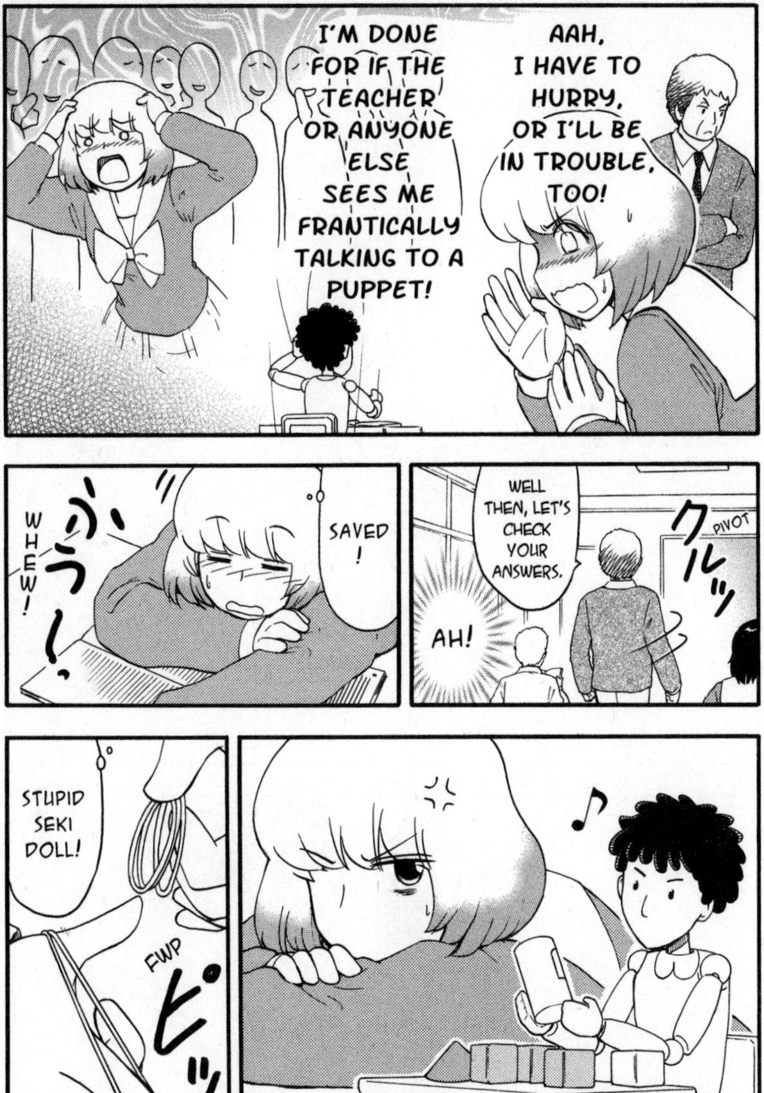
AAH, I HAVE TO HURRY, OR I'LL BE IN TROUBLE, TOO!
I'M DONE FOR IF THE TEACHER OR ANYONE ELSE SEES ME FRANTICALLY TALKING TO A PUPPET!
WELL THEN, LET'S CHECK YOUR ANSWERS.
PIVOT
AH!
SAVED!
WHEW!
STUPID SEKI DOLL!
FWP

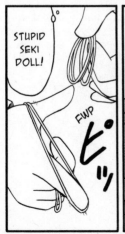

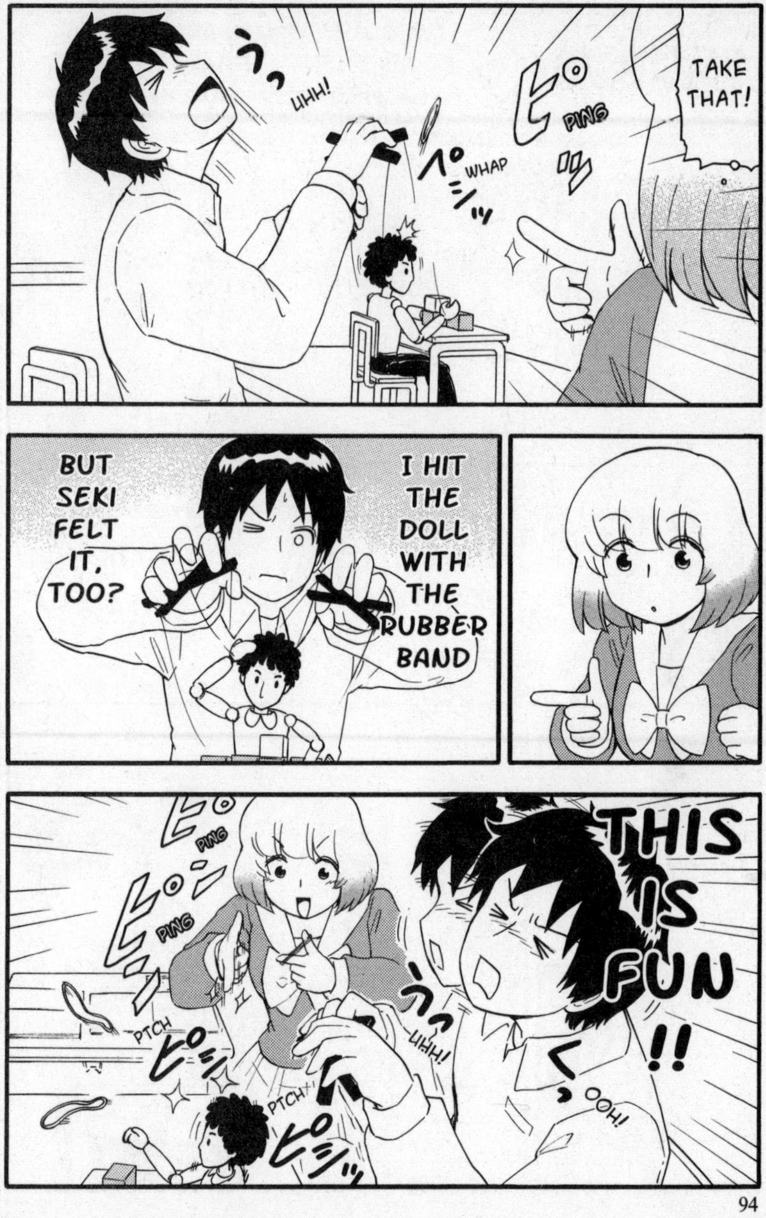
TAKE THAT!
ピッ PING
ペシッ WHAP
うっ UHH!
I HIT THE DOLL WITH THE RUBBER BAND
BUT SEKI FELT IT, TOO?
THIS IS FUN!!
く OOH!
うっ UHH!
ピッ PING
ピッ PING
ピシッ PTCH
ピシッ PTCH

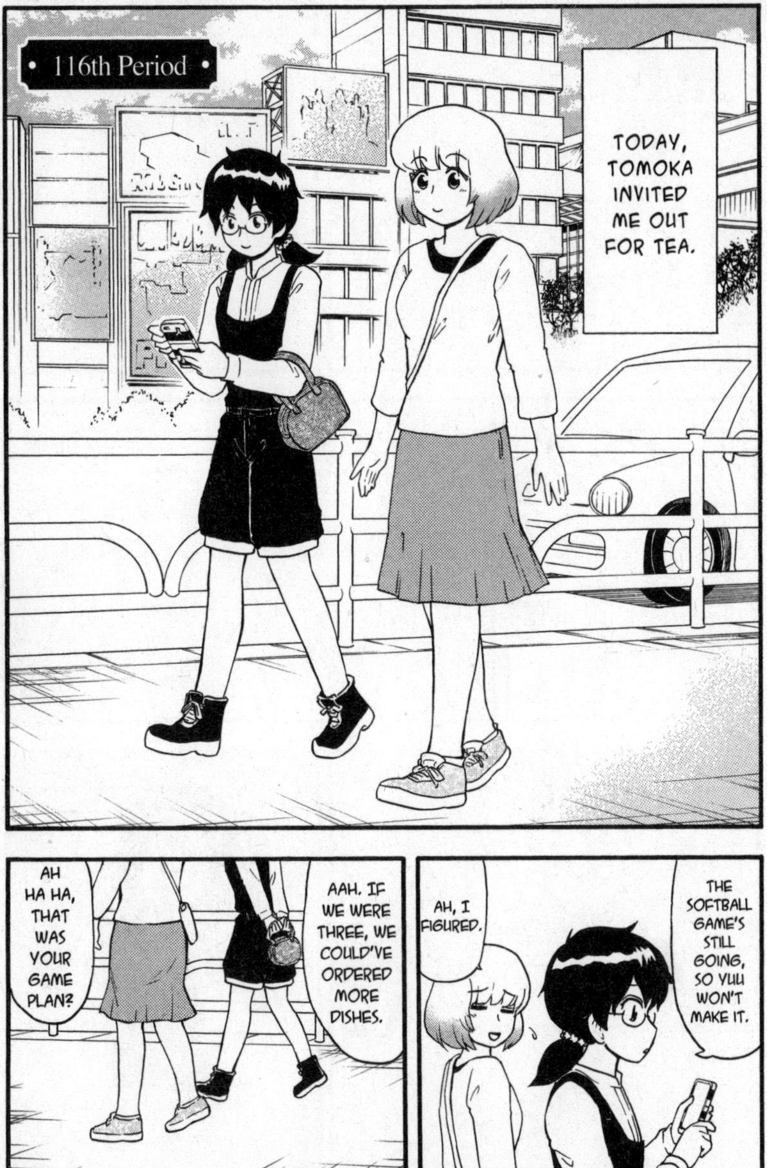

116th Period
TODAY, TOMOKA INVITED ME OUT FOR TEA.
THE SOFTBALL GAME'S STILL GOING, SO YUU WON'T MAKE IT.
AH, I FIGURED.
AAH. IF WE WERE THREE, WE COULD'VE ORDERED MORE DISHES.
AH HA HA, THAT WAS YOUR GAME PLAN?

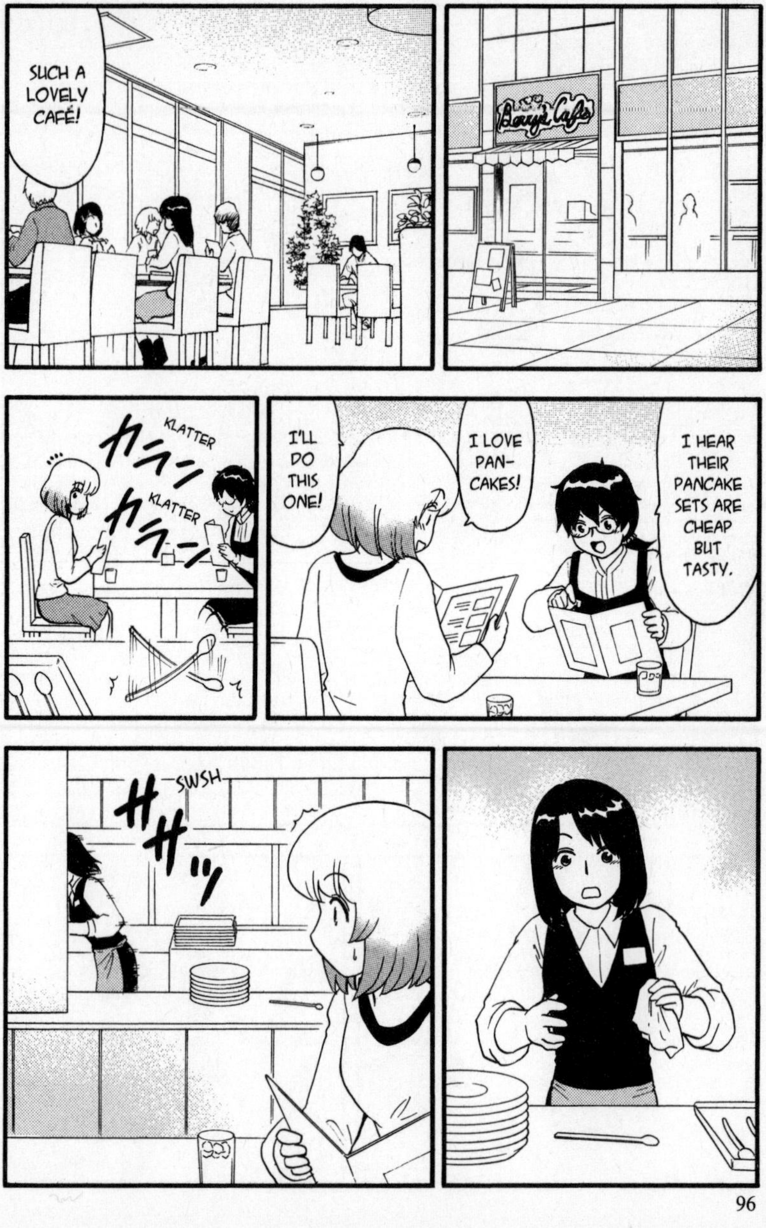
SUCH A LOVELY CAFÉ!
I HEAR THEIR PANCAKE SETS ARE CHEAP BUT TASTY.
I LOVE PAN-CAKES!
I'LL DO THIS ONE!
カラン
KLATTER
カラーン
KLATTER
ザザッ
SWSH

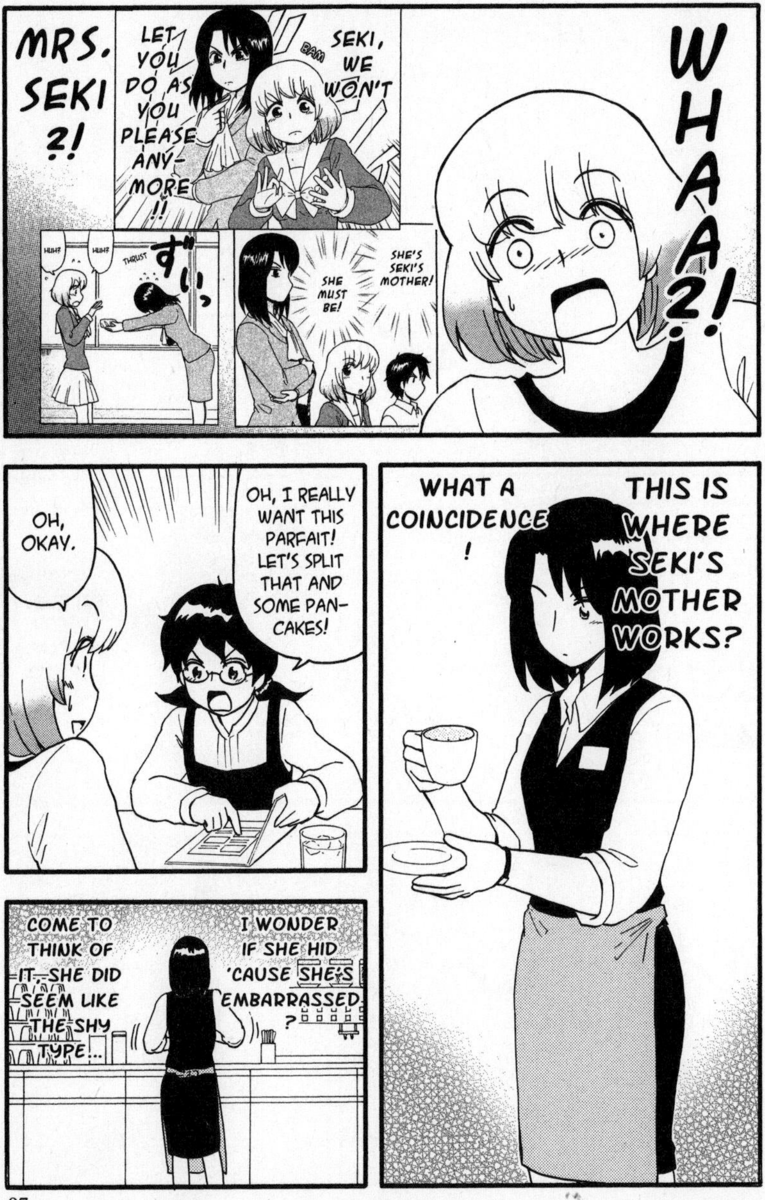
WHAA?!
SEKI, WE WON'T
BAM
LET YOU DO AS YOU PLEASE ANYMORE!!
MRS. SEKI?!
SHE'S SEKI'S MOTHER!
SHE MUST BE!
HUH?
HUH?
THRUST
ずいっ
THIS IS WHERE SEKI'S MOTHER WORKS?
WHAT A COINCIDENCE!
OH, I REALLY WANT THIS PARFAIT! LET'S SPLIT THAT AND SOME PAN-CAKES!
OH, OKAY.
I WONDER IF SHE HID 'CAUSE SHE'S EMBARRASSED?
COME TO THINK OF IT, SHE DID SEEM LIKE THE SHY TYPE...

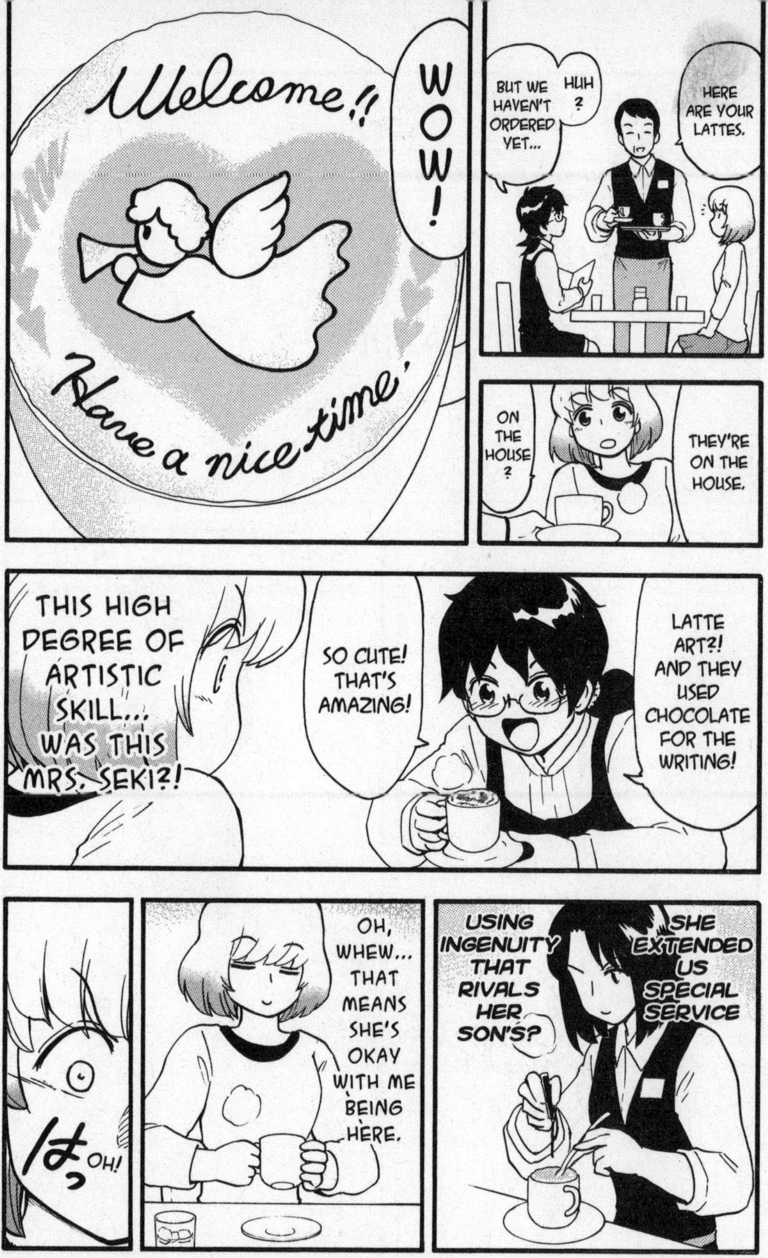
HERE ARE YOUR LATTES.
HUH?
BUT WE HAVEN'T ORDERED YET...
THEY'RE ON THE HOUSE.
ON THE HOUSE?
WOW!
Welcome!!
Have a nice time.
LATTE ART?! AND THEY USED CHOCOLATE FOR THE WRITING!
SO CUTE! THAT'S AMAZING!
THIS HIGH DEGREE OF ARTISTIC SKILL... WAS THIS MRS. SEKI?!
SHE EXTENDED US SPECIAL SERVICE
USING INGENUITY THAT RIVALS HER SON'S?
OH, WHEW... THAT MEANS SHE'S OKAY WITH ME BEING HERE.
はっ
OH!

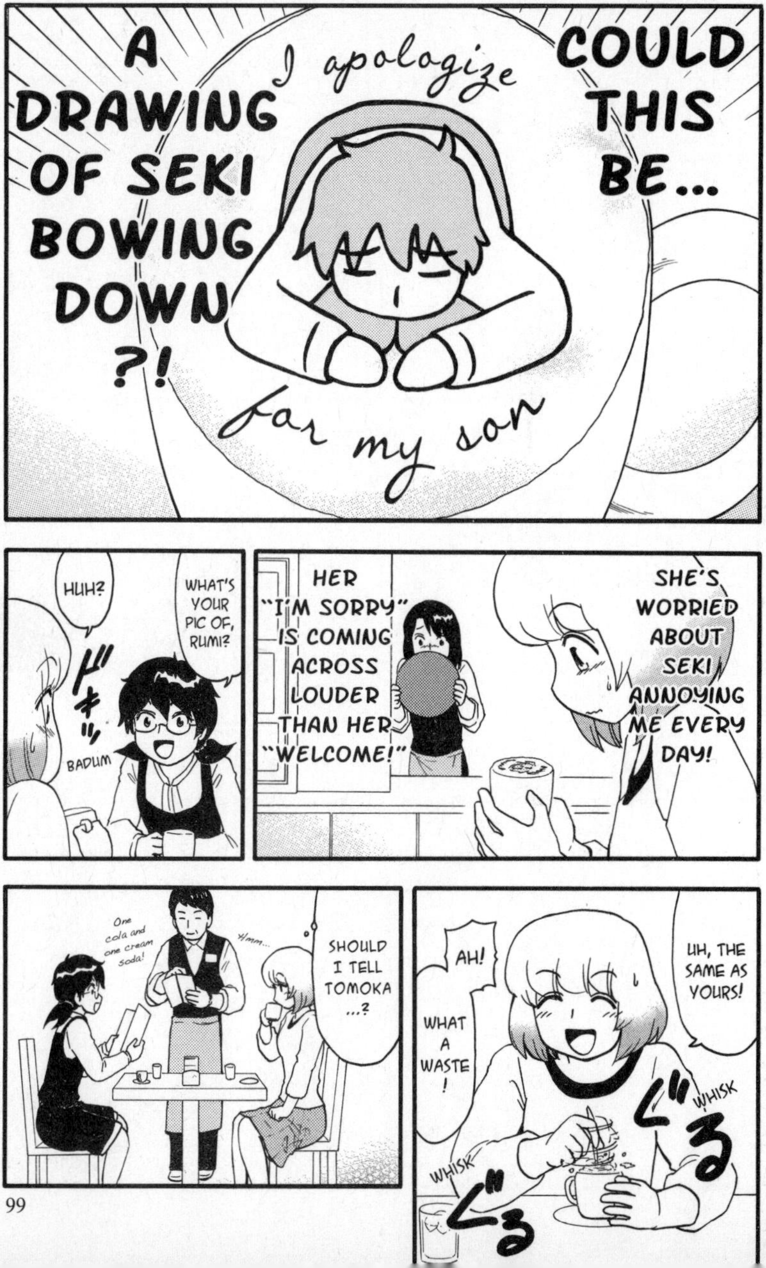
COULD THIS BE...
I apologize
A DRAWING OF SEKI BOWING DOWN ?!
for my son
SHE'S WORRIED ABOUT SEKI ANNOYING ME EVERY DAY!
HER "I'M SORRY" IS COMING ACROSS LOUDER THAN HER "WELCOME!"
WHAT'S YOUR PIC OF, RUMI?
HUH?
ドキッ
BADUM
UH, THE SAME AS YOURS!
AH!
WHAT A WASTE!
ぐる
WHISK
WHISK
ぐる
SHOULD I TELL TOMOKA ...?
Hmm...
One cola and one cream soda!

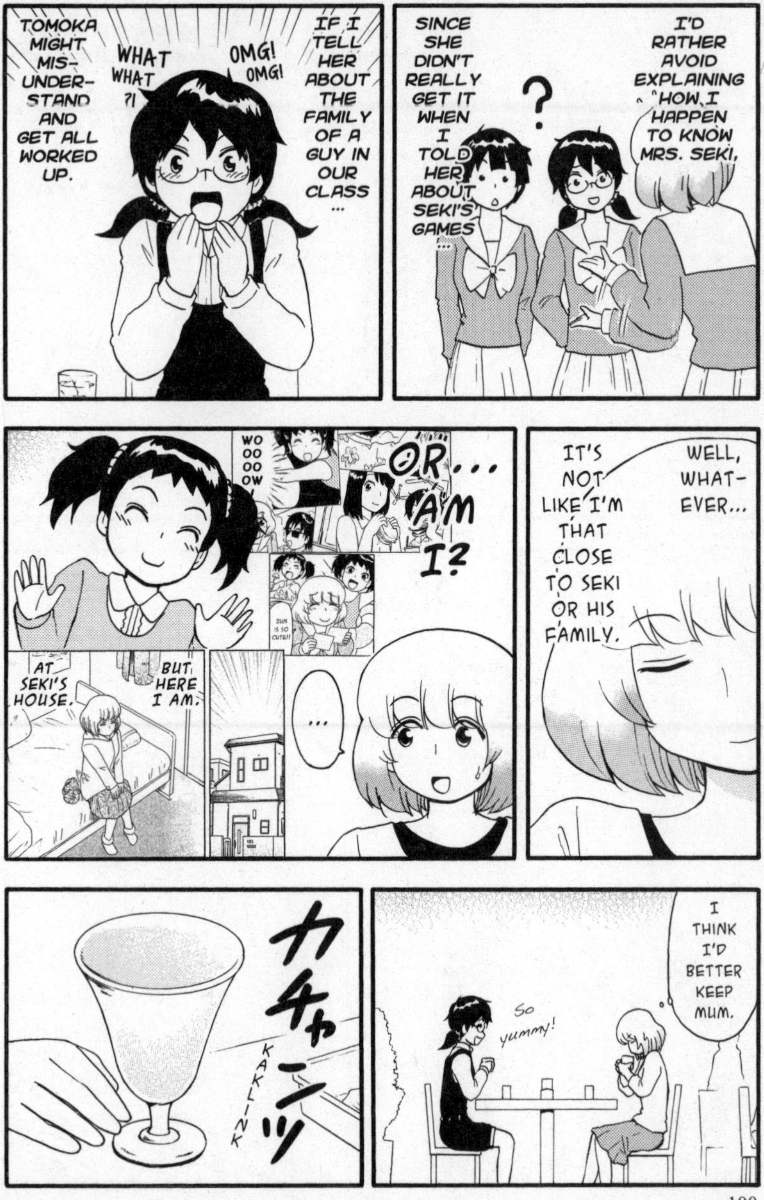
I'D RATHER AVOID EXPLAINING HOW I HAPPEN TO KNOW MRS. SEKI,
SINCE SHE DIDN'T REALLY GET IT WHEN I TOLD HER ABOUT SEKI'S GAMES...
?
IF I TELL HER ABOUT THE FAMILY OF A GUY IN OUR CLASS...
OMG! OMG!
WHAT WHAT ?!
TOMOKA MIGHT MIS-UNDERSTAND AND GET ALL WORKED UP.
WELL, WHAT-EVER...
IT'S NOT LIKE I'M THAT CLOSE TO SEKI OR HIS FAMILY.
OR... AM I?
WOOOOOOOW!
JUN IS SO CUTE!!
...
BUT HERE I AM.
AT SEKI'S HOUSE.
I THINK I'D BETTER KEEP MUM.
So yummy!
カチャーンッ
KAKLINK

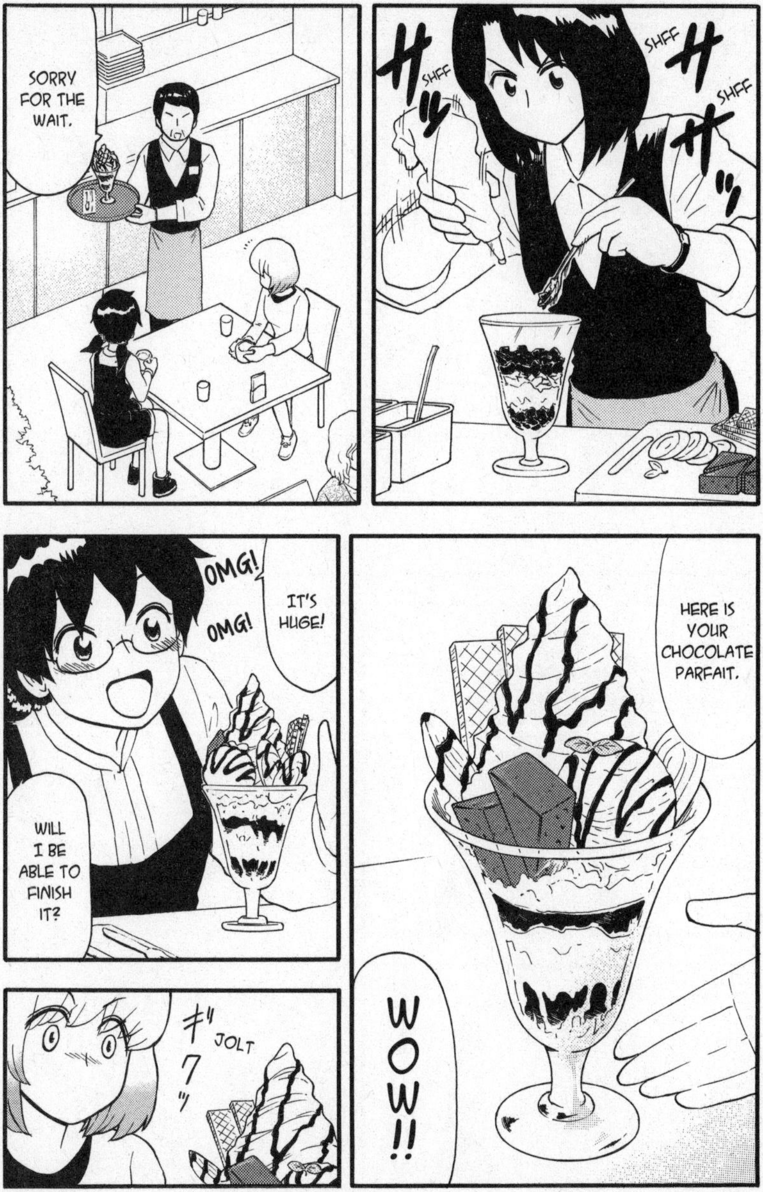
SHFF
SHFF
SHFF
SORRY FOR THE WAIT.
HERE IS YOUR CHOCOLATE PARFAIT.
WOW!!
OMG!
OMG!
IT'S HUGE!
WILL I BE ABLE TO FINISH IT?
ギクッ
JOLT

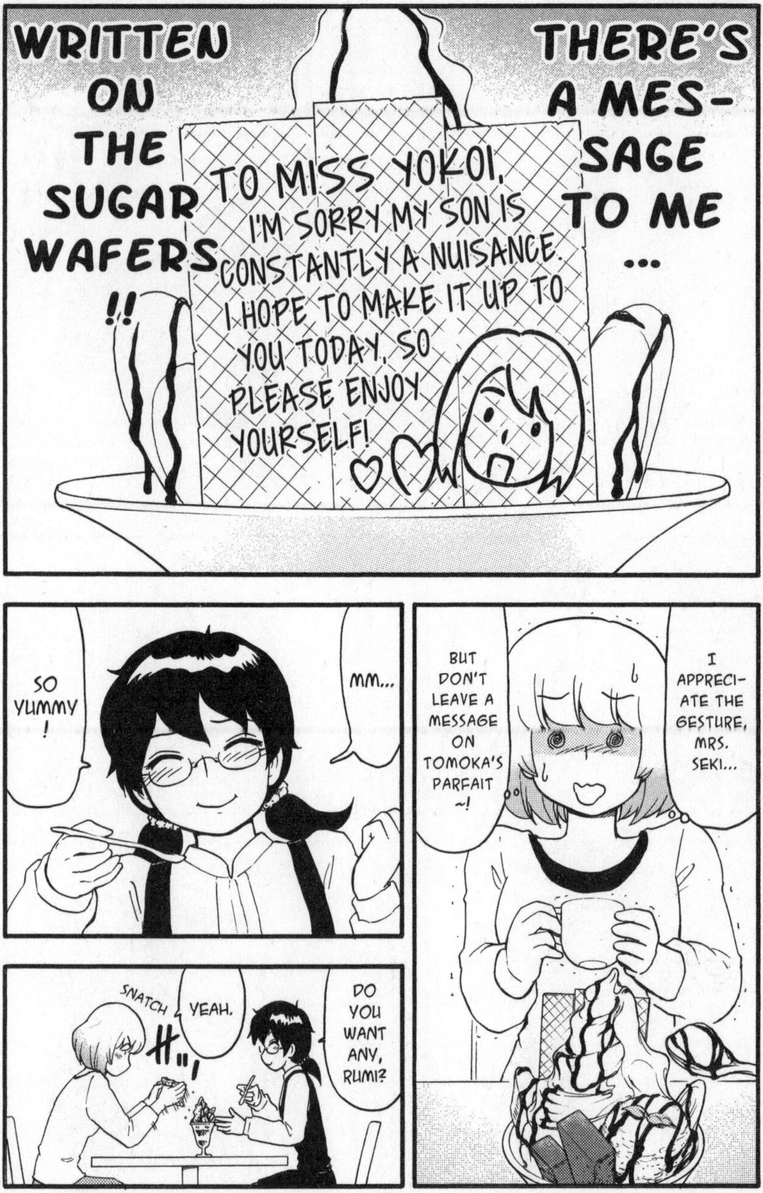
THERE'S A MES-SAGE TO ME...
WRITTEN ON THE SUGAR WAFERS!!
TO MISS YOKOI, I'M SORRY MY SON IS CONSTANTLY A NUISANCE. I HOPE TO MAKE IT UP TO YOU TODAY, SO PLEASE ENJOY YOURSELF! ♡
I APPRECIATE THE GESTURE, MRS. SEKI...
BUT DON'T LEAVE A MESSAGE ON TOMOKA'S PARFAIT~!
MM...
SO YUMMY!
DO YOU WANT ANY, RUMI?
YEAH.
SNATCH

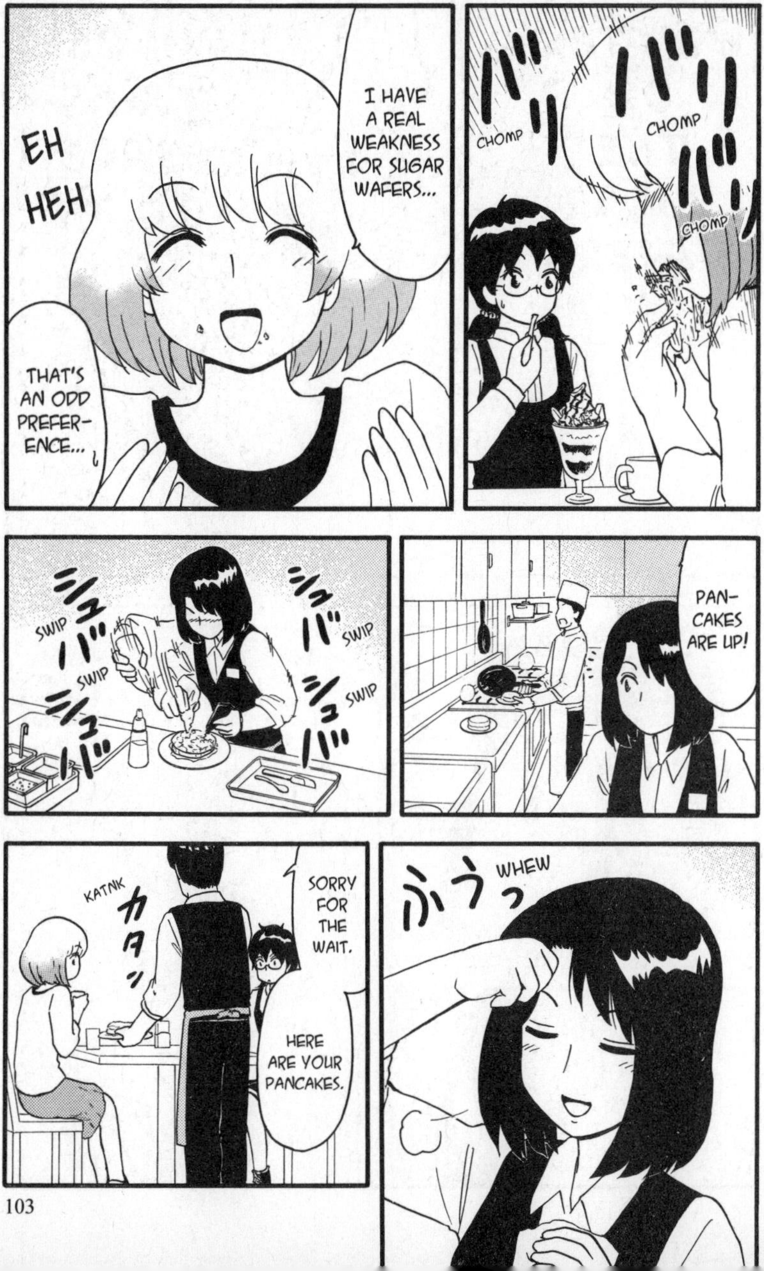
CHOMP
CHOMP
CHOMP
I HAVE A REAL WEAKNESS FOR SUGAR WAFERS...
EH HEH
THAT'S AN ODD PREFERENCE...
PAN-CAKES ARE UP!
SWIP
SWIP
SWIP
SWIP
ふうっ
WHEW
SORRY FOR THE WAIT.
HERE ARE YOUR PANCAKES.
カタン
KATNK

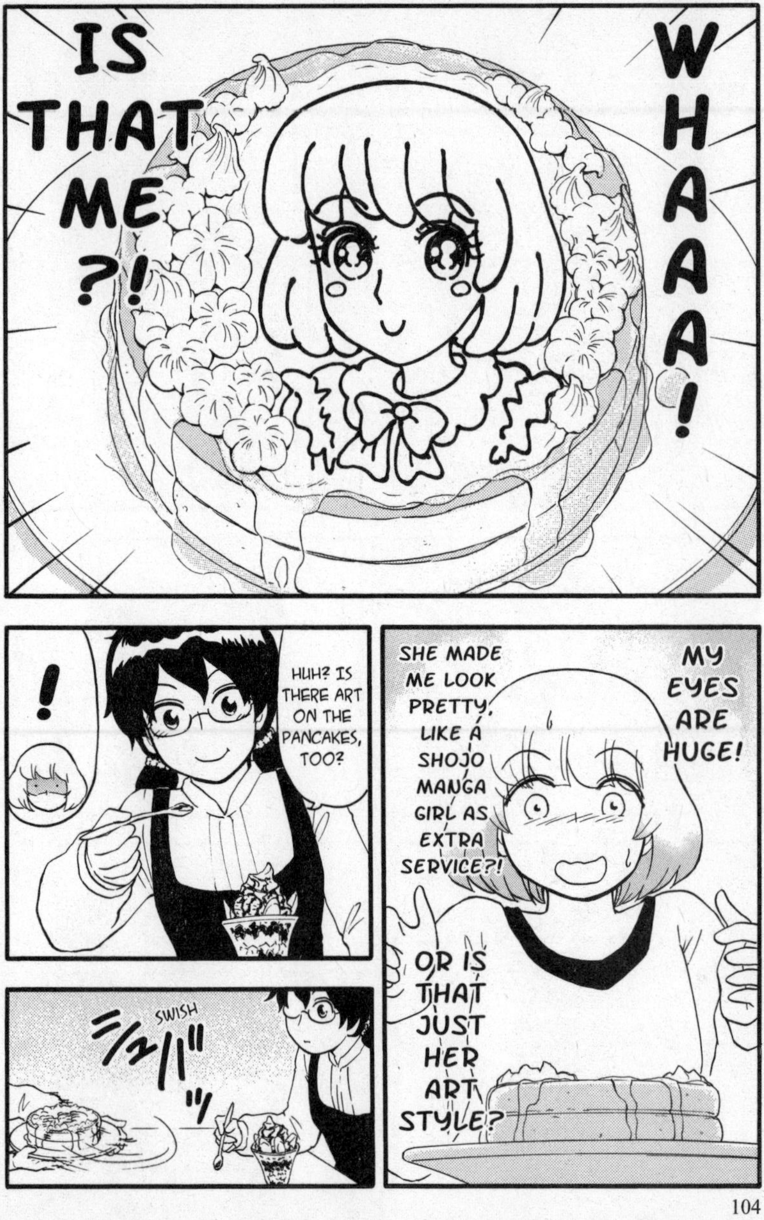
WHAAAA!
IS THAT ME?!
MY EYES ARE HUGE!
SHE MADE ME LOOK PRETTY, LIKE A SHOJO MANGA GIRL AS EXTRA SERVICE?!
OR IS THAT JUST HER ART STYLE?
HUH? IS THERE ART ON THE PANCAKES, TOO?
!
SWISH

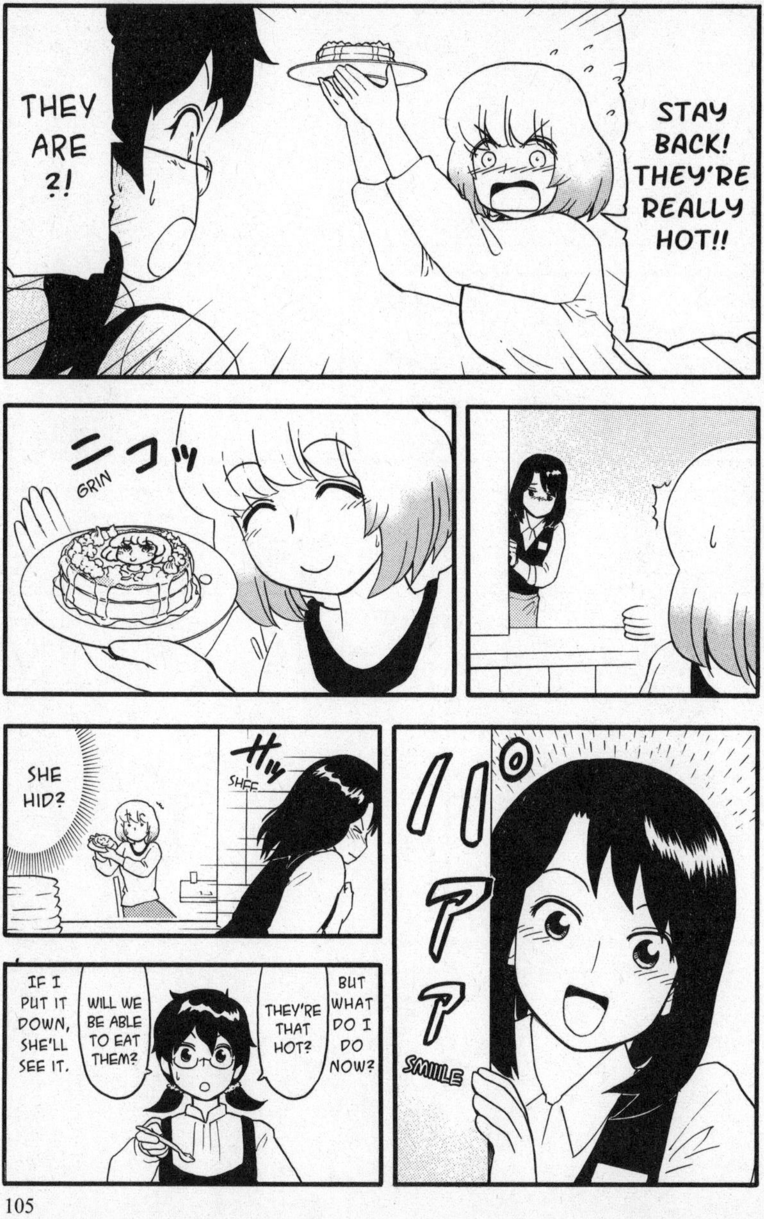
STAY BACK! THEY'RE REALLY HOT!!
THEY ARE ?!
ニコッ
GRIN
パァァ
SMIIILE
ハッ
SHFF
SHE HID?
BUT WHAT DO I DO NOW?
THEY'RE THAT HOT?
WILL WE BE ABLE TO EAT THEM?
IF I PUT IT DOWN, SHE'LL SEE IT.

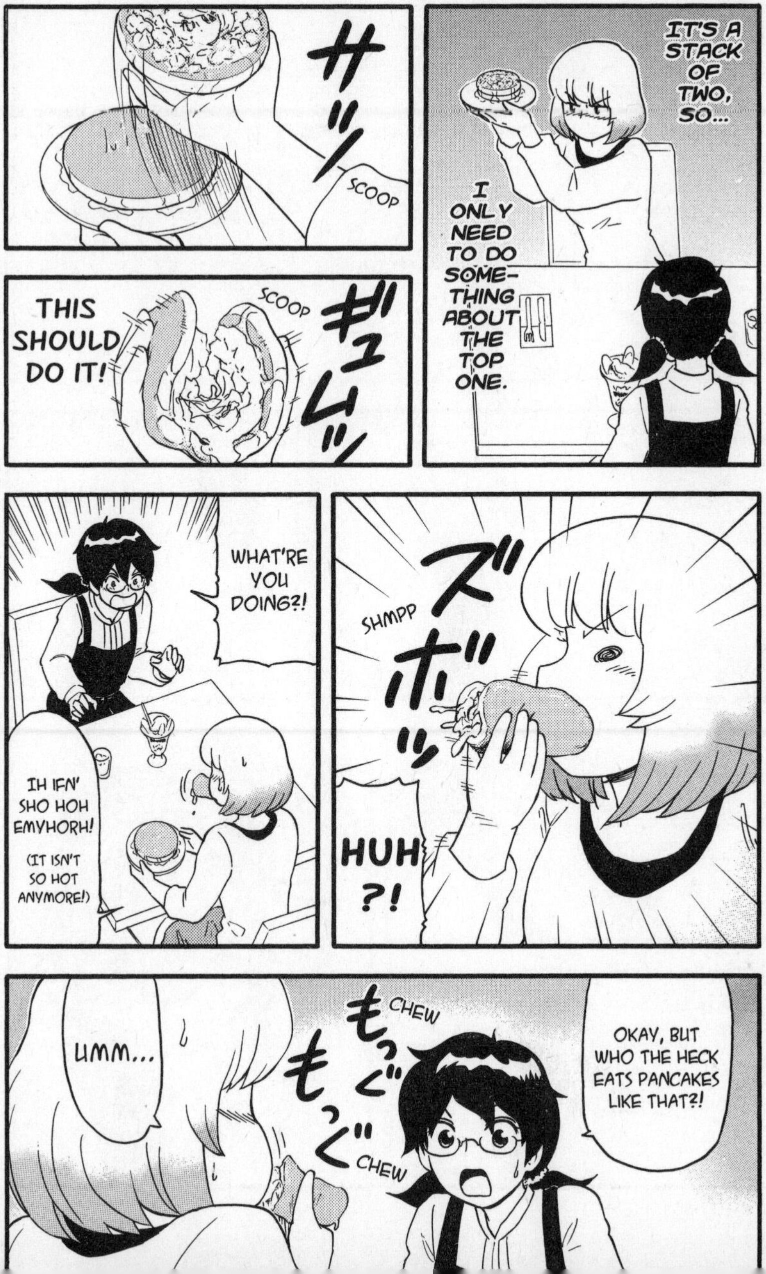
IT'S A STACK OF TWO, SO...
I ONLY NEED TO DO SOME-THING ABOUT THE TOP ONE.
サッ
SCOOP
ギュムッ
SCOOP
THIS SHOULD DO IT!
ズボッ
SHMPP
HUH?!
WHAT'RE YOU DOING?!
IH IFN' SHO HOH EMYHORH!
(IT ISN'T SO HOT ANYMORE!)
OKAY, BUT WHO THE HECK EATS PANCAKES LIKE THAT?!
もっぐ
CHEW
もっぐ
CHEW
UMM...

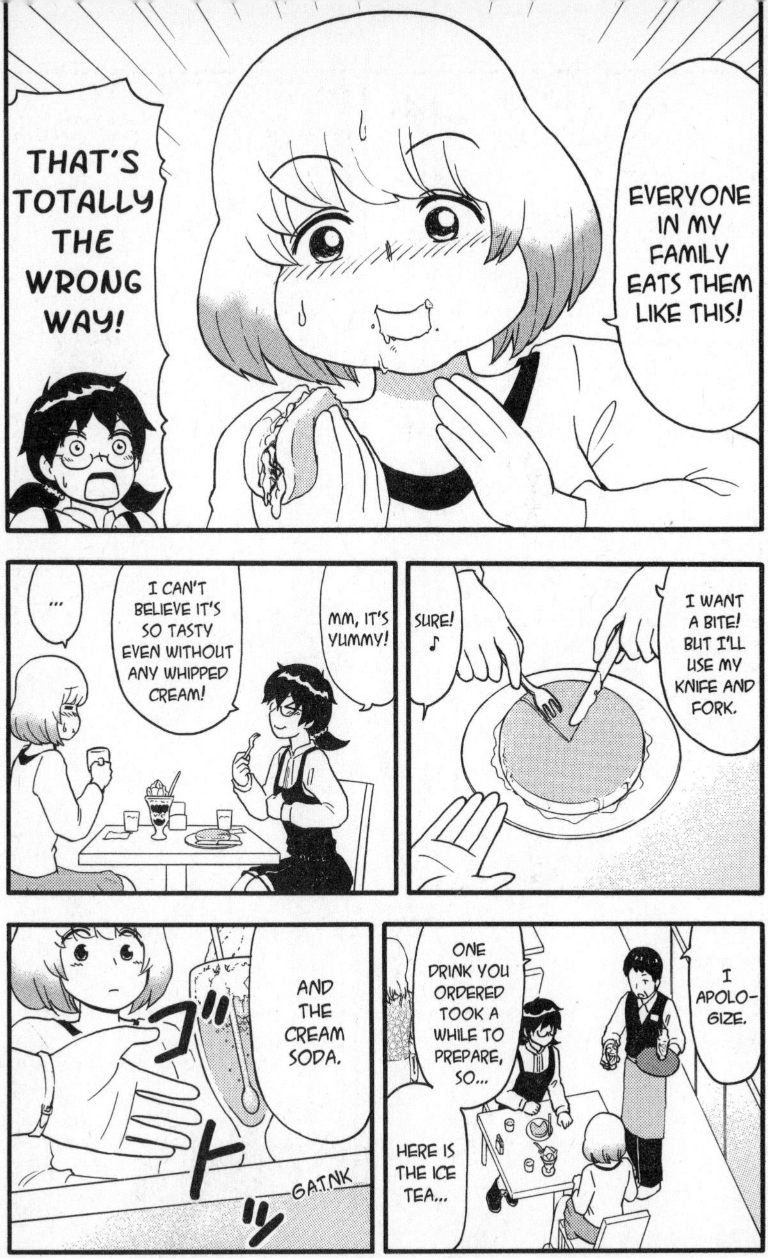
EVERYONE IN MY FAMILY EATS THEM LIKE THIS!
THAT'S TOTALLY THE WRONG WAY!
I WANT A BITE! BUT I'LL USE MY KNIFE AND FORK.
SURE! ♪
MM, IT'S YUMMY!
I CAN'T BELIEVE IT'S SO TASTY EVEN WITHOUT ANY WHIPPED CREAM!
...
I APOLOGIZE.
ONE DRINK YOU ORDERED TOOK A WHILE TO PREPARE, SO...
HERE IS THE ICE TEA...
AND THE CREAM SODA.
GATNK

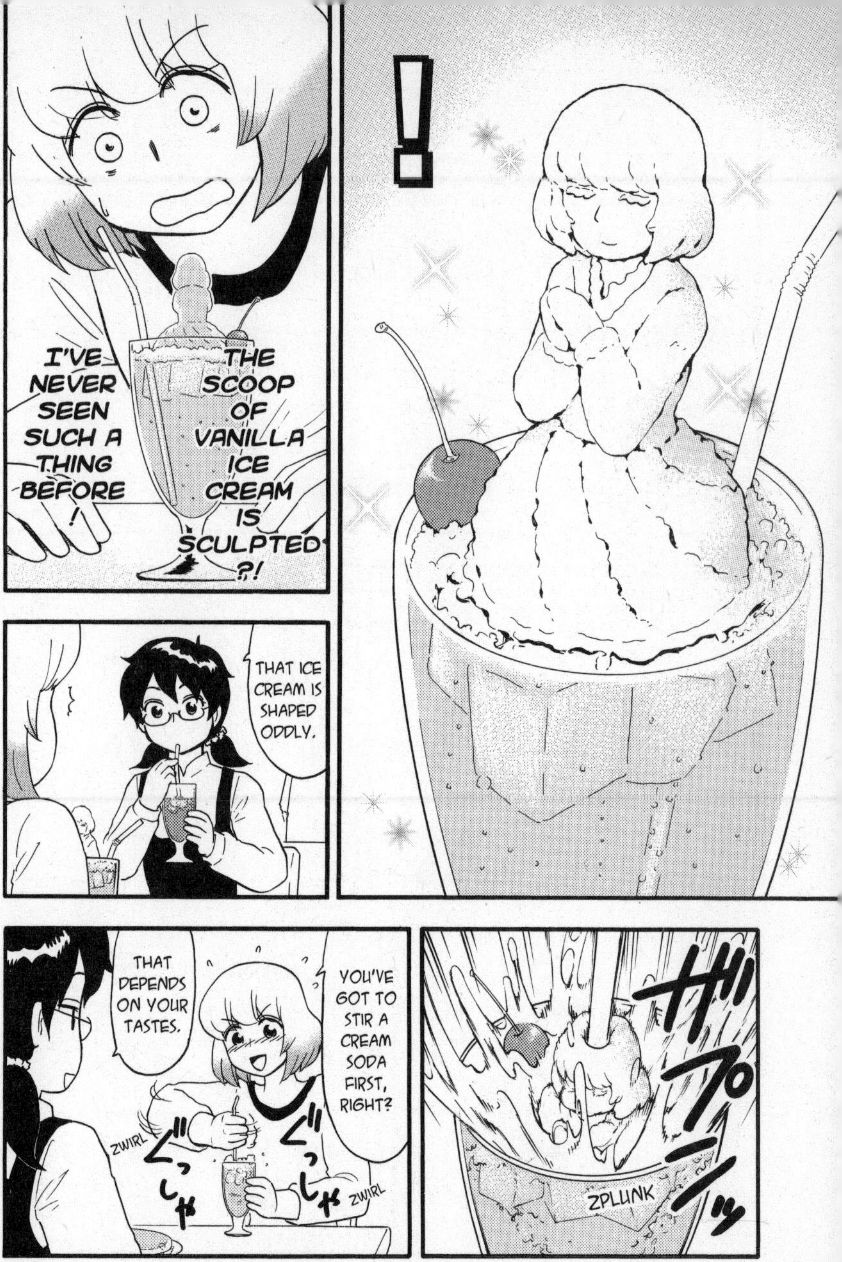
!
THE SCOOP OF VANILLA ICE CREAM IS SCULPTED?!
I'VE NEVER SEEN SUCH A THING BEFORE!
THAT ICE CREAM IS SHAPED ODDLY.
ザプンッ
ZPLUNK
YOU'VE GOT TO STIR A CREAM SODA FIRST, RIGHT?
ぐっしゃ
ZWIRL
THAT DEPENDS ON YOUR TASTES.
ぐっしゃ
ZWIRL

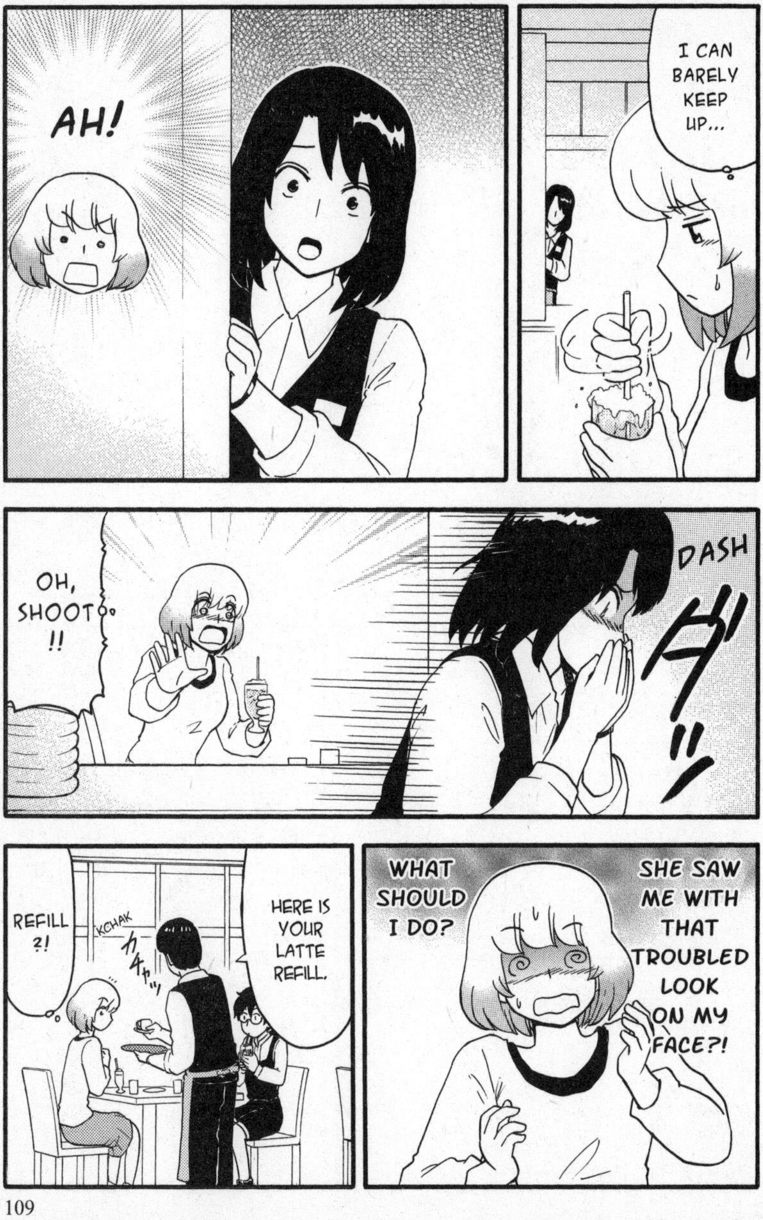
I CAN BARELY KEEP UP...
AH!
DASH
OH, SHOOT..!!
SHE SAW ME WITH THAT TROUBLED LOOK ON MY FACE?!
WHAT SHOULD I DO?
HERE IS YOUR LATTE REFILL.
KCHAK
REFILL?!

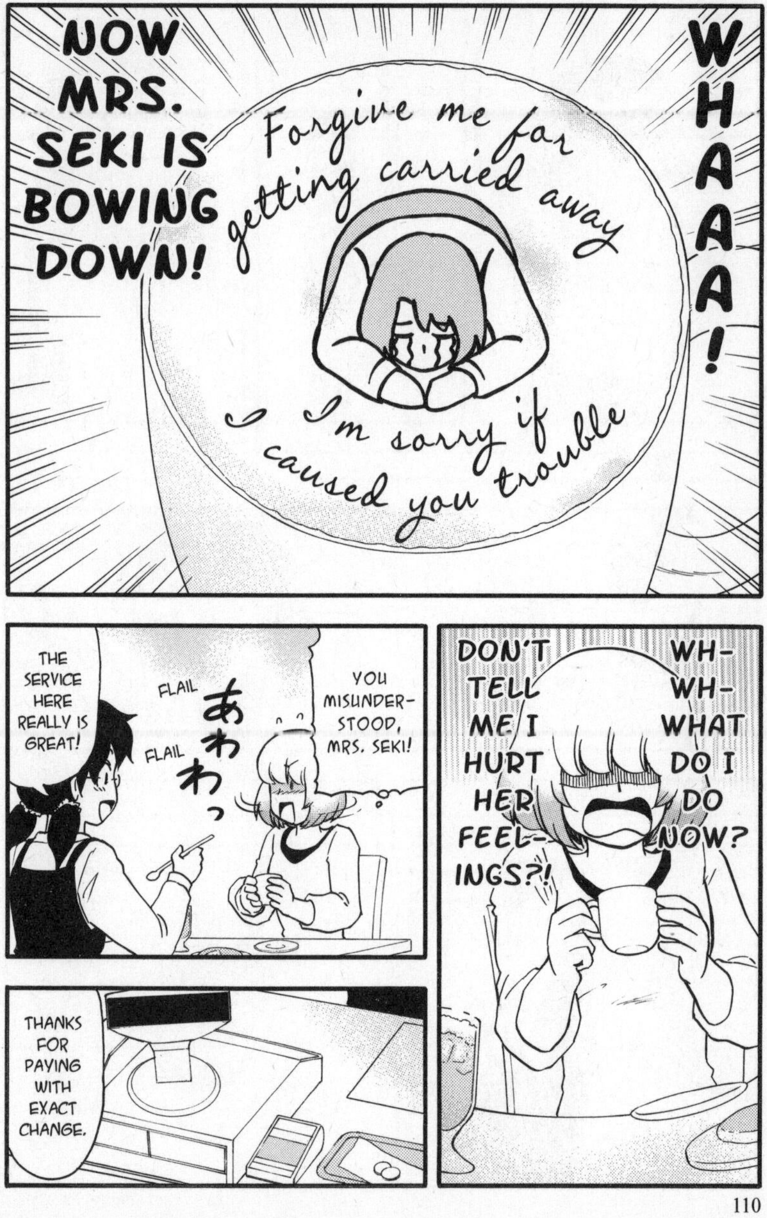
WHAAAA!
NOW MRS. SEKI IS BOWING DOWN!
Forgive me for getting carried away
I'm sorry if I caused you trouble
WH-WH-WHAT DO I DO NOW?
DON'T TELL ME I HURT HER FEEL-INGS?!
YOU MISUNDER-STOOD, MRS. SEKI!
あわわっ
FLAIL
FLAIL
THE SERVICE HERE REALLY IS GREAT!
THANKS FOR PAYING WITH EXACT CHANGE.

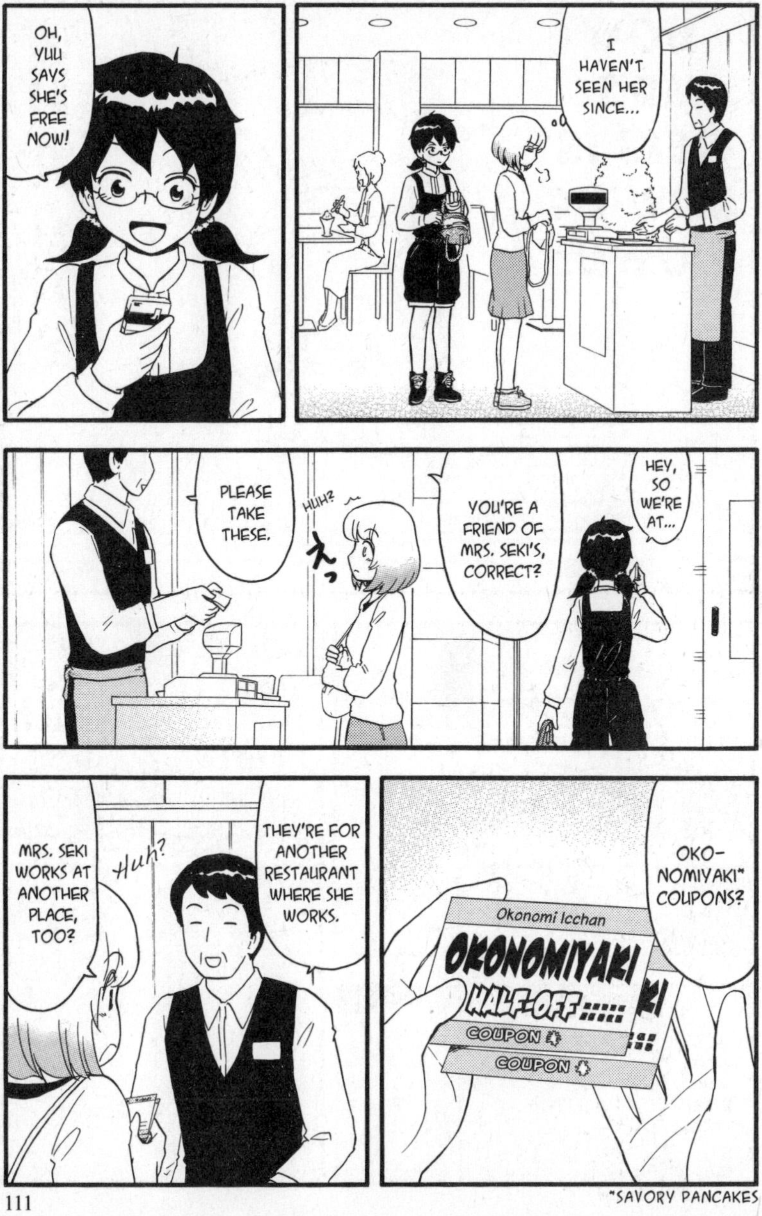

I HAVEN'T SEEN HER SINCE...
OH, YUU SAYS SHE'S FREE NOW!
HEY, SO WE'RE AT...
YOU'RE A FRIEND OF MRS. SEKI'S, CORRECT?
HUH? ~
えっ
PLEASE TAKE THESE.
OKO-NOMIYAKI* COUPONS?
Okonomi Icchan
OKONOMIYAKI
HALF-OFF
COUPON
COUPON
THEY'RE FOR ANOTHER RESTAURANT WHERE SHE WORKS.
Huh?
MRS. SEKI WORKS AT ANOTHER PLACE, TOO?

*SAVORY PANCAKES

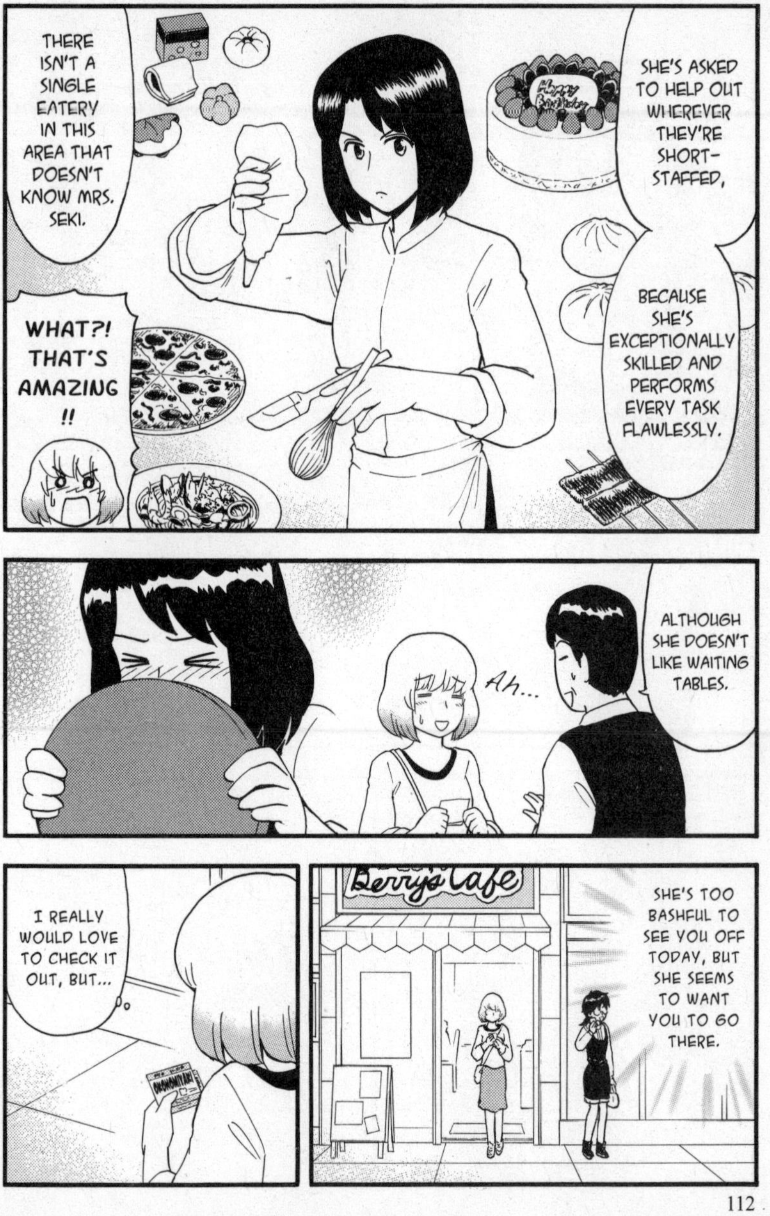
SHE'S ASKED TO HELP OUT WHEREVER THEY'RE SHORT-STAFFED,
BECAUSE SHE'S EXCEPTIONALLY SKILLED AND PERFORMS EVERY TASK FLAWLESSLY.
THERE ISN'T A SINGLE EATERY IN THIS AREA THAT DOESN'T KNOW MRS. SEKI.
WHAT?! THAT'S AMAZING !!
ALTHOUGH SHE DOESN'T LIKE WAITING TABLES.
Ah...
Berry's Cafe
SHE'S TOO BASHFUL TO SEE YOU OFF TODAY, BUT SHE SEEMS TO WANT YOU TO GO THERE.
I REALLY WOULD LOVE TO CHECK IT OUT, BUT...

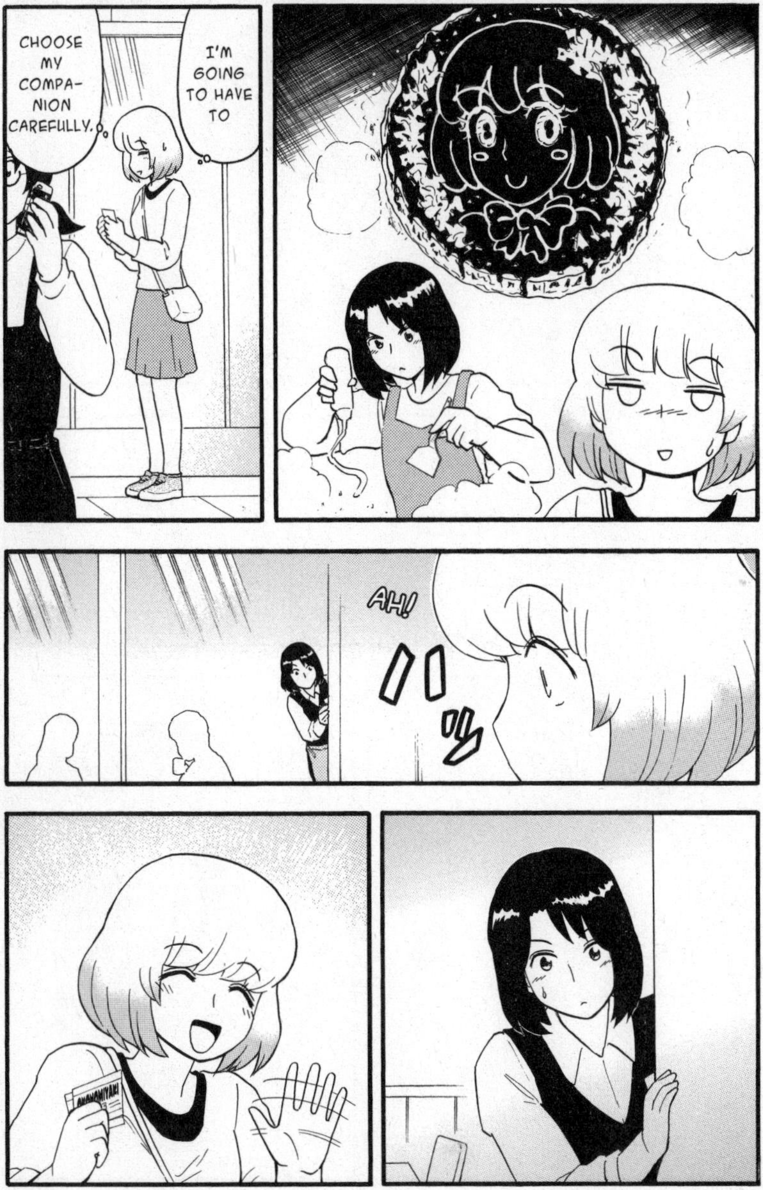
I'M GOING TO HAVE TO
CHOOSE MY COMPANION CAREFULLY.
AH!

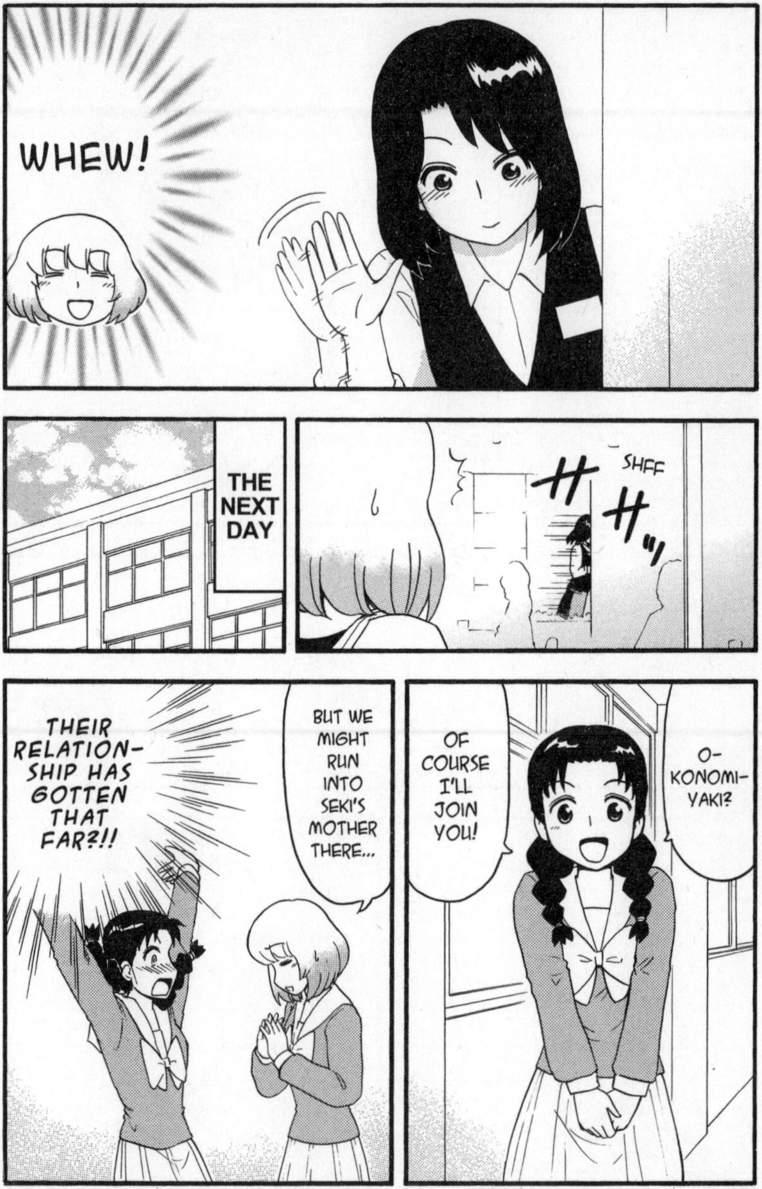
WHEW!
SHFF
THE NEXT DAY
O-KONOMI-YAKI?
OF COURSE I'LL JOIN YOU!
BUT WE MIGHT RUN INTO SEKI'S MOTHER THERE...
THEIR RELATION-SHIP HAS GOTTEN THAT FAR?!!

My Neighbor Seki

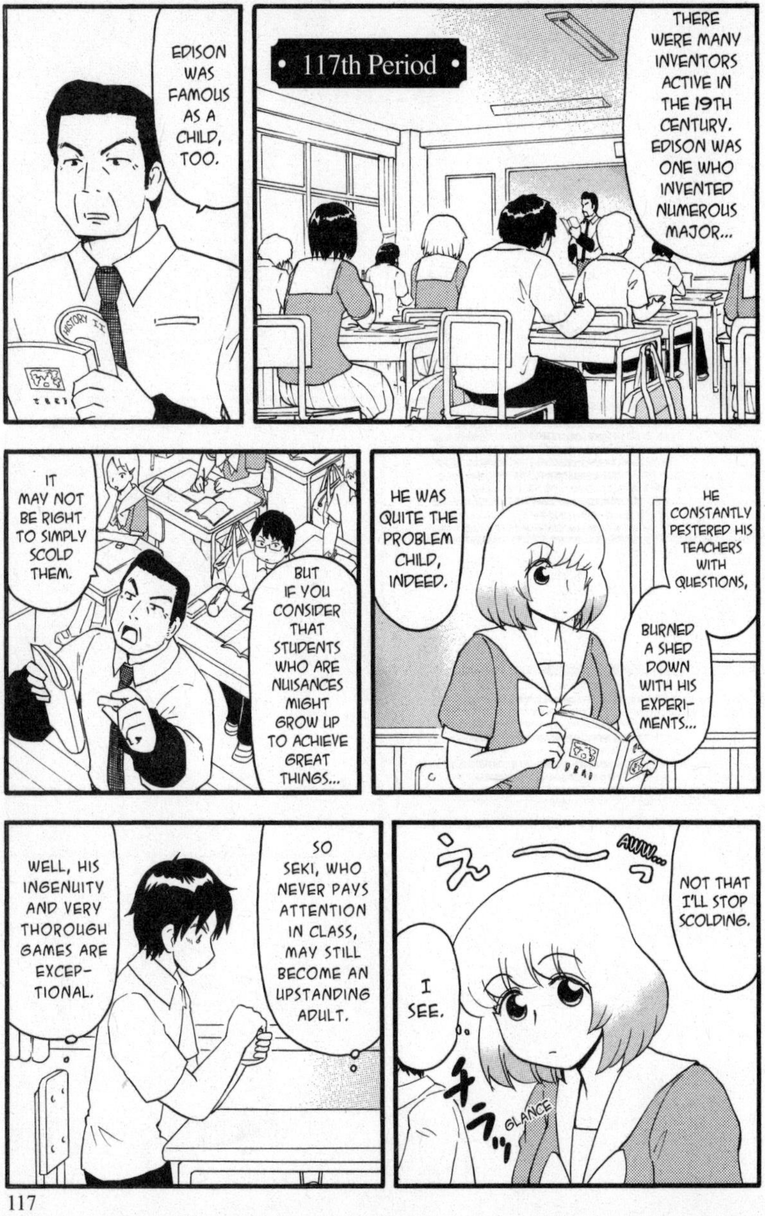

117th Period
THERE WERE MANY INVENTORS ACTIVE IN THE 19TH CENTURY. EDISON WAS ONE WHO INVENTED NUMEROUS MAJOR...
EDISON WAS FAMOUS AS A CHILD, TOO.
HE CONSTANTLY PESTERED HIS TEACHERS WITH QUESTIONS,
BURNED A SHED DOWN WITH HIS EXPERIMENTS...
HE WAS QUITE THE PROBLEM CHILD, INDEED.
BUT IF YOU CONSIDER THAT STUDENTS WHO ARE NUISANCES MIGHT GROW UP TO ACHIEVE GREAT THINGS...
IT MAY NOT BE RIGHT TO SIMPLY SCOLD THEM.
AWW...
NOT THAT I'LL STOP SCOLDING.
I SEE.
GLANCE
SO SEKI, WHO NEVER PAYS ATTENTION IN CLASS, MAY STILL BECOME AN UPSTANDING ADULT.
WELL, HIS INGENUITY AND VERY THOROUGH GAMES ARE EXCEP-TIONAL.

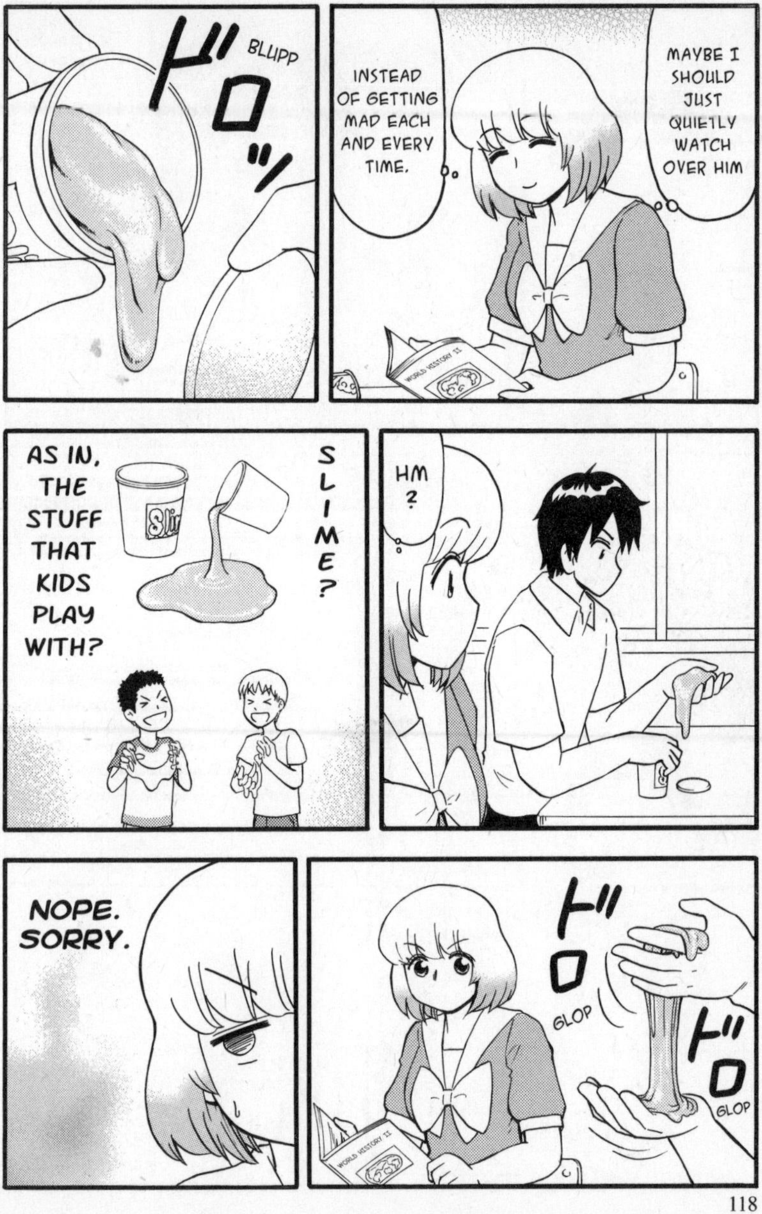
MAYBE I SHOULD JUST QUIETLY WATCH OVER HIM
INSTEAD OF GETTING MAD EACH AND EVERY TIME.
WORLD HISTORY II
ドロッ
BLUPP
HM?
SLIME?
AS IN, THE STUFF THAT KIDS PLAY WITH?
ドロ
GLOP
ドロ
GLOP
WORLD HISTORY II
NOPE. SORRY.

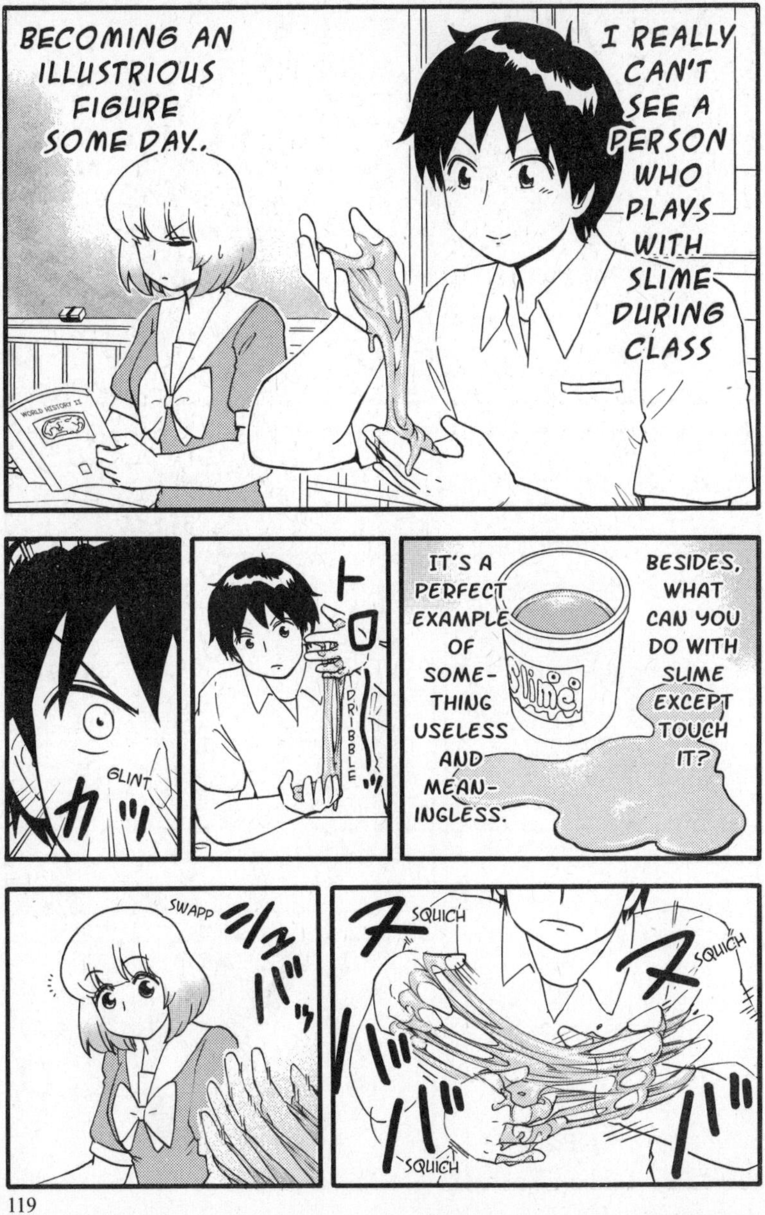
I REALLY CAN'T SEE A PERSON WHO PLAYS WITH SLIME DURING CLASS
BECOMING AN ILLUSTRIOUS FIGURE SOME DAY..
BESIDES, WHAT CAN YOU DO WITH SLIME EXCEPT TOUCH IT?
Slime
IT'S A PERFECT EXAMPLE OF SOME-THING USELESS AND MEAN-INGLESS.
トロ
DRIBBLE
ッ
GLINT
カッ
ヌ
SQUICH
ヌ
SQUICH
バ
バ
バ
SQUICH
SWAPP
シュバッ

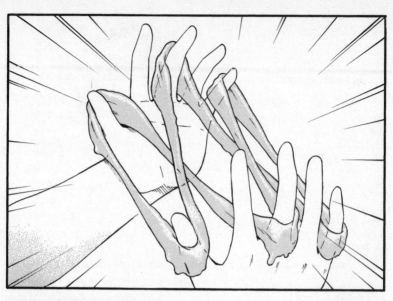

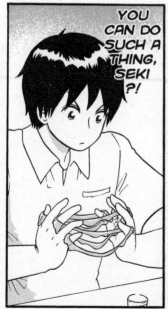

COULD THAT BE...
CAT'S CRADLE?!
HUH? BUT SLIME IS ALL RUNNY!!
YET HE STRETCHED IT OUT INTO STRINGS...?!
YOU CAN DO SUCH A THING, SEKI?!

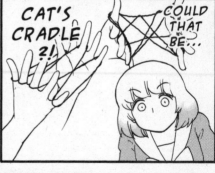

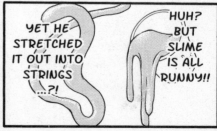

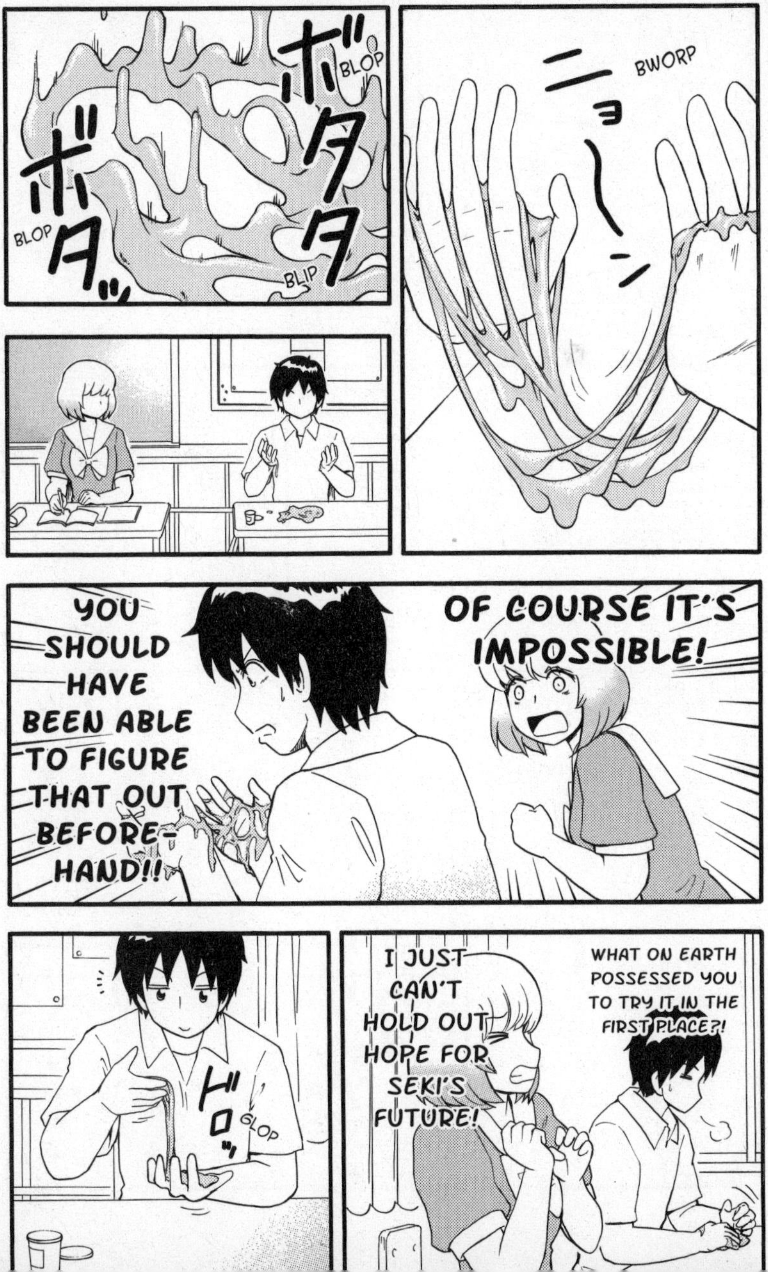

BWORP
BLOP
BLOP
BLIP
OF COURSE IT'S IMPOSSIBLE!
YOU SHOULD HAVE BEEN ABLE TO FIGURE THAT OUT BEFORE-HAND!!
WHAT ON EARTH POSSESSED YOU TO TRY IT IN THE FIRST PLACE?!
I JUST CAN'T HOLD OUT HOPE FOR SEKI'S FUTURE!
GLOP

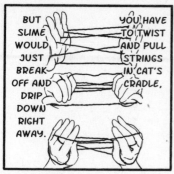

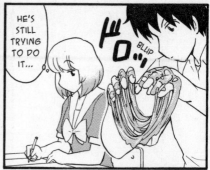

HE'S STILL TRYING TO DO IT...
BLUP
YOU HAVE TO TWIST AND PULL STRINGS IN CAT'S CRADLE.
BUT SLIME WOULD JUST BREAK OFF AND DRIP DOWN RIGHT AWAY.
HE LOOKS SO SERI- OUS.
AH, PERHAPS SEKI WANTS TO FIND EVEN ONE USE FOR SLIME?
IN WHICH CASE, WHAT HE'S DOING IS MEANINGFUL?
BLOP
BLIP
SPINN
SPINN
DANGLE
HM ?

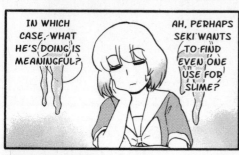

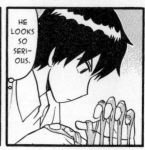

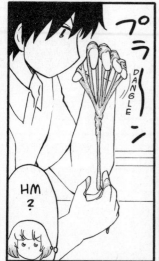

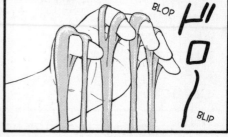

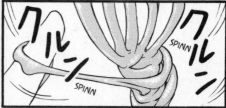

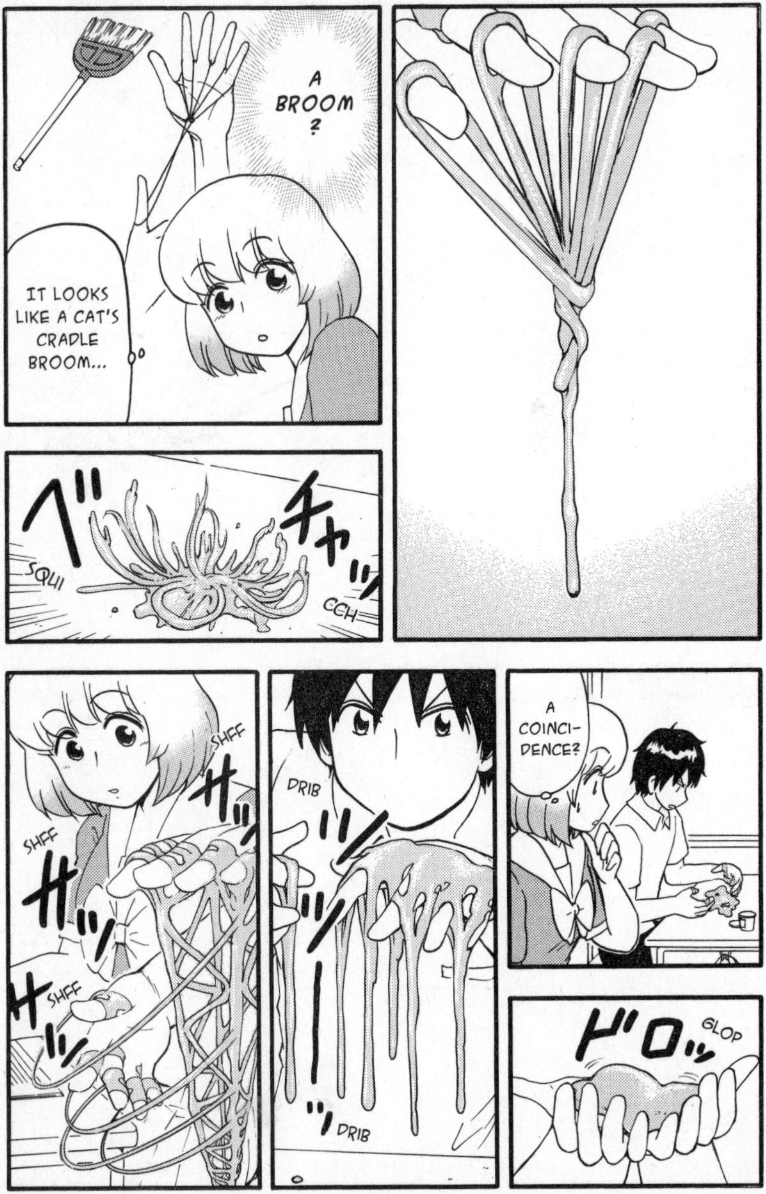
A BROOM?
IT LOOKS LIKE A CAT'S CRADLE BROOM...
ベチャッ
SQUI
CCH
A COINCI-DENCE?
ドロッ
GLOP
ズルーッ
DRIB
DRIB
ザッ
SHFF
ザッ
SHFF
ザッ
SHFF

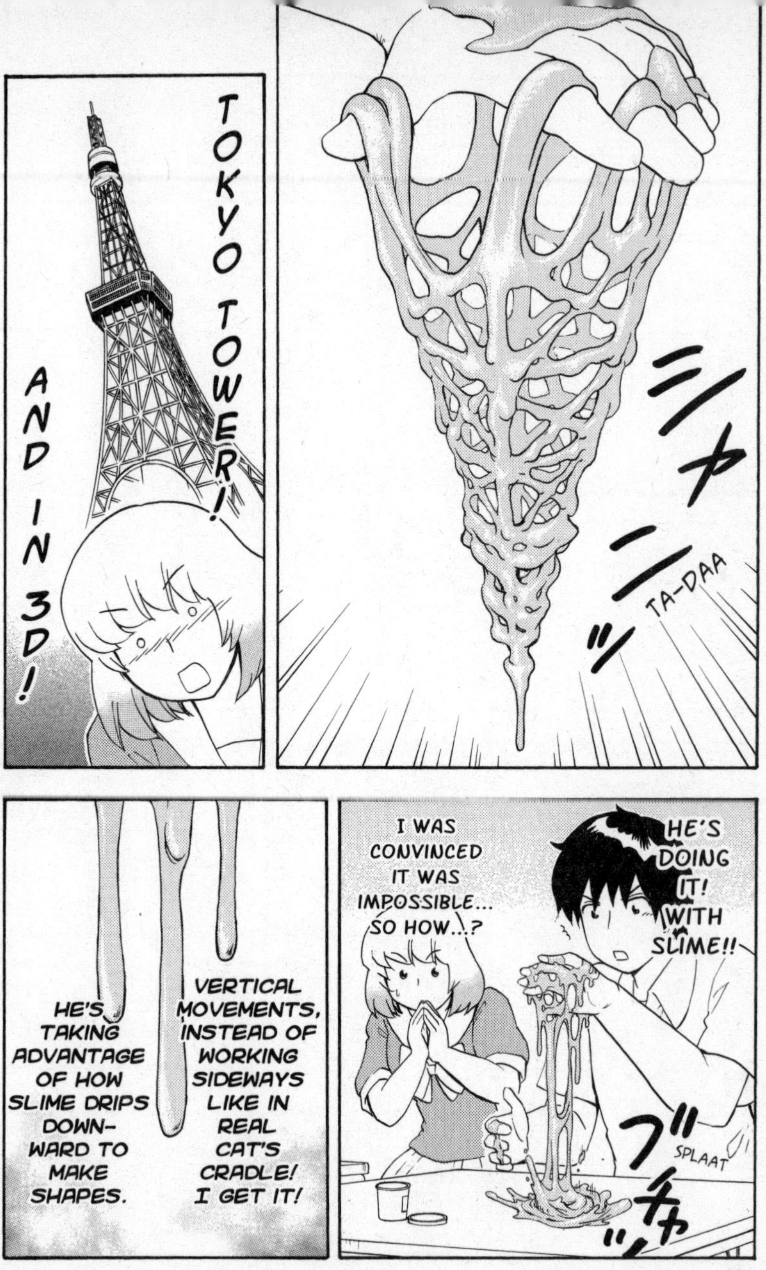
TA-DAA
TOKYO TOWER!
AND IN 3D!
HE'S DOING IT! WITH SLIME!!
I WAS CONVINCED IT WAS IMPOSSIBLE... SO HOW...?
SPLAAT
VERTICAL MOVEMENTS, INSTEAD OF WORKING SIDEWAYS LIKE IN REAL CAT'S CRADLE! I GET IT!
HE'S TAKING ADVANTAGE OF HOW SLIME DRIPS DOWNWARD TO MAKE SHAPES.

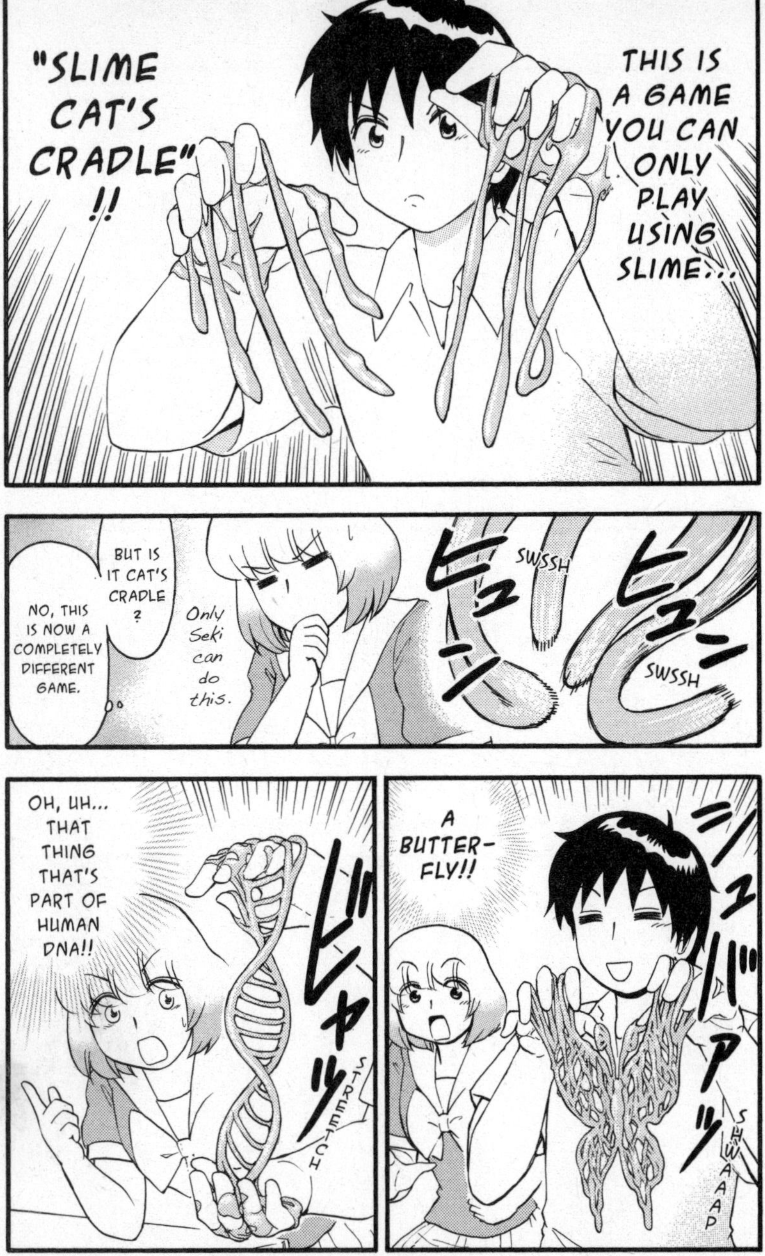
THIS IS A GAME YOU CAN ONLY PLAY USING SLIME...
"SLIME CAT'S CRADLE" !!
SWSSH
SWSSH
Only Seki can do this.
BUT IS IT CAT'S CRADLE ?
NO, THIS IS NOW A COMPLETELY DIFFERENT GAME.
SHWAAAP
A BUTTERFLY!!
STREETCH
OH, UH... THAT THING THAT'S PART OF HUMAN DNA!!

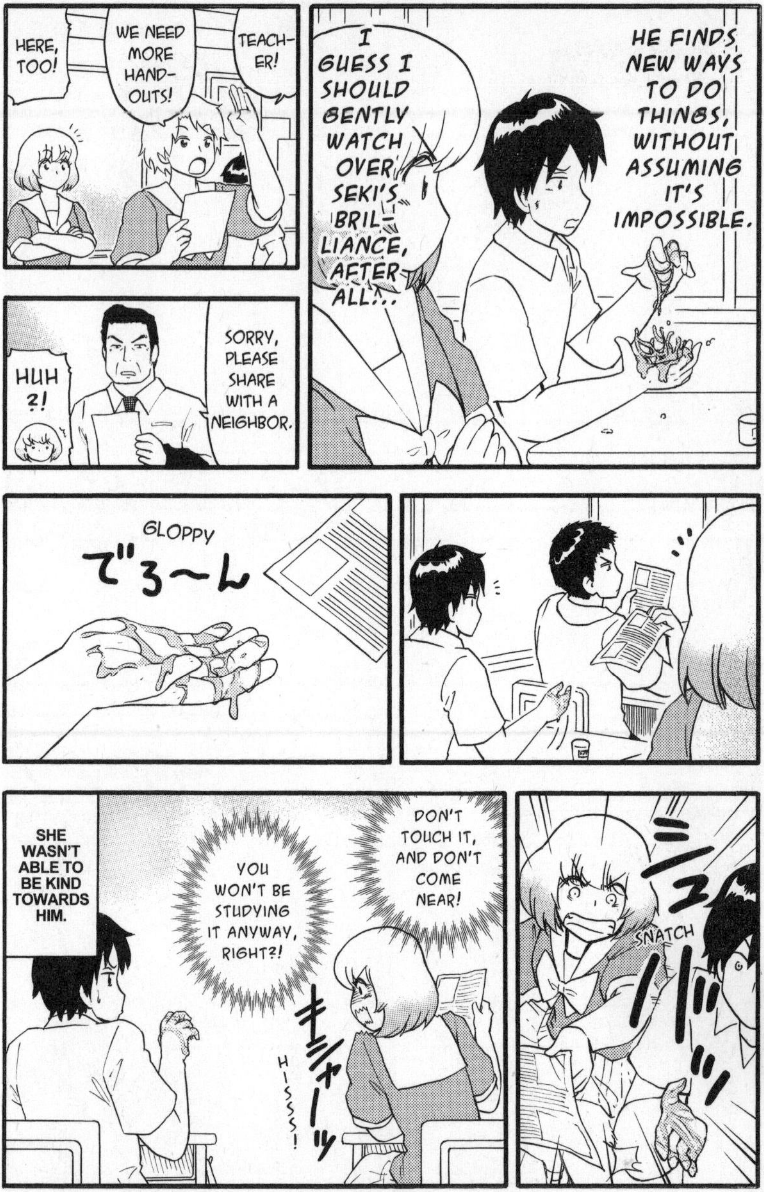
HE FINDS NEW WAYS TO DO THINGS, WITHOUT ASSUMING IT'S IMPOSSIBLE.
I GUESS I SHOULD GENTLY WATCH OVER SEKI'S BRILLIANCE, AFTER ALL...
TEACHER!
WE NEED MORE HANDOUTS!
HERE, TOO!
SORRY, PLEASE SHARE WITH A NEIGHBOR.
HUH?!
GLOPPY
でろ～ん
SNATCH
DON'T TOUCH IT, AND DON'T COME NEAR!
YOU WON'T BE STUDYING IT ANYWAY, RIGHT?!
HISSS!
SHE WASN'T ABLE TO BE KIND TOWARDS HIM.

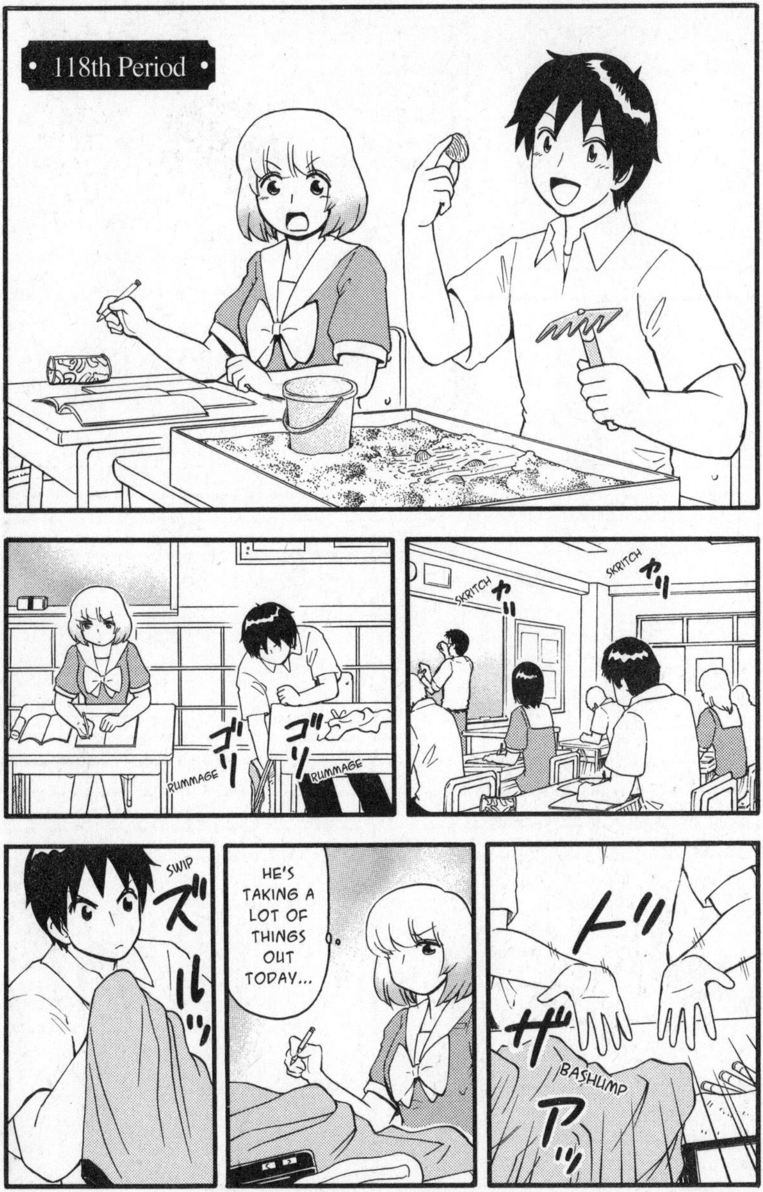
• 118th Period •
SKRITCH
SKRITCH
RUMMAGE
RUMMAGE
BASHUMP
HE'S TAKING A LOT OF THINGS OUT TODAY...
SWIP

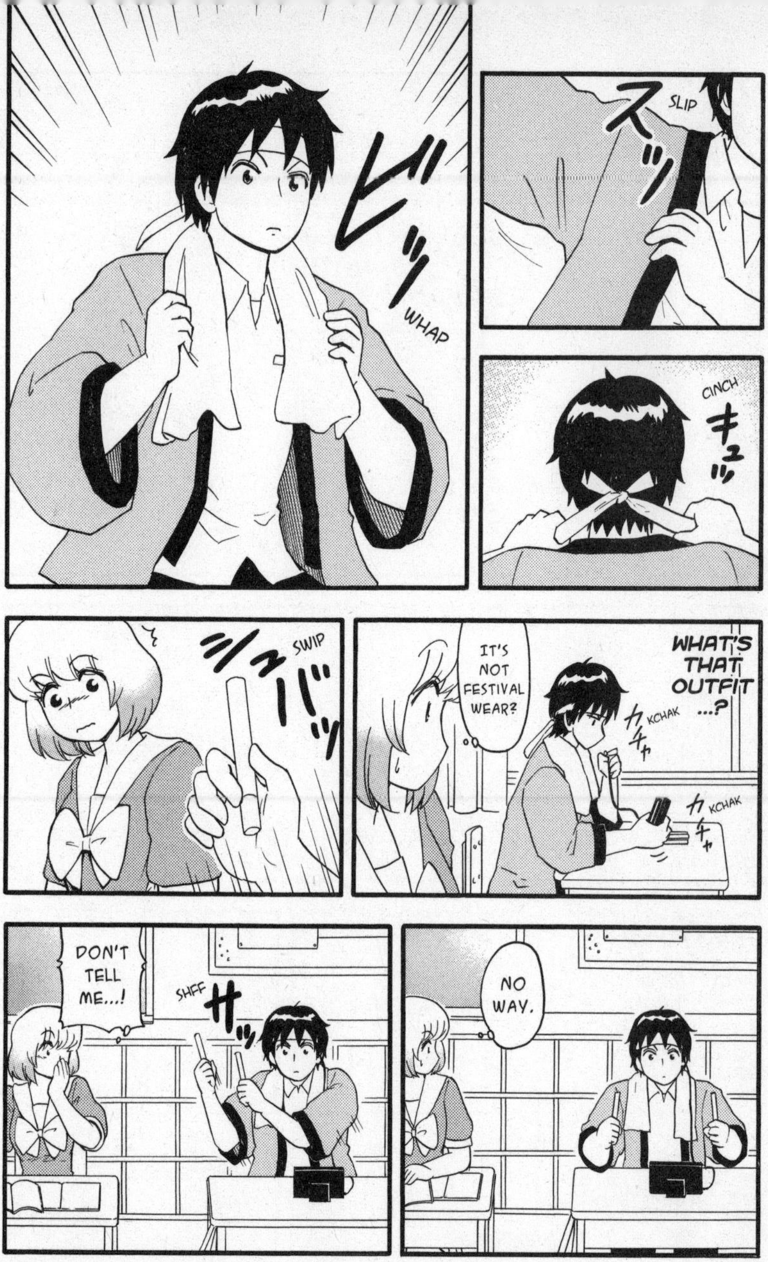

スッ
SLIP
キュッ
CINCH
ビッ
WHAP
WHAT'S THAT OUTFIT ...?
IT'S NOT FESTIVAL WEAR?
カチャ
KCHAK
カチャ
KCHAK
シュバッ
SWIP
NO WAY.
DON'T TELL ME...!
サッ
SHFF

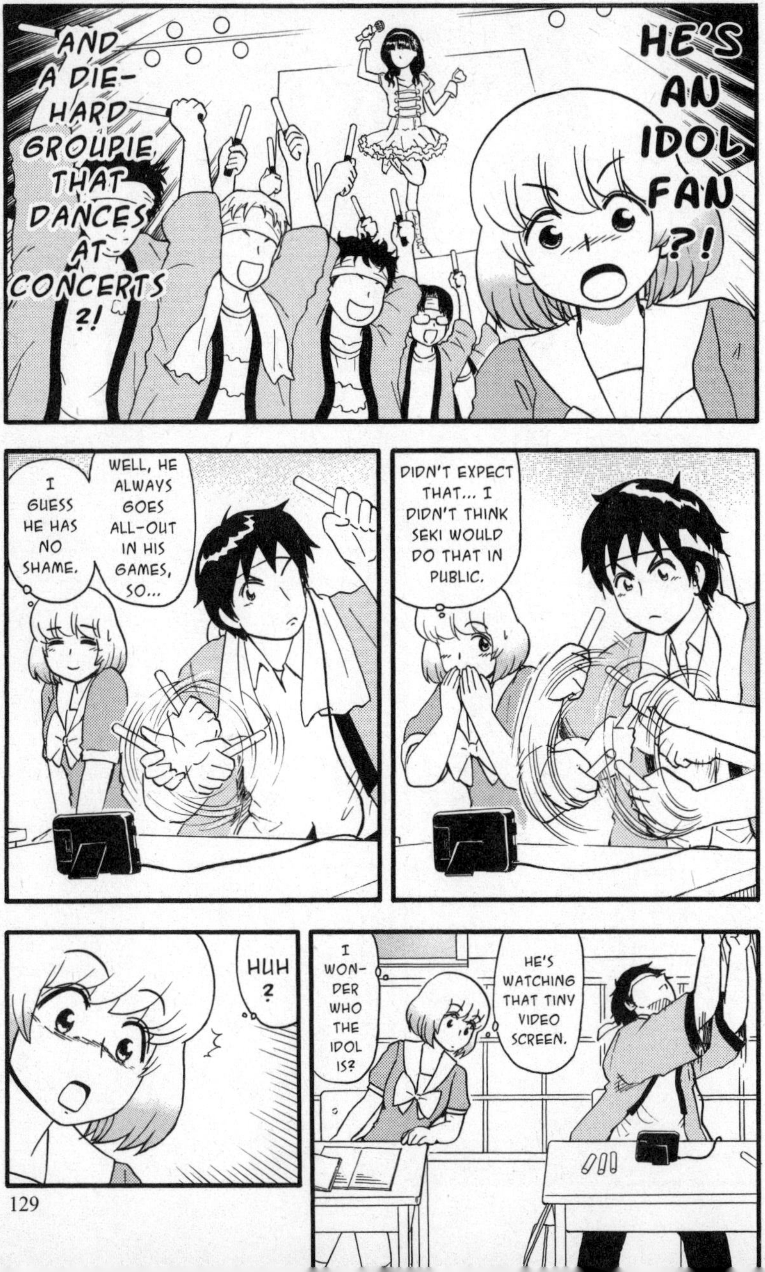
HE'S AN IDOL FAN?!
AND A DIE-HARD GROUPIE THAT DANCES AT CONCERTS?!
DIDN'T EXPECT THAT... I DIDN'T THINK SEKI WOULD DO THAT IN PUBLIC.
WELL, HE ALWAYS GOES ALL-OUT IN HIS GAMES, SO...
I GUESS HE HAS NO SHAME.
HE'S WATCHING THAT TINY VIDEO SCREEN.
I WONDER WHO THE IDOL IS?
HUH?

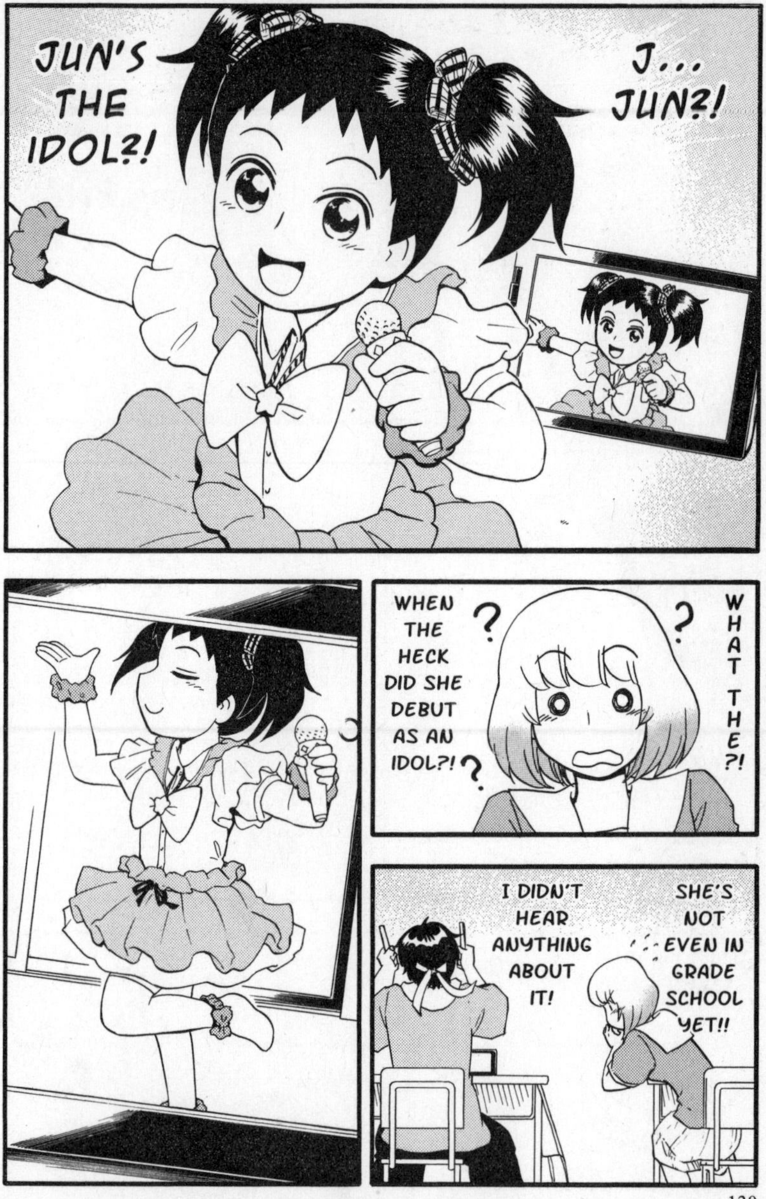
J... JUN?!
JUN'S THE IDOL?!
WHAT THE?!
WHEN THE HECK DID SHE DEBUT AS AN IDOL?!
SHE'S NOT EVEN IN GRADE SCHOOL YET!!
I DIDN'T HEAR ANYTHING ABOUT IT!

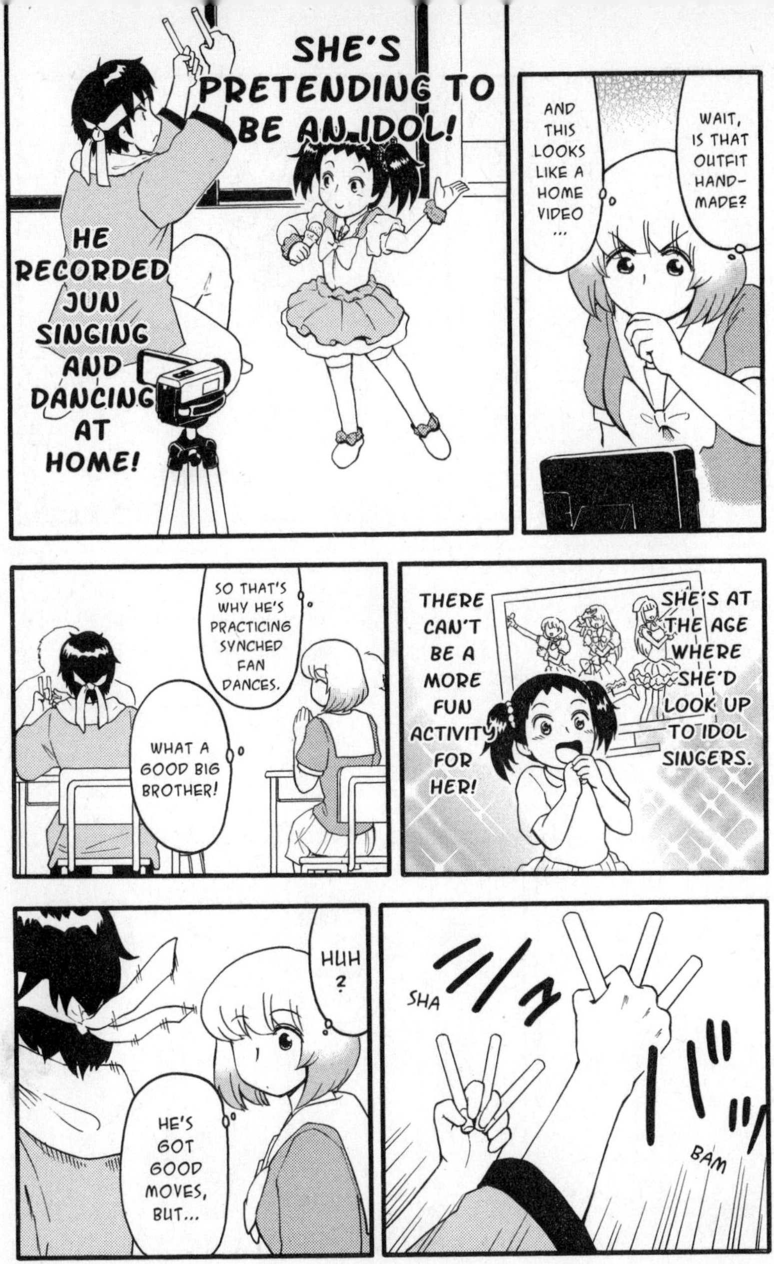
WAIT, IS THAT OUTFIT HAND-MADE?
AND THIS LOOKS LIKE A HOME VIDEO...
SHE'S PRETENDING TO BE AN IDOL!
HE RECORDED JUN SINGING AND DANCING AT HOME!
SHE'S AT THE AGE WHERE SHE'D LOOK UP TO IDOL SINGERS.
THERE CAN'T BE A MORE FUN ACTIVITY FOR HER!
SO THAT'S WHY HE'S PRACTICING SYNCHED FAN DANCES.
WHAT A GOOD BIG BROTHER!
SHA
BAM
HUH?
HE'S GOT GOOD MOVES, BUT...

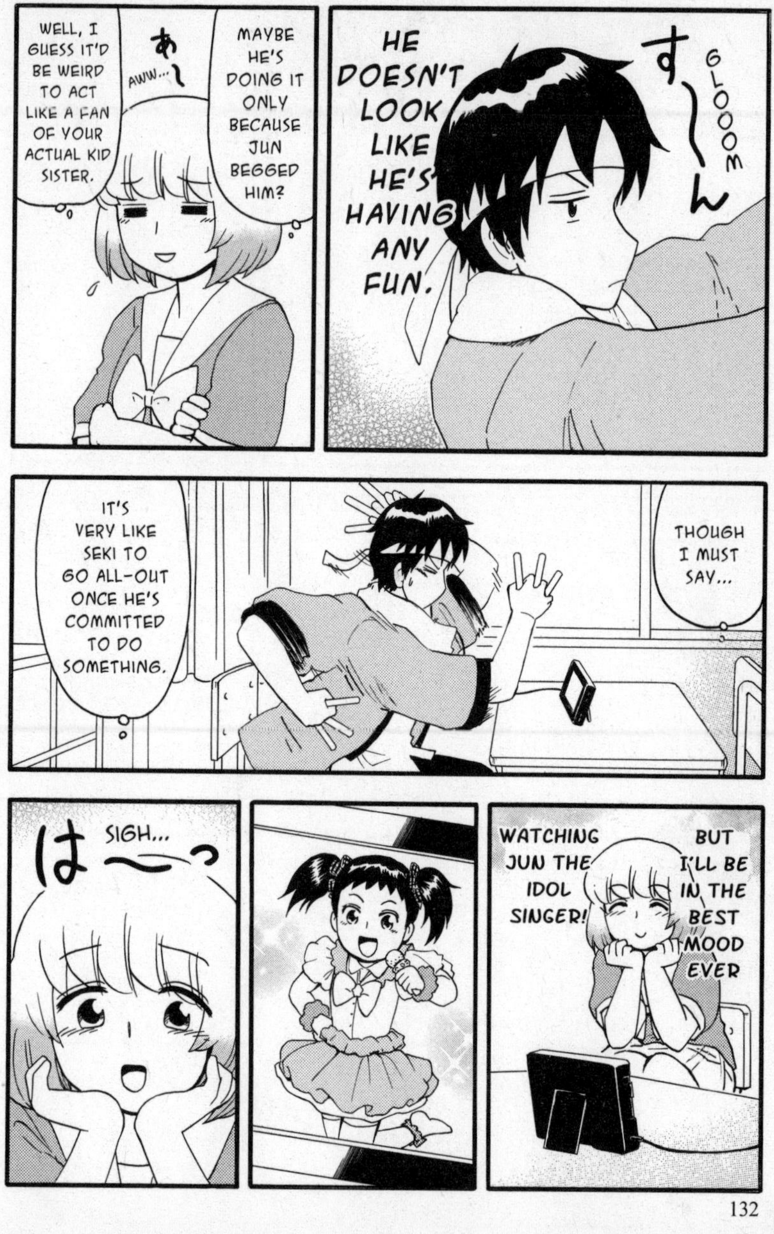
HE DOESN'T LOOK LIKE HE'S HAVING ANY FUN.
す～ん
GLOOOM
MAYBE HE'S DOING IT ONLY BECAUSE JUN BEGGED HIM?
あ～
AWW...
WELL, I GUESS IT'D BE WEIRD TO ACT LIKE A FAN OF YOUR ACTUAL KID SISTER.
THOUGH I MUST SAY...
IT'S VERY LIKE SEKI TO GO ALL-OUT ONCE HE'S COMMITTED TO DO SOMETHING.
BUT I'LL BE IN THE BEST MOOD EVER
WATCHING JUN THE IDOL SINGER!
は～っ
SIGH...

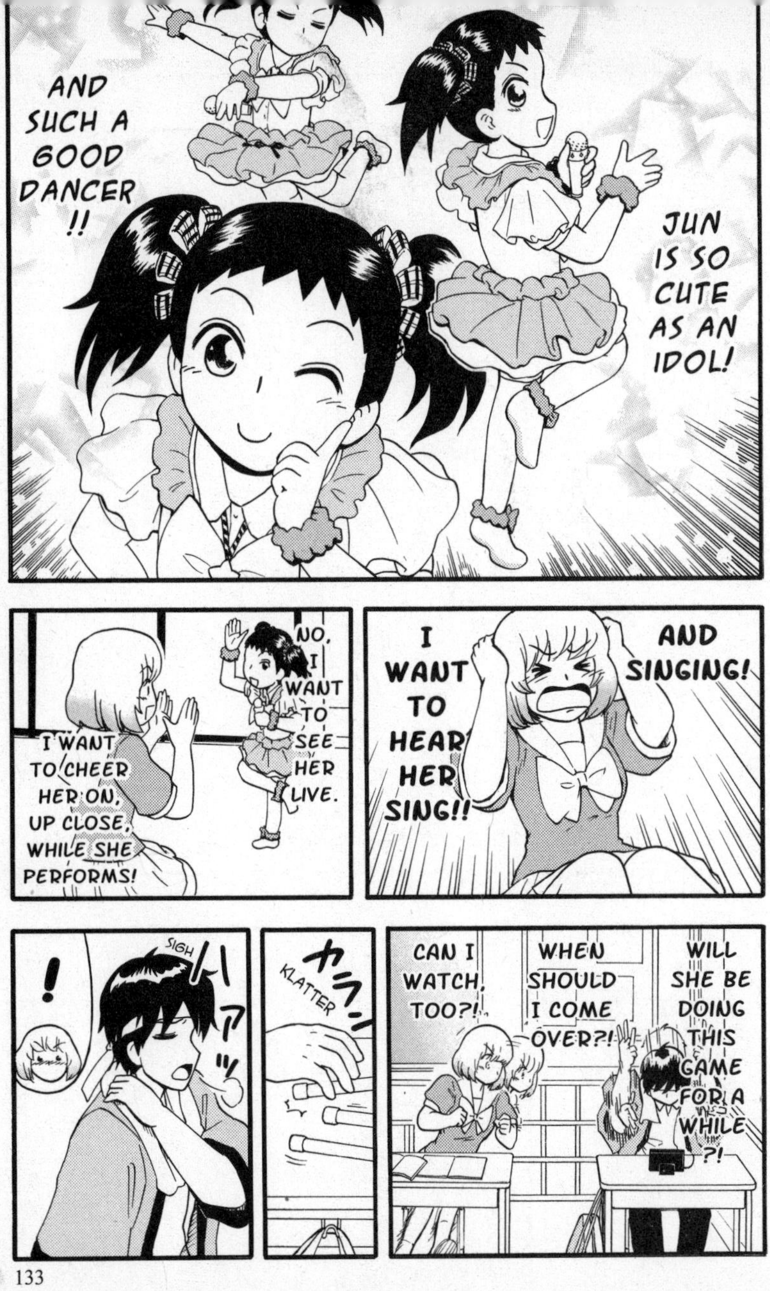

JUN IS SO CUTE AS AN IDOL!
AND SUCH A GOOD DANCER!!
AND SINGING!
I WANT TO HEAR HER SING!!
NO, I WANT TO SEE HER LIVE.
I WANT TO CHEER HER ON, UP CLOSE, WHILE SHE PERFORMS!
WILL SHE BE DOING THIS GAME FOR A WHILE?!
WHEN SHOULD I COME OVER?!
CAN I WATCH, TOO?!
KLATTER
SIGH
!

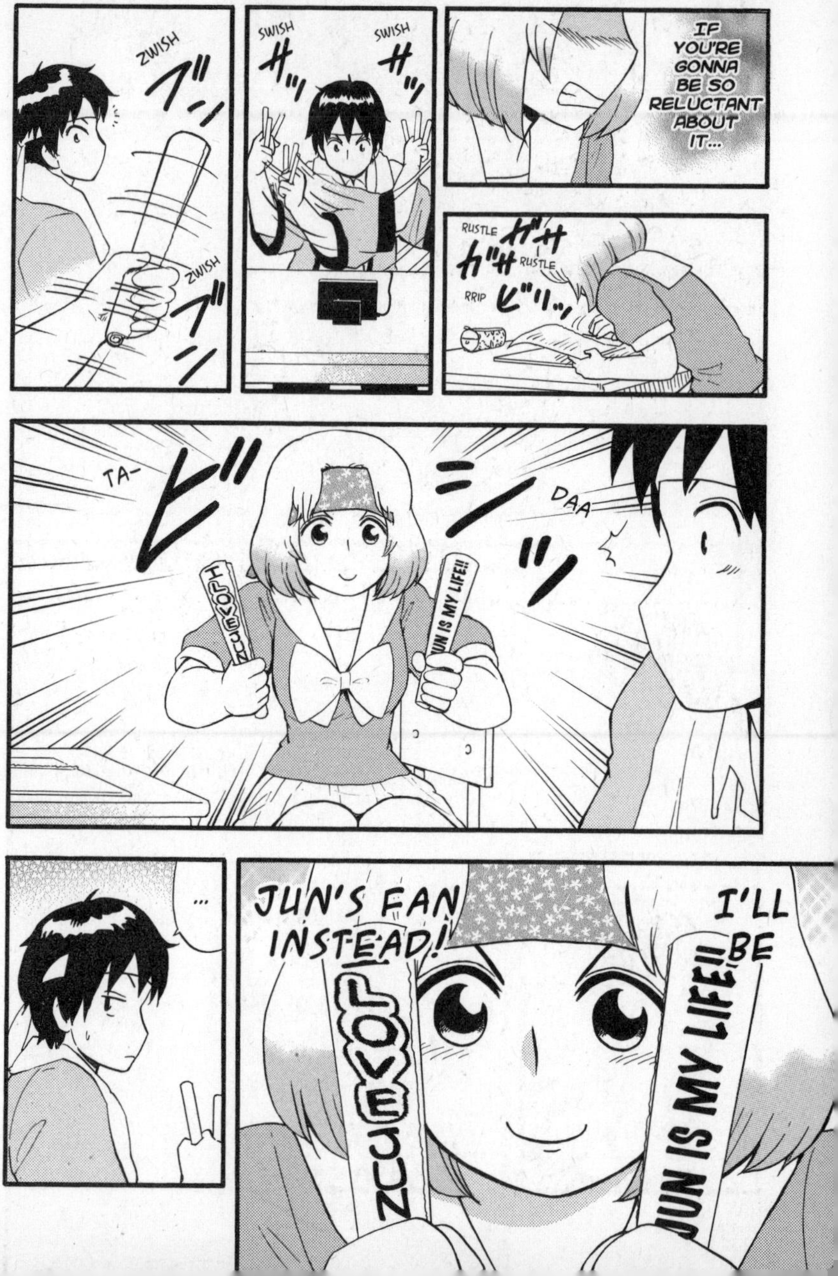

IF YOU'RE GONNA BE SO RELUCTANT ABOUT IT...
RUSTLE
RUSTLE
RRIP
SWISH
SWISH
ZWISH
ZWISH
TA-
DAA
I LOVE JUN
JUN IS MY LIFE!!
I'LL BE
JUN'S FAN INSTEAD!
JUN IS MY LIFE!!
LOVE JUN
...

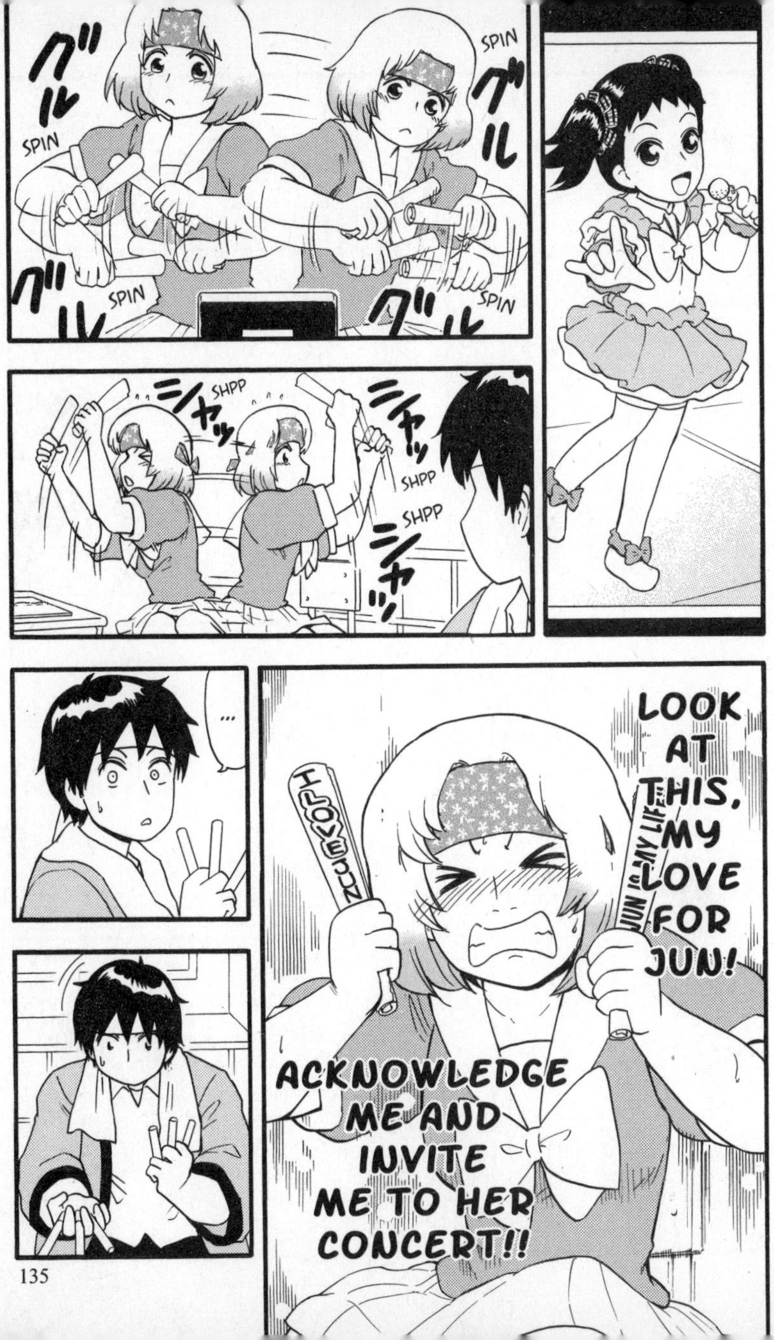
SPIN
グル
SPIN
グル
SPIN
グル
SPIN
グル
SHPP
シャッ
SHPP
シャッ
SHPP
シャッ
LOOK AT THIS, MY LOVE FOR JUN!
I LOVE JUN
JUN is MY LIFE
ACKNOWLEDGE ME AND INVITE ME TO HER CONCERT!!
...

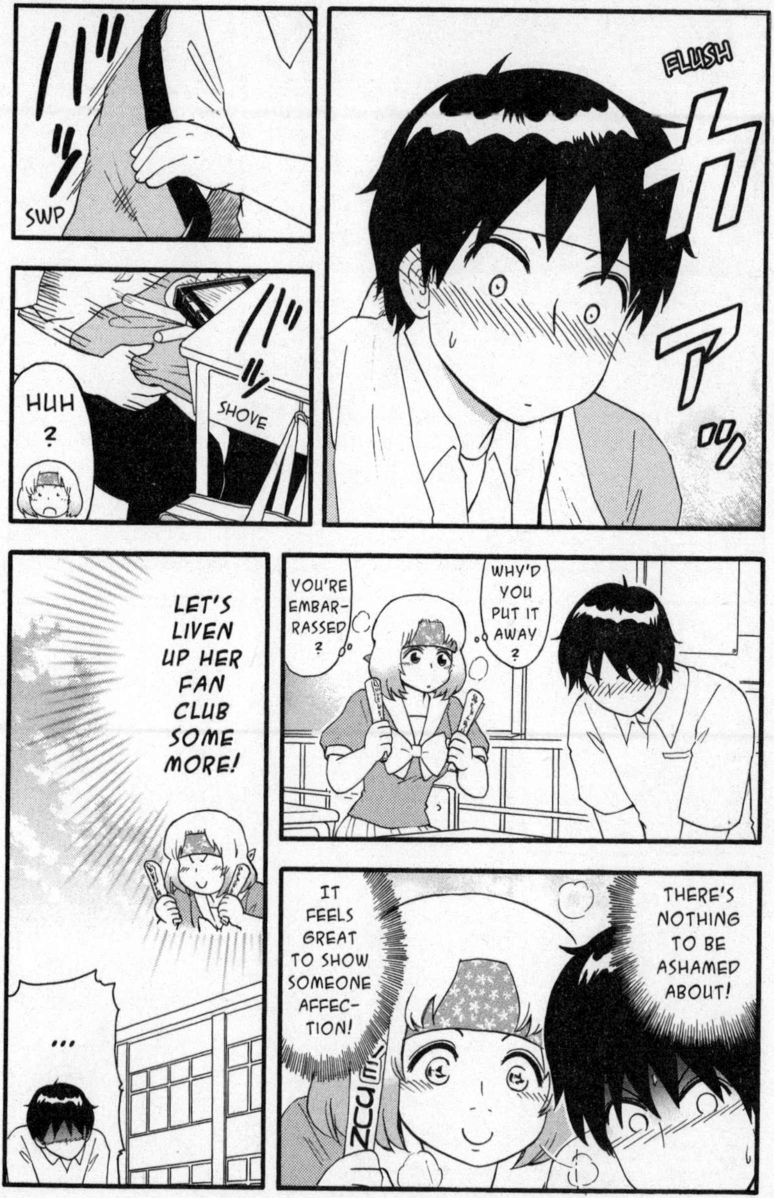
FLUSH
カァッ
バッ
SWP
バッ
SHOVE
HUH?
WHY'D YOU PUT IT AWAY?
YOU'RE EMBARRASSED?
THERE'S NOTHING TO BE ASHAMED ABOUT!
IT FEELS GREAT TO SHOW SOMEONE AFFECTION!
LET'S LIVEN UP HER FAN CLUB SOME MORE!
...

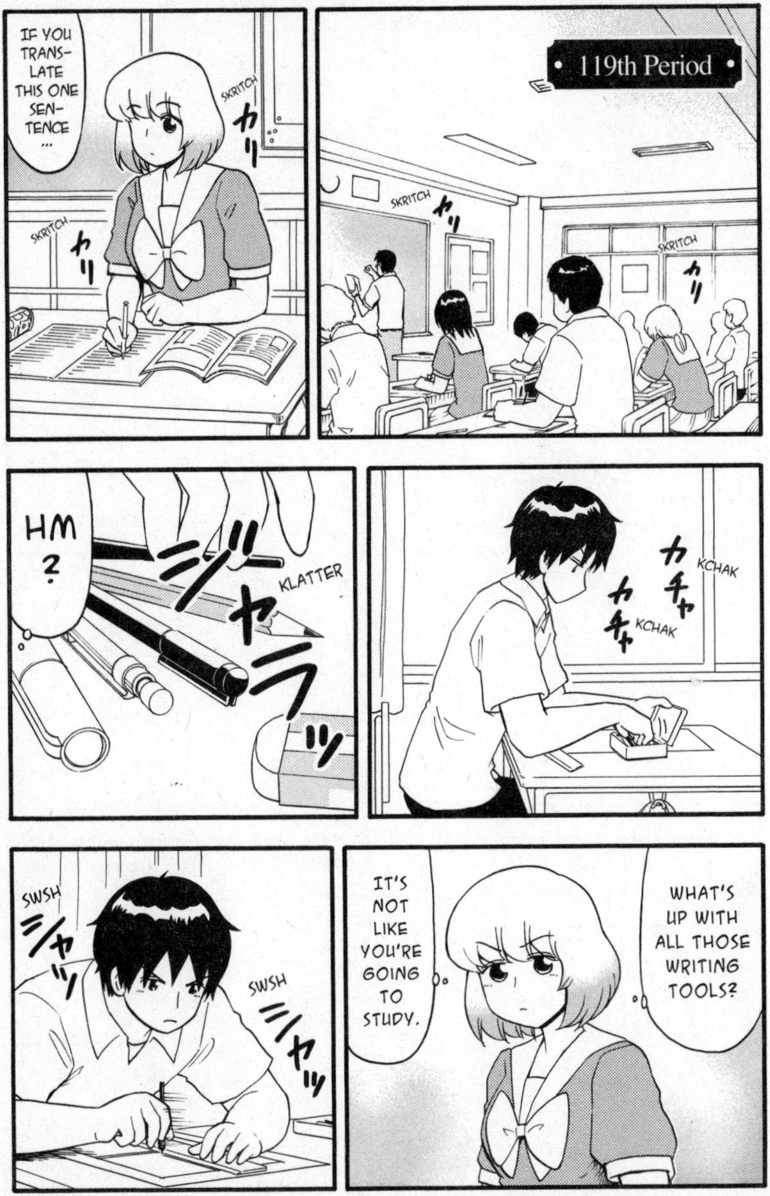
• 119th Period •
SKRITCH カリ
SKRITCH カリ
IF YOU TRANSLATE THIS ONE SENTENCE ...
SKRITCH カリ
SKRITCH カリ
KCHAK カチャ
KCHAK カチャ
HM?
KLATTER ジャラッ
WHAT'S UP WITH ALL THOSE WRITING TOOLS?
IT'S NOT LIKE YOU'RE GOING TO STUDY.
SWSH シャッ
SWSH シャッ

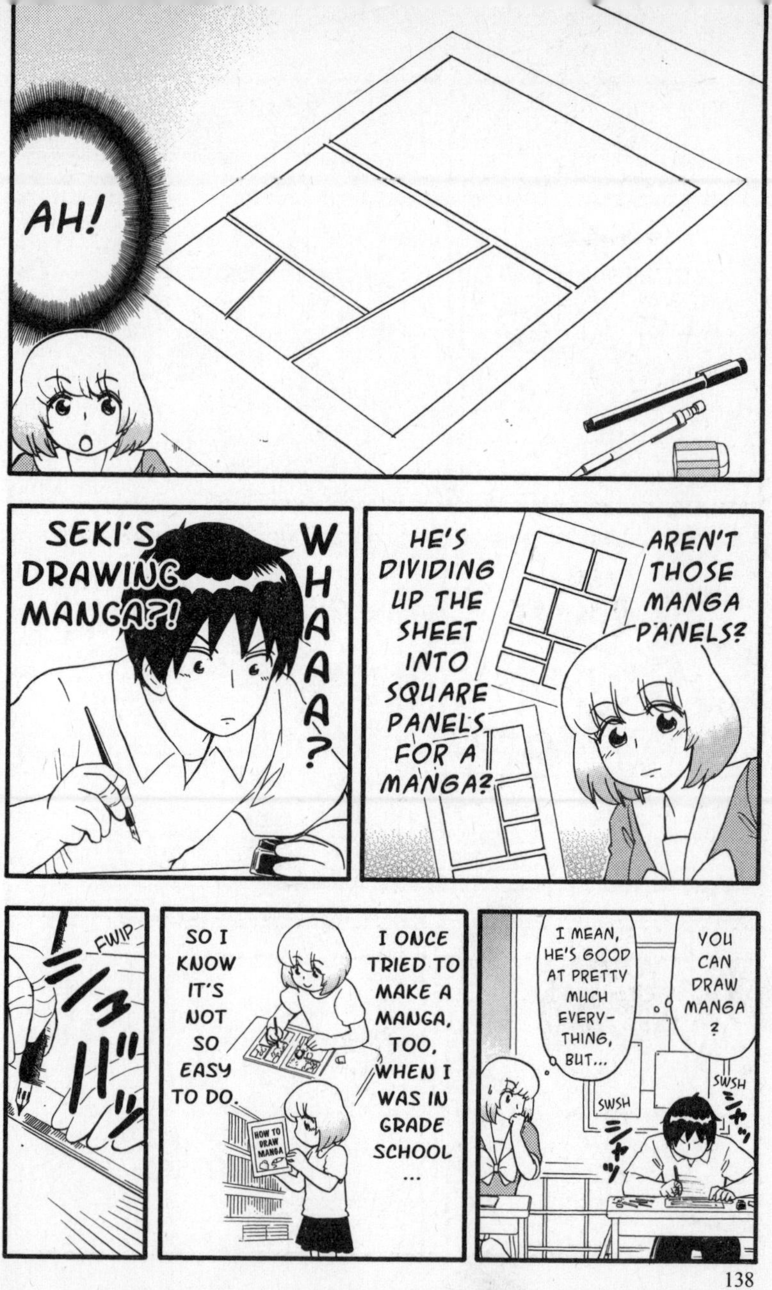
AH!
AREN'T THOSE MANGA PANELS?
HE'S DIVIDING UP THE SHEET INTO SQUARE PANELS FOR A MANGA?
WHAAAA?
SEKI'S DRAWING MANGA?!
YOU CAN DRAW MANGA?
I MEAN, HE'S GOOD AT PRETTY MUCH EVERY-THING, BUT...
SWSH
SWSH
I ONCE TRIED TO MAKE A MANGA, TOO, WHEN I WAS IN GRADE SCHOOL ...
SO I KNOW IT'S NOT SO EASY TO DO.
HOW TO DRAW MANGA
FWIP

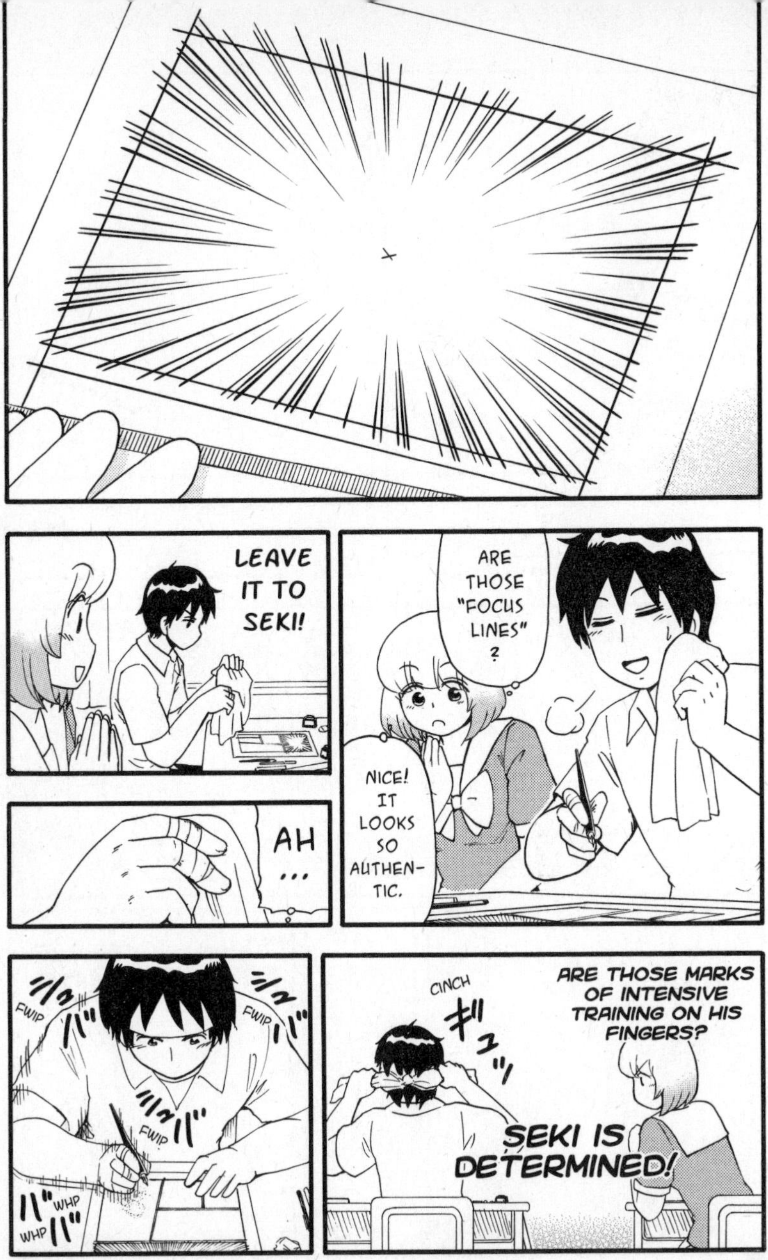
ARE THOSE "FOCUS LINES"?
NICE! IT LOOKS SO AUTHEN-TIC.
LEAVE IT TO SEKI!
AH...
ARE THOSE MARKS OF INTENSIVE TRAINING ON HIS FINGERS?
CINCH
SEKI IS DETERMINED!
FWIP
FWIP
FWIP
WHP
WHP

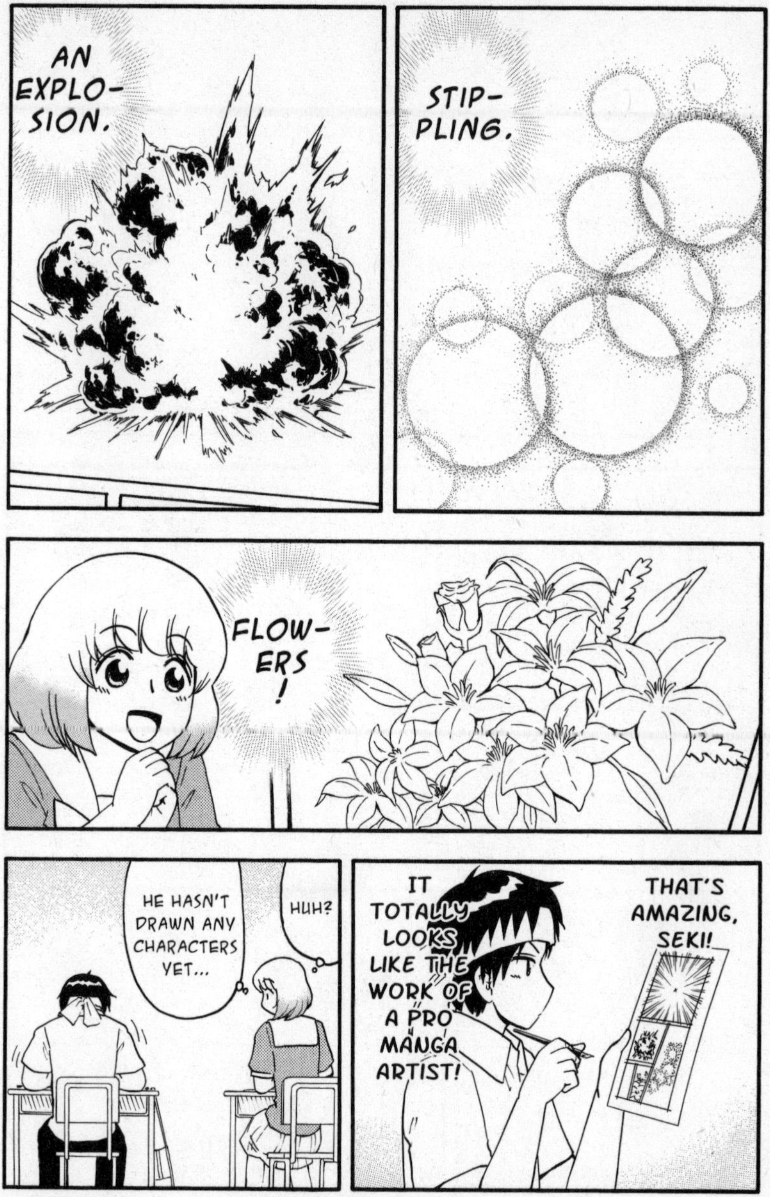
STIP-
PLING.
AN
EXPLO-
SION.
FLOW-
ERS
!
THAT'S AMAZING, SEKI!
IT TOTALLY LOOKS LIKE THE WORK OF A PRO MANGA ARTIST!
HUH?
HE HASN'T DRAWN ANY CHARACTERS YET...

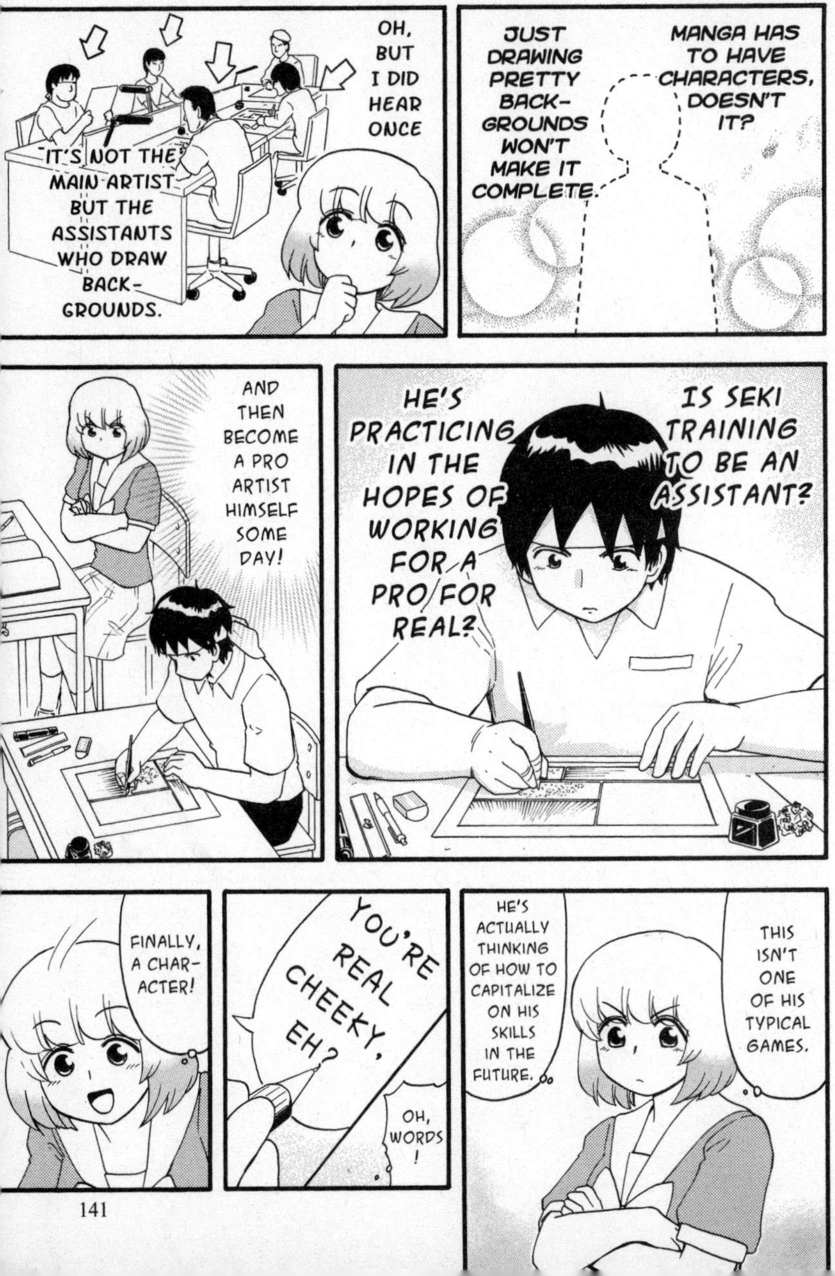

MANGA HAS TO HAVE CHARACTERS, DOESN'T IT?
JUST DRAWING PRETTY BACKGROUNDS WON'T MAKE IT COMPLETE.
OH, BUT I DID HEAR ONCE
IT'S NOT THE MAIN ARTIST BUT THE ASSISTANTS WHO DRAW BACKGROUNDS.
IS SEKI TRAINING TO BE AN ASSISTANT?
HE'S PRACTICING IN THE HOPES OF WORKING FOR A PRO FOR REAL?
AND THEN BECOME A PRO ARTIST HIMSELF SOME DAY!
THIS ISN'T ONE OF HIS TYPICAL GAMES.
HE'S ACTUALLY THINKING OF HOW TO CAPITALIZE ON HIS SKILLS IN THE FUTURE.
YOU'RE REAL CHEEKY, EH?
OH, WORDS!
FINALLY, A CHARACTER!

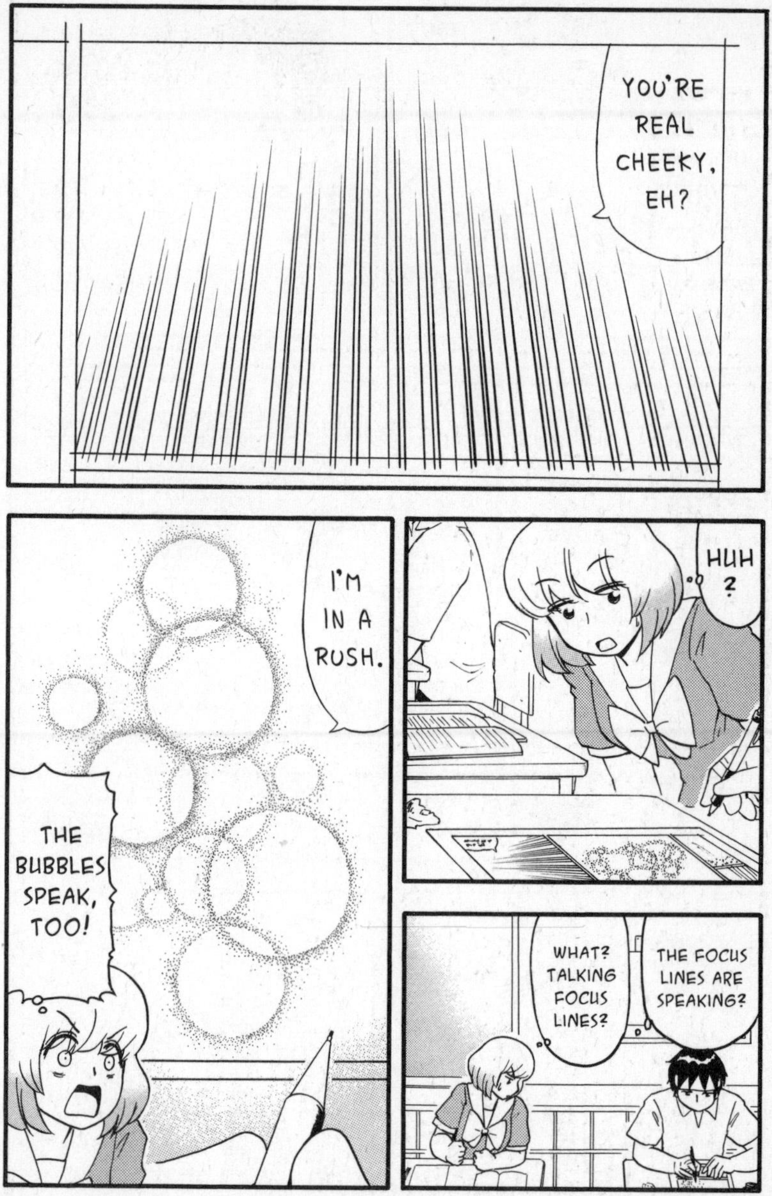

YOU'RE REAL CHEEKY, EH?
HUH?
THE FOCUS LINES ARE SPEAKING?
WHAT? TALKING FOCUS LINES?
I'M IN A RUSH.
THE BUBBLES SPEAK, TOO!

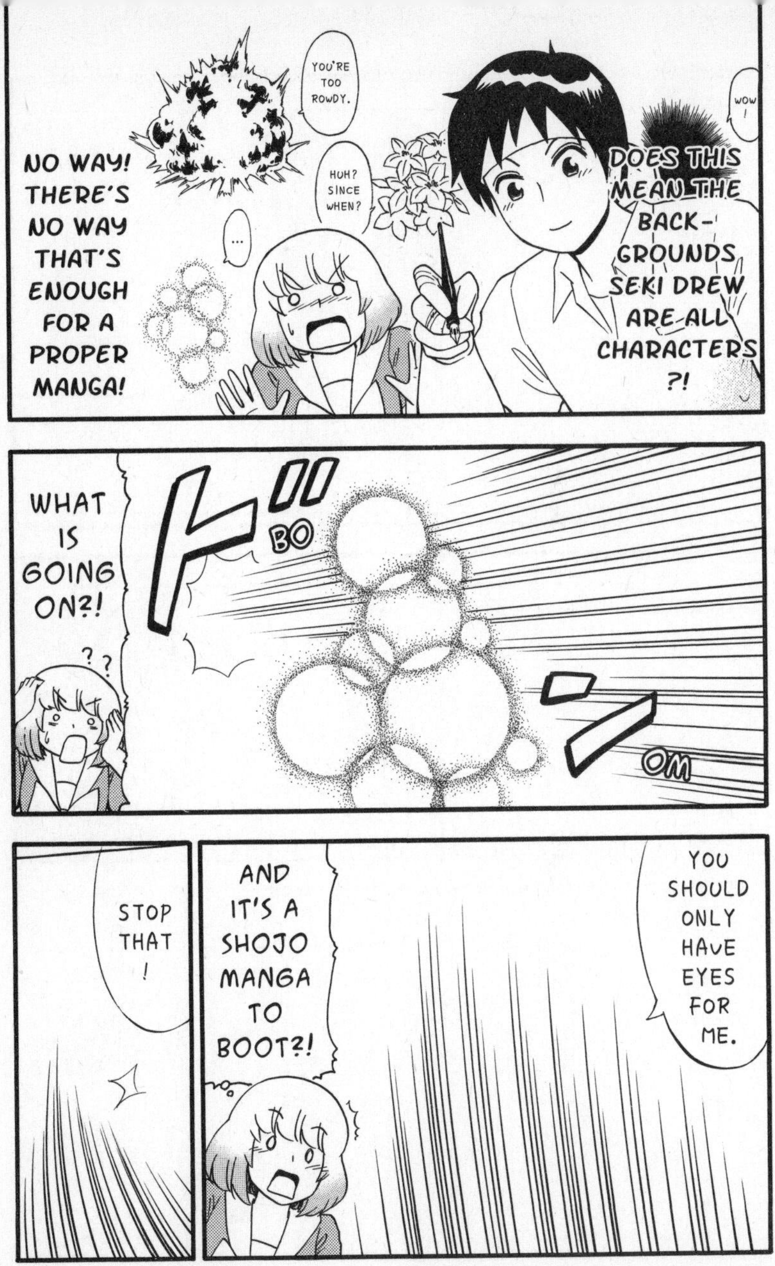
WOW!
DOES THIS MEAN THE BACKGROUNDS SEKI DREW ARE ALL CHARACTERS?!
YOU'RE TOO ROWDY.
HUH? SINCE WHEN?
...
NO WAY! THERE'S NO WAY THAT'S ENOUGH FOR A PROPER MANGA!
BO
OM
WHAT IS GOING ON?!
??
YOU SHOULD ONLY HAVE EYES FOR ME.
AND IT'S A SHOJO MANGA TO BOOT?!
STOP THAT!

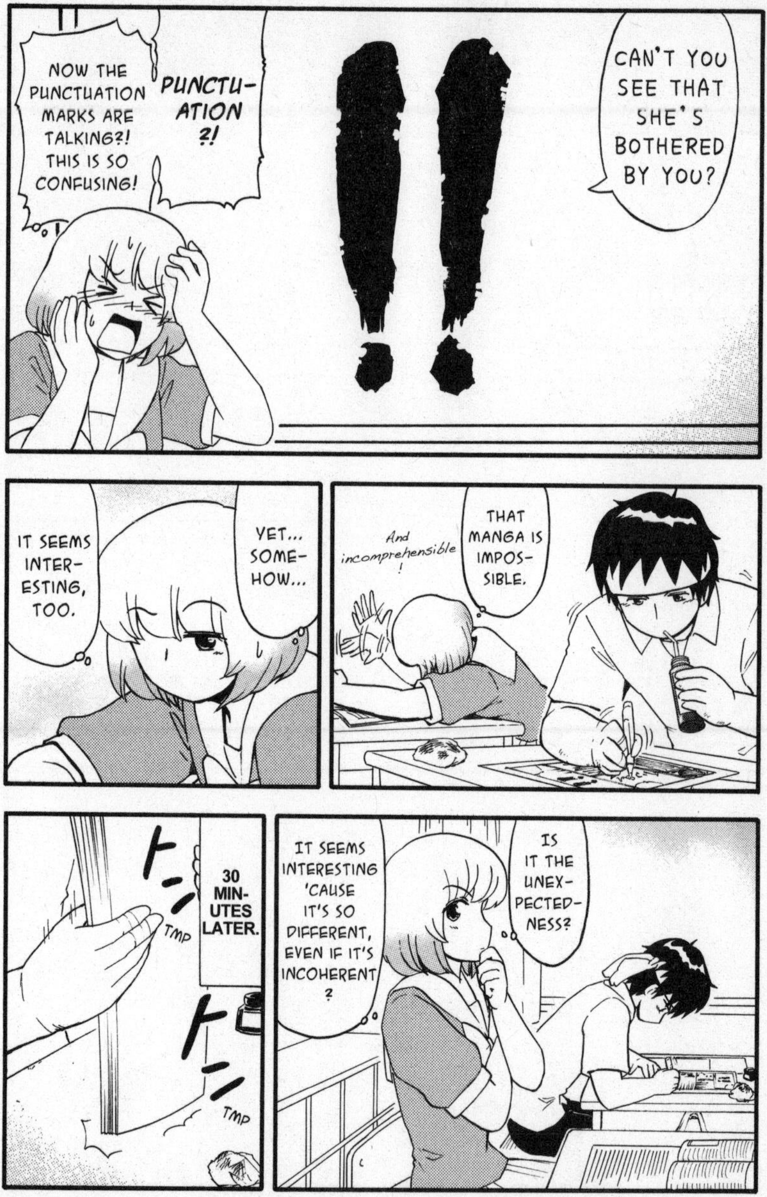
CAN'T YOU SEE THAT SHE'S BOTHERED BY YOU?
PUNCTUATION ?!
NOW THE PUNCTUATION MARKS ARE TALKING?! THIS IS SO CONFUSING!
THAT MANGA IS IMPOSSIBLE.
And incomprehensible!
YET... SOMEHOW...
IT SEEMS INTERESTING, TOO.
IS IT THE UNEXPECTEDNESS?
IT SEEMS INTERESTING 'CAUSE IT'S SO DIFFERENT, EVEN IF IT'S INCOHERENT?
30 MINUTES LATER.
TMP
TMP

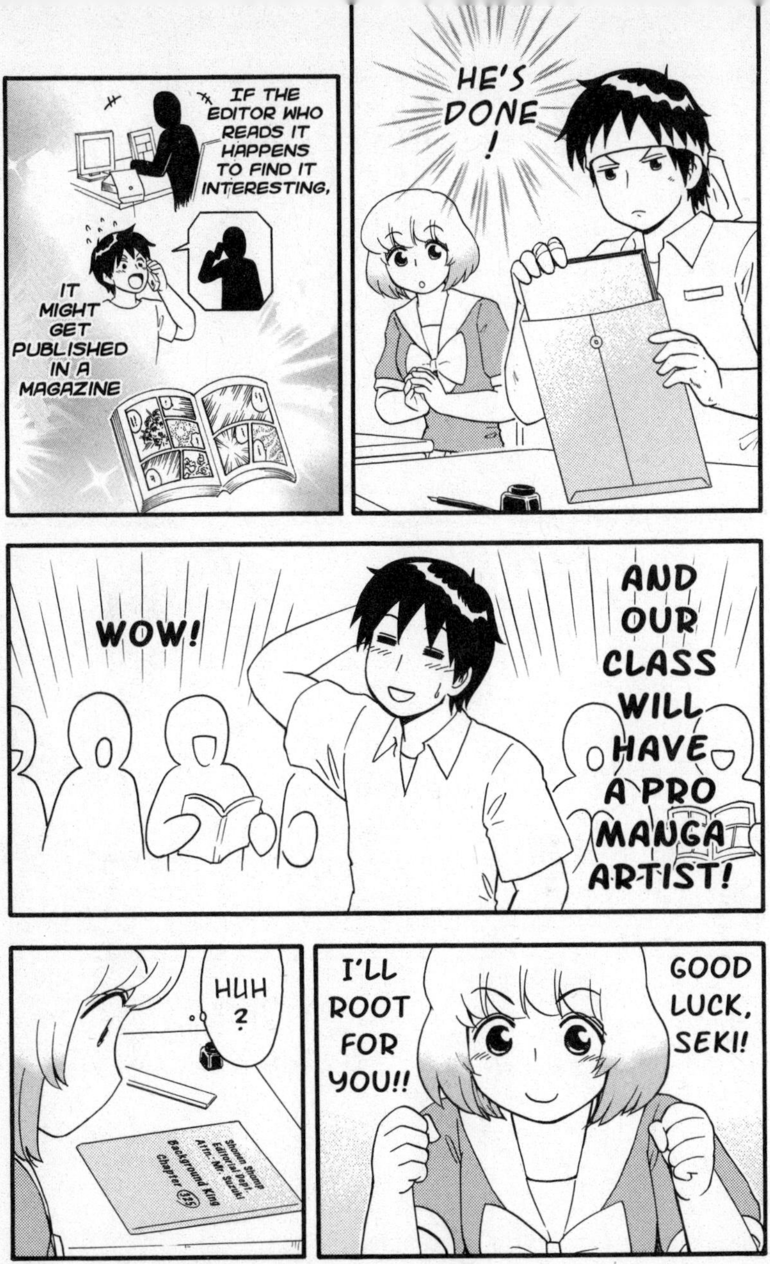
HE'S DONE!
IF THE EDITOR WHO READS IT HAPPENS TO FIND IT INTERESTING,
IT MIGHT GET PUBLISHED IN A MAGAZINE
AND OUR CLASS WILL HAVE A PRO MANGA ARTIST!
WOW!
GOOD LUCK, SEKI!
I'LL ROOT FOR YOU!!
HUH?
Shonen Shomp Editorial Dept. Attn.: Mr. Suzuki Background King Chapter 325

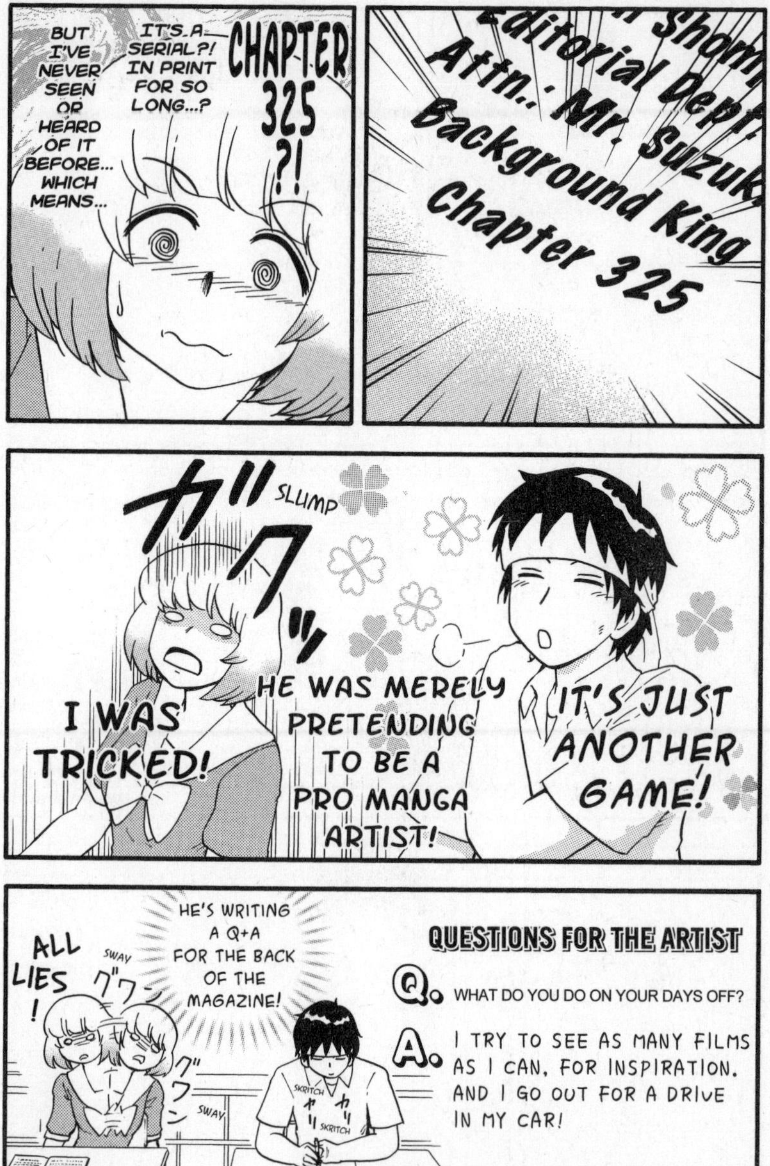
Editorial Dept.
Attn.: Mr. Suzuk
Background King
Chapter 325
CHAPTER 325 ?!
IT'S A SERIAL?! IN PRINT FOR SO LONG...?
BUT I'VE NEVER SEEN OR HEARD OF IT BEFORE... WHICH MEANS...
IT'S JUST ANOTHER GAME!
ガクッ
SLUMP
HE WAS MERELY PRETENDING TO BE A PRO MANGA ARTIST!
I WAS TRICKED!
QUESTIONS FOR THE ARTIST
Q. WHAT DO YOU DO ON YOUR DAYS OFF?
A. I TRY TO SEE AS MANY FILMS AS I CAN, FOR INSPIRATION. AND I GO OUT FOR A DRIVE IN MY CAR!
カリ
SKRITCH
カリ
SKRITCH
HE'S WRITING A Q+A FOR THE BACK OF THE MAGAZINE!
グワン
SWAY
グワン
SWAY
ALL LIES!

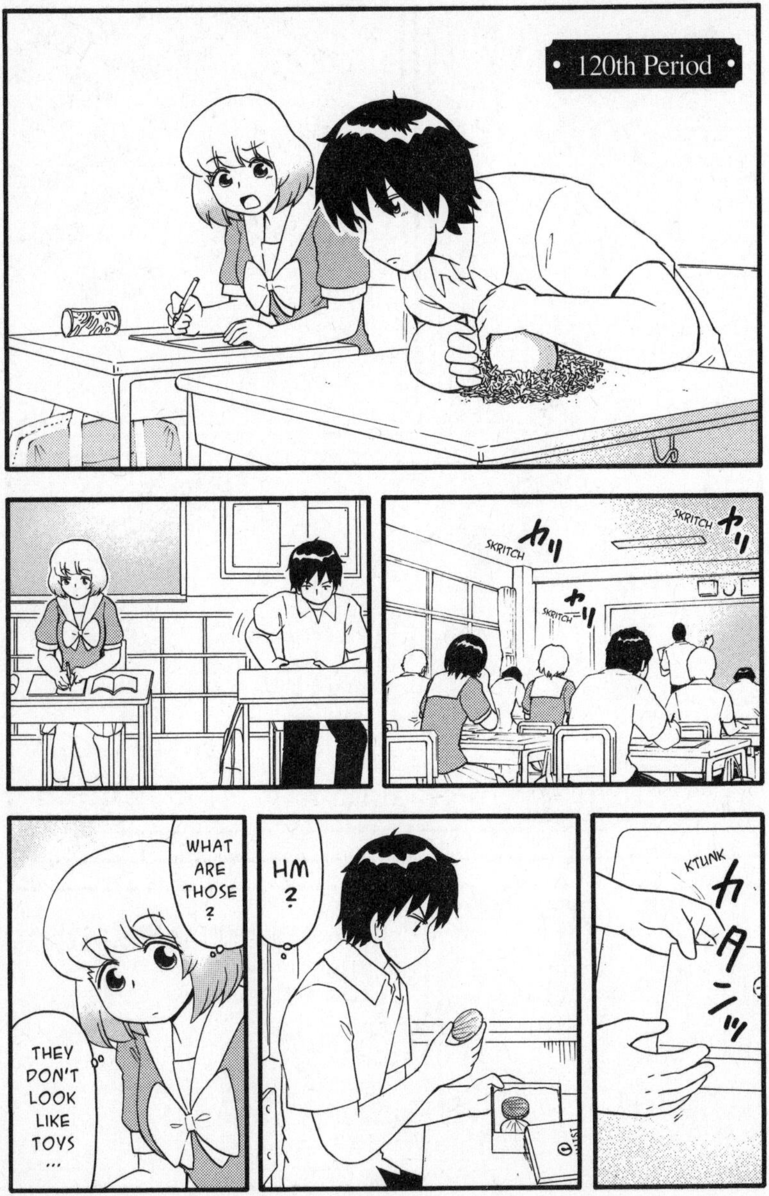
120th Period
SKRITCH
SKRITCH
SKRITCH
KTUNK
カタンッ
HM ?
WHAT ARE THOSE ?
THEY DON'T LOOK LIKE TOYS ...

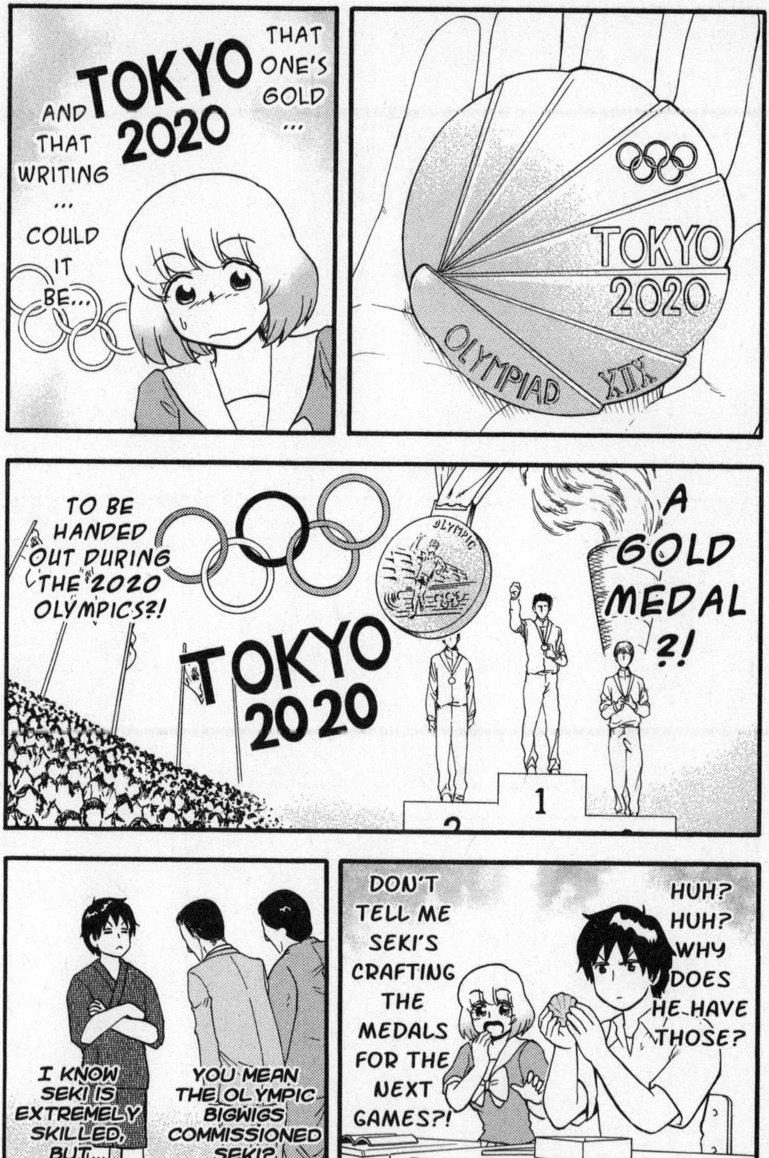
TOKYO 2020
OLYMPIAD
THAT ONE'S GOLD...
AND THAT WRITING... TOKYO 2020 ... COULD IT BE...
A GOLD MEDAL?!
OLYMPIC
TOKYO 2020
TO BE HANDED OUT DURING THE 2020 OLYMPICS?!
1
HUH? HUH? WHY DOES HE HAVE THOSE?
DON'T TELL ME SEKI'S CRAFTING THE MEDALS FOR THE NEXT GAMES?!
YOU MEAN THE OLYMPIC BIGWIGS COMMISSIONED SEKI?
I KNOW SEKI IS EXTREMELY SKILLED, BUT...

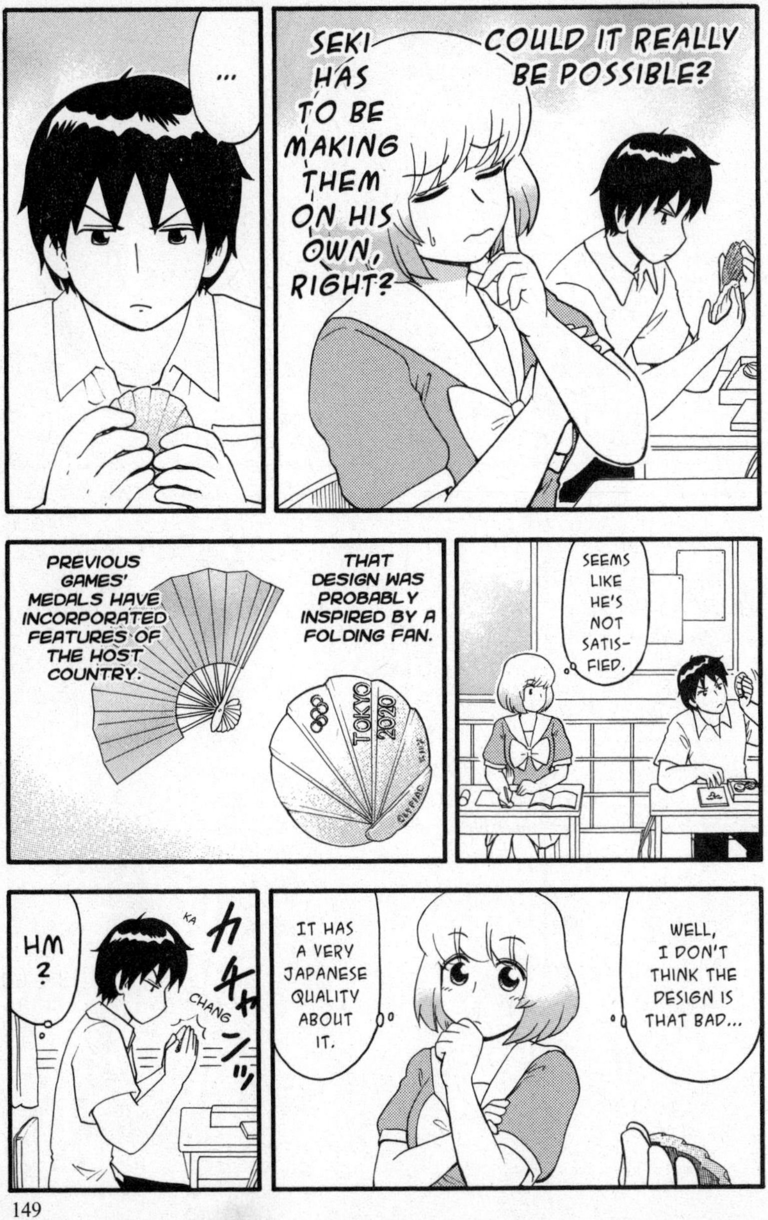
COULD IT REALLY BE POSSIBLE?
SEKI HAS TO BE MAKING THEM ON HIS OWN, RIGHT?
...
SEEMS LIKE HE'S NOT SATIS-FIED.
THAT DESIGN WAS PROBABLY INSPIRED BY A FOLDING FAN.
PREVIOUS GAMES' MEDALS HAVE INCORPORATED FEATURES OF THE HOST COUNTRY.
TOKYO 2020
WELL, I DON'T THINK THE DESIGN IS THAT BAD...
IT HAS A VERY JAPANESE QUALITY ABOUT IT.
KA
カチャーンッ
CHANG
HM?

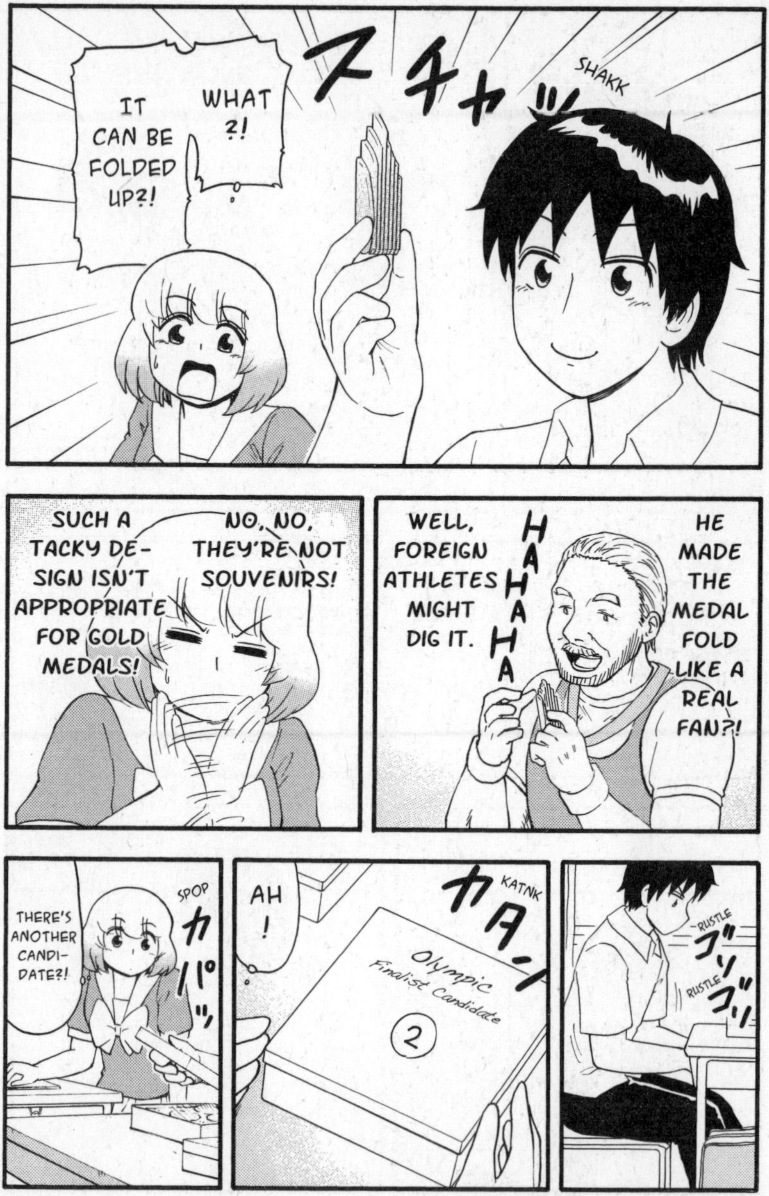
SHAKK
WHAT?!
IT CAN BE FOLDED UP?!
HE MADE THE MEDAL FOLD LIKE A REAL FAN?!
HAHAHAHA
WELL, FOREIGN ATHLETES MIGHT DIG IT.
NO, NO, THEY'RE NOT SOUVENIRS!
SUCH A TACKY DE-SIGN ISN'T APPROPRIATE FOR GOLD MEDALS!
RUSTLE
RUSTLE
KATNK
Olympic Finalist Candidate
2
AH!
SPOP
THERE'S ANOTHER CANDI-DATE?!

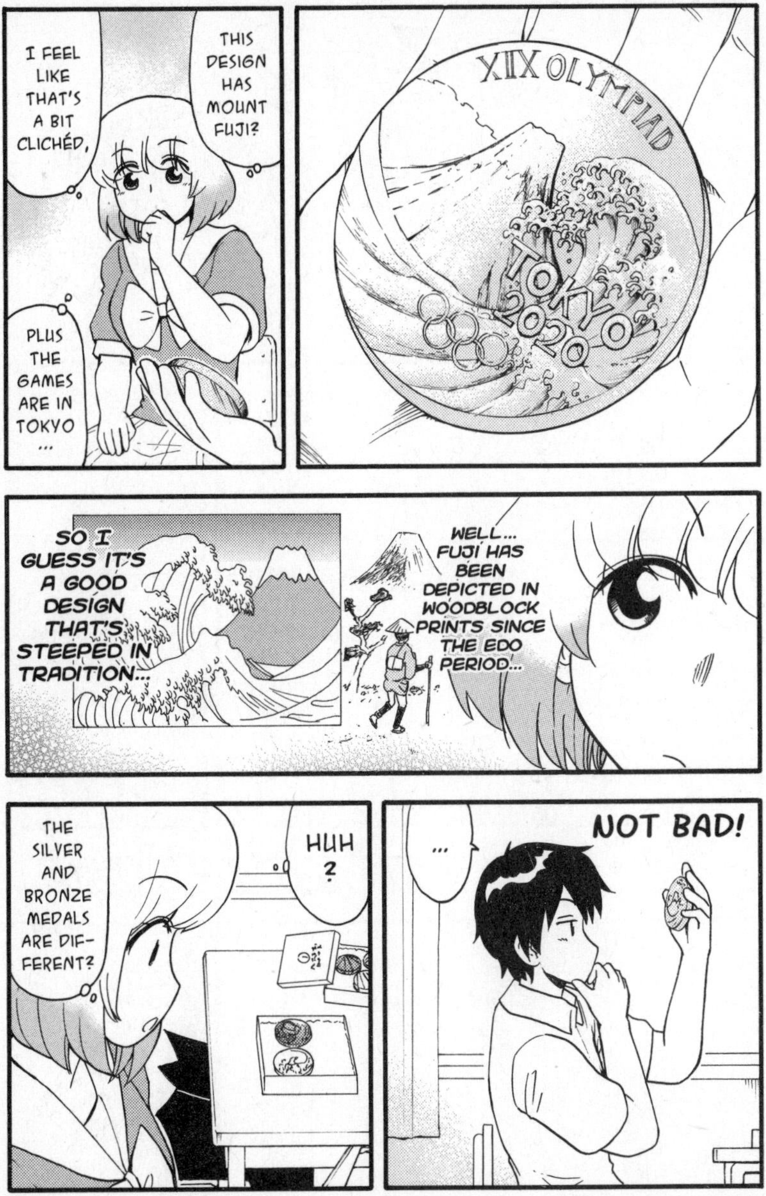
XIX OLYMPIAD
TOKYO 2020
THIS DESIGN HAS MOUNT FUJI?
I FEEL LIKE THAT'S A BIT CLICHÉD,
PLUS THE GAMES ARE IN TOKYO ...
WELL... FUJI HAS BEEN DEPICTED IN WOODBLOCK PRINTS SINCE THE EDO PERIOD...
SO I GUESS IT'S A GOOD DESIGN THAT'S STEEPED IN TRADITION...
NOT BAD!
...
HUH ?
THE SILVER AND BRONZE MEDALS ARE DIFFERENT?

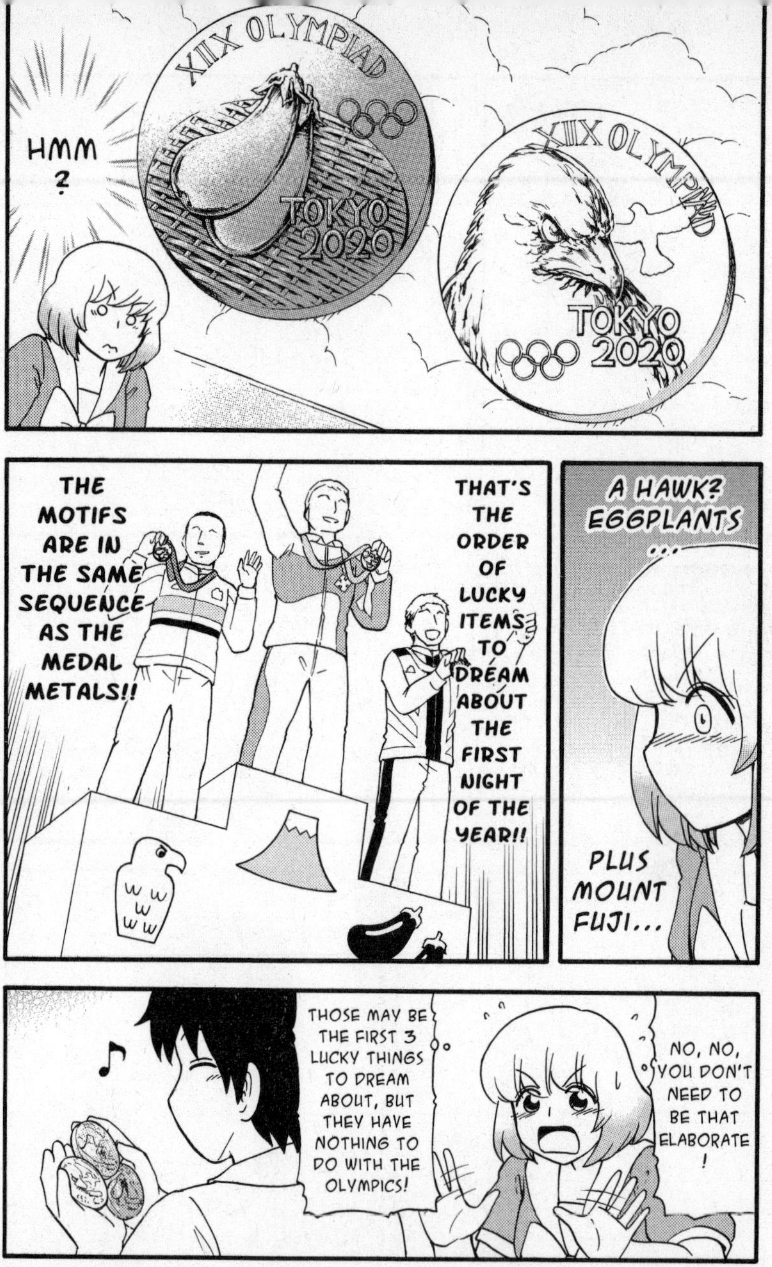
HMM ?
XIIX OLYMPIAD
TOKYO 2020
XIIX OLYMPIAD
TOKYO 2020
A HAWK? EGGPLANTS ...
PLUS MOUNT FUJI...
THAT'S THE ORDER OF LUCKY ITEMS TO DREAM ABOUT THE FIRST NIGHT OF THE YEAR!!
THE MOTIFS ARE IN THE SAME SEQUENCE AS THE MEDAL METALS!!
NO, NO, YOU DON'T NEED TO BE THAT ELABORATE !
THOSE MAY BE THE FIRST 3 LUCKY THINGS TO DREAM ABOUT, BUT THEY HAVE NOTHING TO DO WITH THE OLYMPICS!

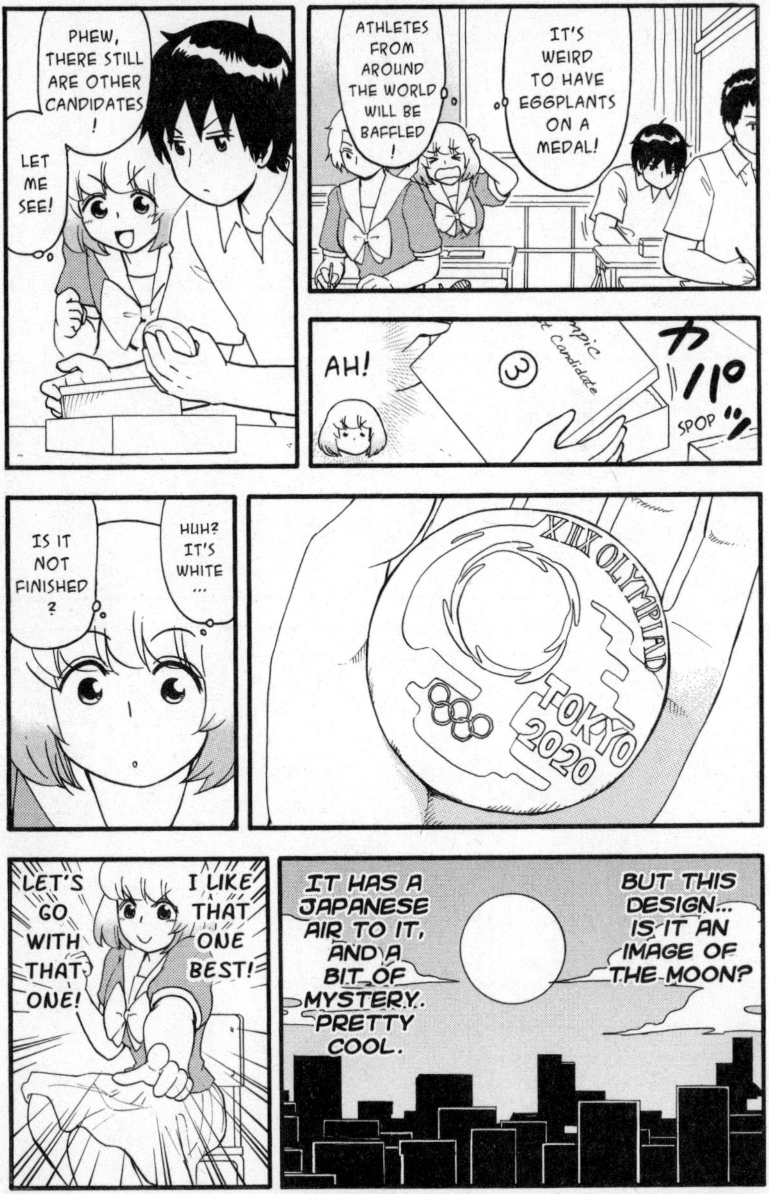
IT'S WEIRD TO HAVE EGGPLANTS ON A MEDAL!
ATHLETES FROM AROUND THE WORLD WILL BE BAFFLED!
カパッ
SPOP
AH!
PHEW, THERE STILL ARE OTHER CANDIDATES!
LET ME SEE!
XIIX OLYMPIAD
TOKYO 2020
HUH? IT'S WHITE...
IS IT NOT FINISHED?
BUT THIS DESIGN... IS IT AN IMAGE OF THE MOON?
IT HAS A JAPANESE AIR TO IT, AND A BIT OF MYSTERY. PRETTY COOL.
I LIKE THAT ONE BEST!
LET'S GO WITH THAT ONE!

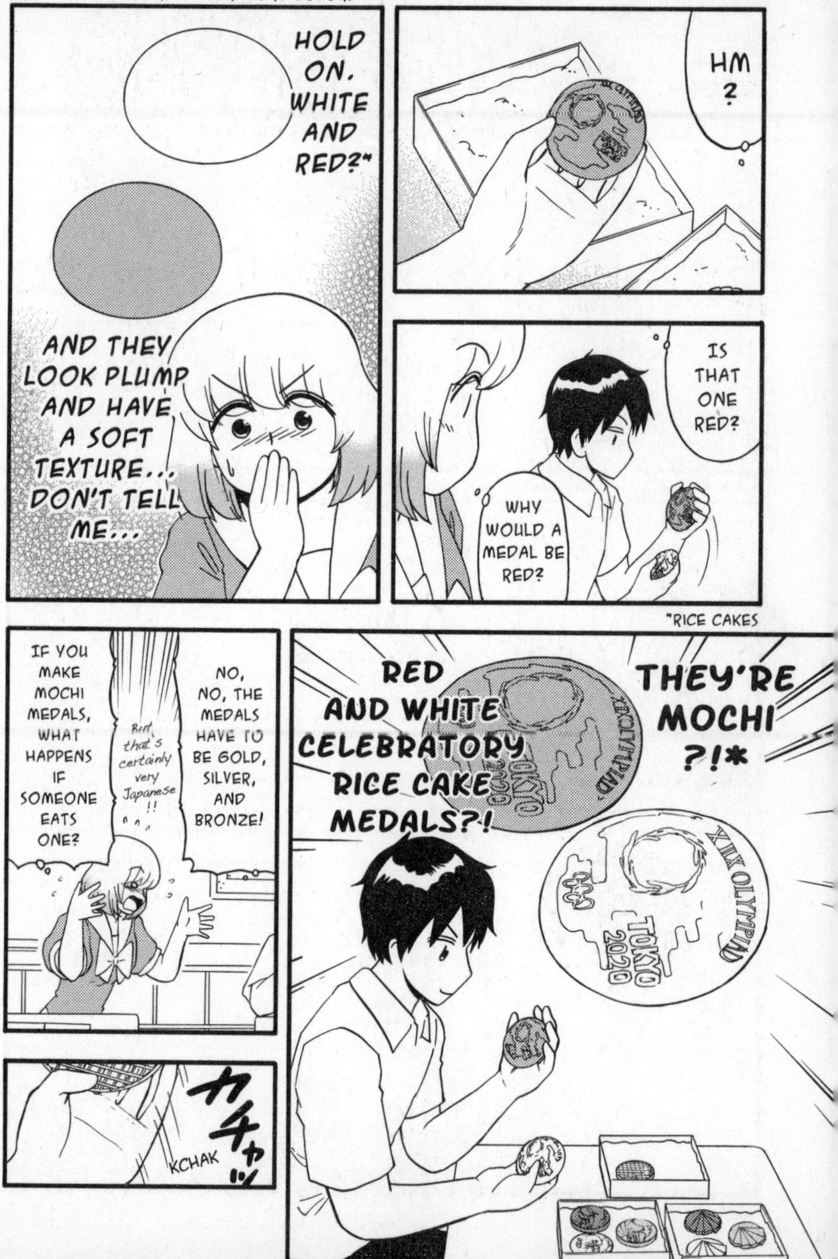
HM?
IS THAT ONE RED?
WHY WOULD A MEDAL BE RED?
HOLD ON. WHITE AND RED?*
AND THEY LOOK PLUMP AND HAVE A SOFT TEXTURE... DON'T TELL ME...
THEY'RE MOCHI?!*
RED AND WHITE CELEBRATORY RICE CAKE MEDALS?!
XIX OLYMPIAD
TOKYO 2020
NO, NO, THE MEDALS HAVE TO BE GOLD, SILVER, AND BRONZE!
But that's certainly very Japanese!!
IF YOU MAKE MOCHI MEDALS, WHAT HAPPENS IF SOMEONE EATS ONE?
カチャッ
KCHAK

*RED AND WHITE ARE CELEBRATORY COLORS

*RICE CAKES

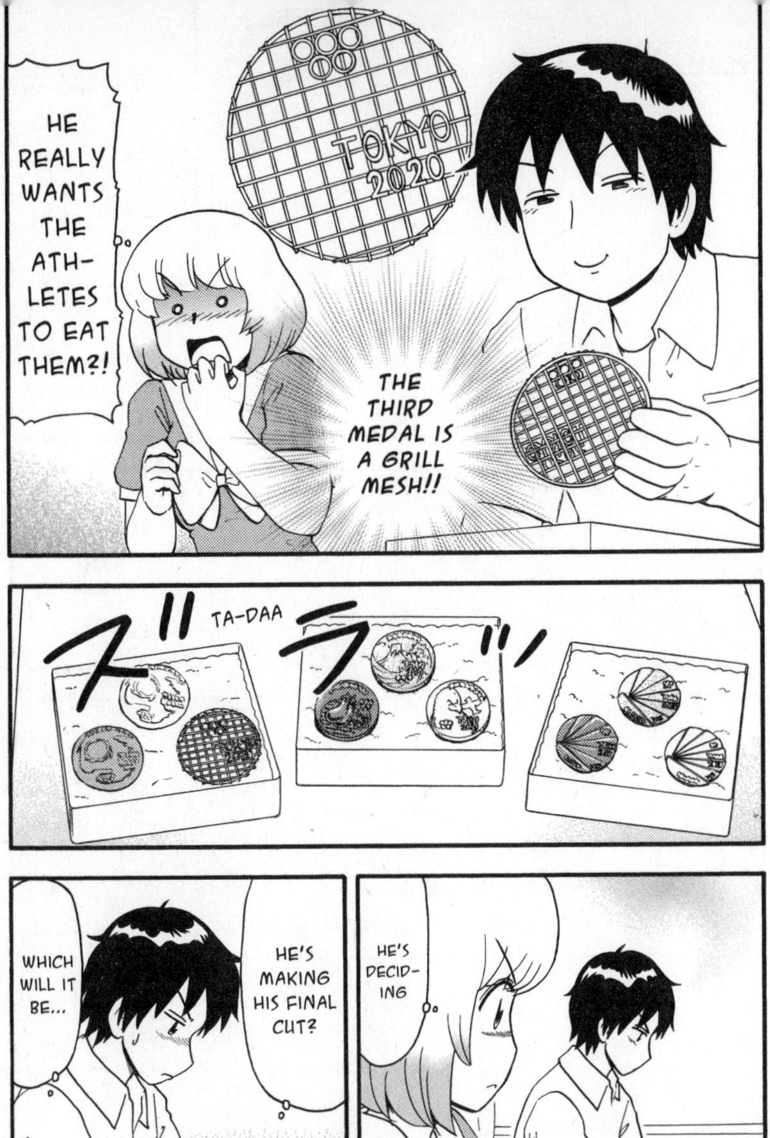

TOKYO 2020
THE THIRD MEDAL IS A GRILL MESH!!
HE REALLY WANTS THE ATH-LETES TO EAT THEM?!
ズラリ
TA-DAA
HE'S DECID-ING
HE'S MAKING HIS FINAL CUT?
WHICH WILL IT BE...

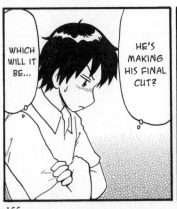

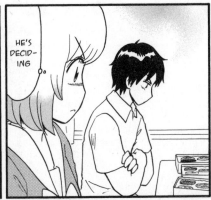

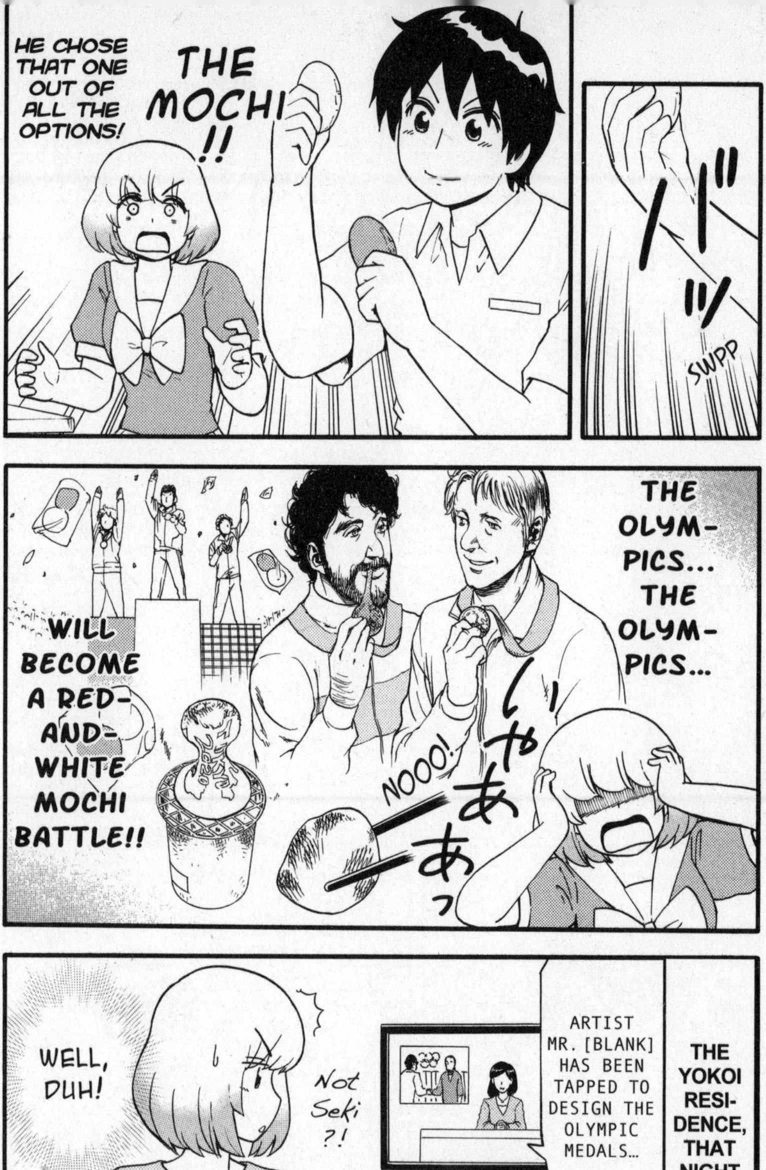
SWPP
THE MOCHI!!
HE CHOSE THAT ONE OUT OF ALL THE OPTIONS!
THE OLYMPICS... THE OLYMPICS...
いやあぁっ
NOOO!
WILL BECOME A RED-AND-WHITE MOCHI BATTLE!!
THE YOKOI RESIDENCE, THAT NIGHT
ARTIST MR. [BLANK] HAS BEEN TAPPED TO DESIGN THE OLYMPIC MEDALS...
Not Seki?!
WELL, DUH!

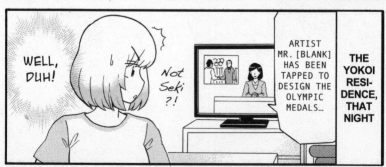

Continued in My Neighbor Seki Volume 10

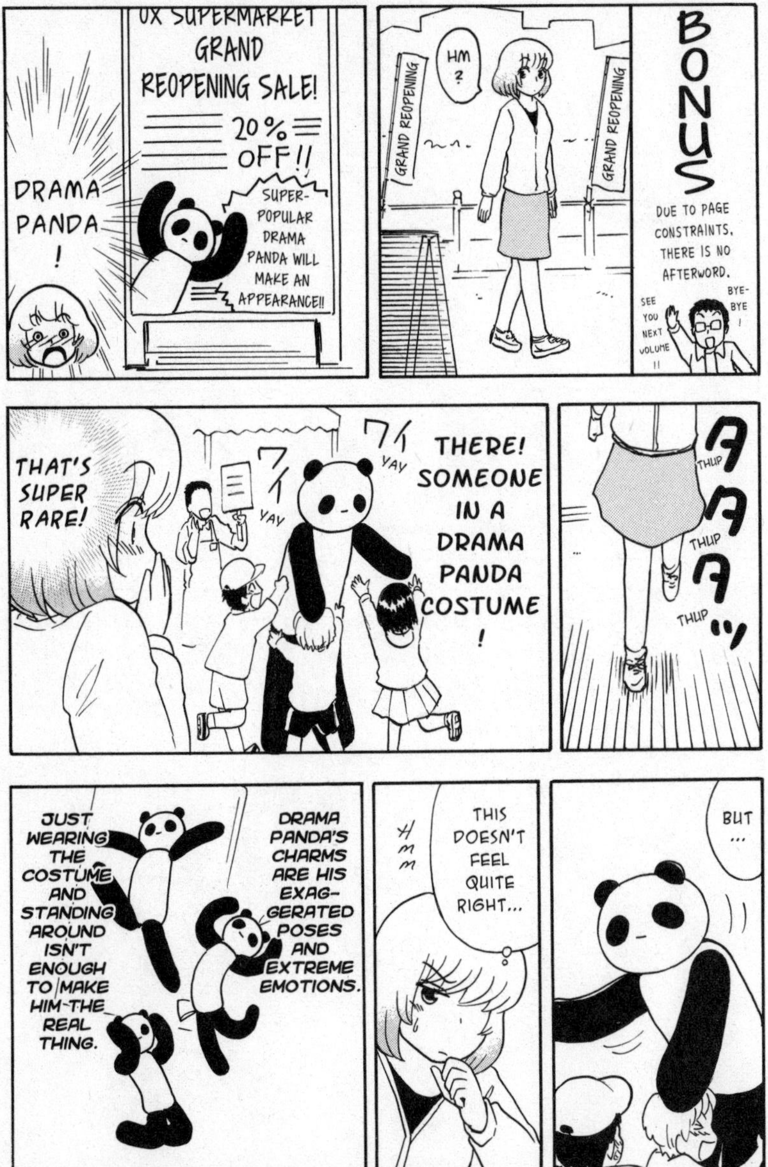
BONUS
DUE TO PAGE CONSTRAINTS, THERE IS NO AFTERWORD.
BYE-BYE!
SEE YOU NEXT VOLUME!!
HM?
GRAND REOPENING
GRAND REOPENING
OX SUPERMARKET GRAND REOPENING SALE!
20% OFF!!
SUPER-POPULAR DRAMA PANDA WILL MAKE AN APPEARANCE!!
DRAMA PANDA!
THUP
THUP
THUP
...
THERE! SOMEONE IN A DRAMA PANDA COSTUME!
YAY
YAY
THAT'S SUPER RARE!
BUT...
THIS DOESN'T FEEL QUITE RIGHT...
HMM
DRAMA PANDA'S CHARMS ARE HIS EXAGGERATED POSES AND EXTREME EMOTIONS.
JUST WEARING THE COSTUME AND STANDING AROUND ISN'T ENOUGH TO MAKE HIM THE REAL THING.

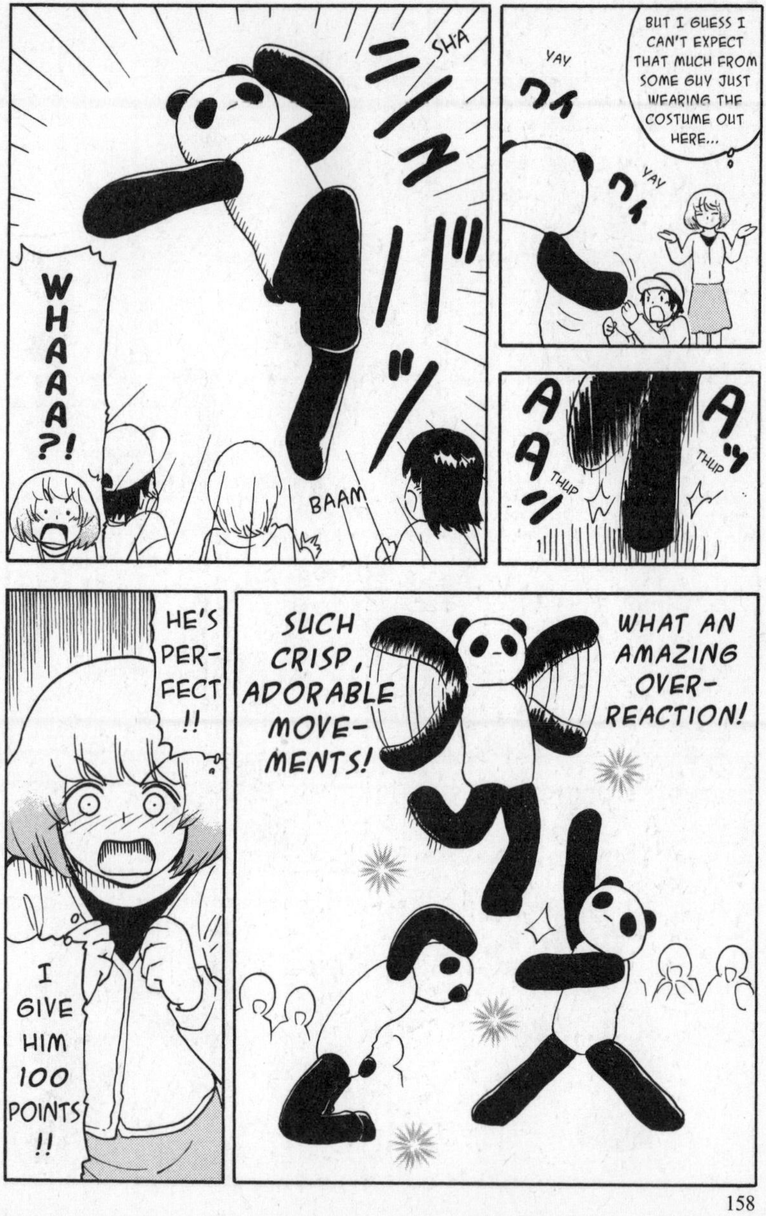
YAY
ワィ
YAY
ワィ
BUT I GUESS I CAN'T EXPECT THAT MUCH FROM SOME GUY JUST WEARING THE COSTUME OUT HERE...
アタッ
THUP
アッ
THUP
SHA
シュバッ
WHAAAA?!
BAAM
WHAT AN AMAZING OVER-REACTION!
SUCH CRISP, ADORABLE MOVE-MENTS!
HE'S PER-FECT!!
I GIVE HIM 100 POINTS!!

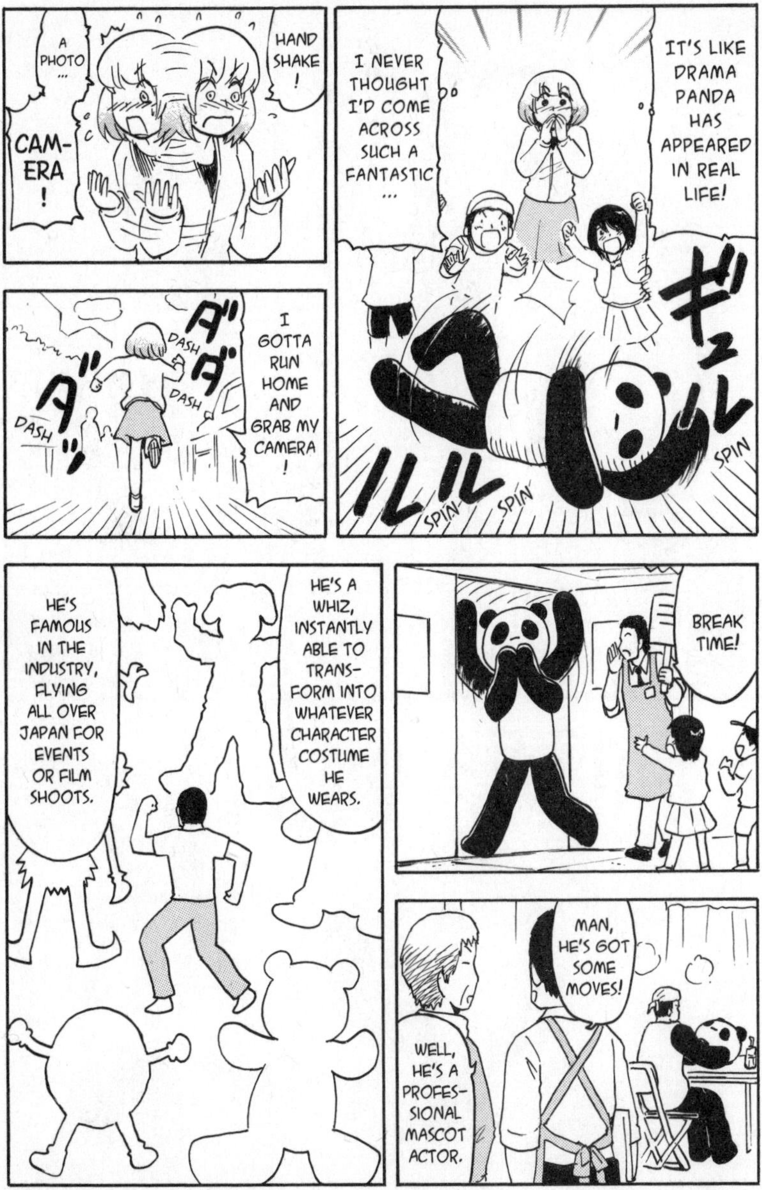
IT'S LIKE DRAMA PANDA HAS APPEARED IN REAL LIFE!
I NEVER THOUGHT I'D COME ACROSS SUCH A FANTASTIC ...
ギュルルル
SPIN
SPIN
SPIN
HAND SHAKE!
A PHOTO ...
CAM-ERA!
I GOTTA RUN HOME AND GRAB MY CAMERA!
ダダダッ
DASH
DASH
DASH
BREAK TIME!
MAN, HE'S GOT SOME MOVES!
WELL, HE'S A PROFES-SIONAL MASCOT ACTOR.
HE'S A WHIZ, INSTANTLY ABLE TO TRANS-FORM INTO WHATEVER CHARACTER COSTUME HE WEARS.
HE'S FAMOUS IN THE INDUSTRY, FLYING ALL OVER JAPAN FOR EVENTS OR FILM SHOOTS.

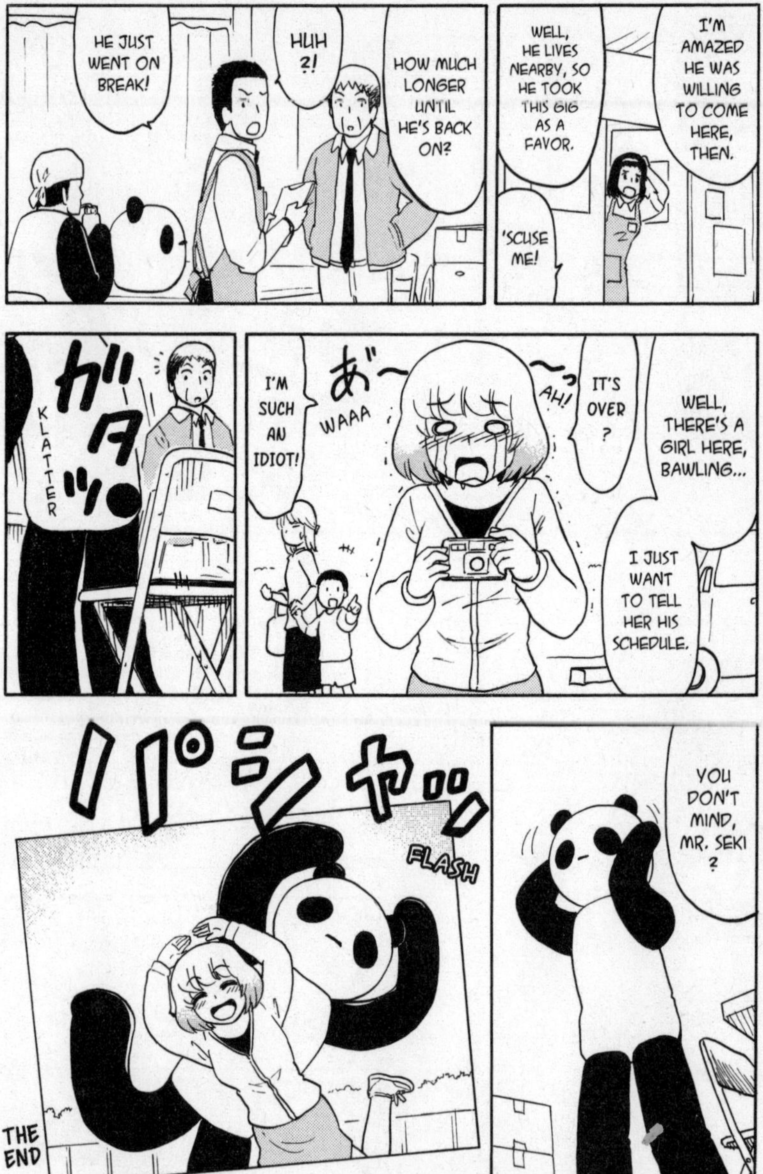
I'M AMAZED HE WAS WILLING TO COME HERE, THEN.
WELL, HE LIVES NEARBY, SO HE TOOK THIS GIG AS A FAVOR.
'SCUSE ME!
HOW MUCH LONGER UNTIL HE'S BACK ON?
HUH?!
HE JUST WENT ON BREAK!
WELL, THERE'S A GIRL HERE, BAWLING...
I JUST WANT TO TELL HER HIS SCHEDULE.
IT'S OVER?
AH!
あ〜
WAAA
I'M SUCH AN IDIOT!
ガタッ
KLATTER
YOU DON'T MIND, MR. SEKI?
パシャ
FLASH
THE END

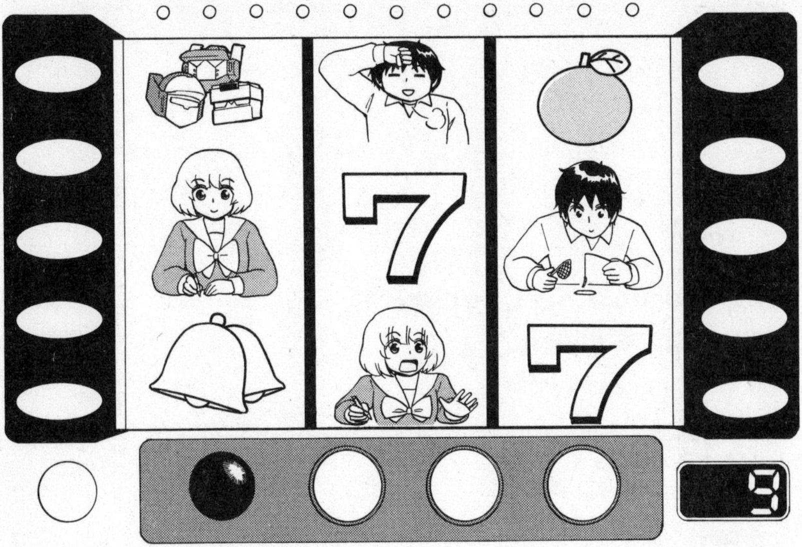
9

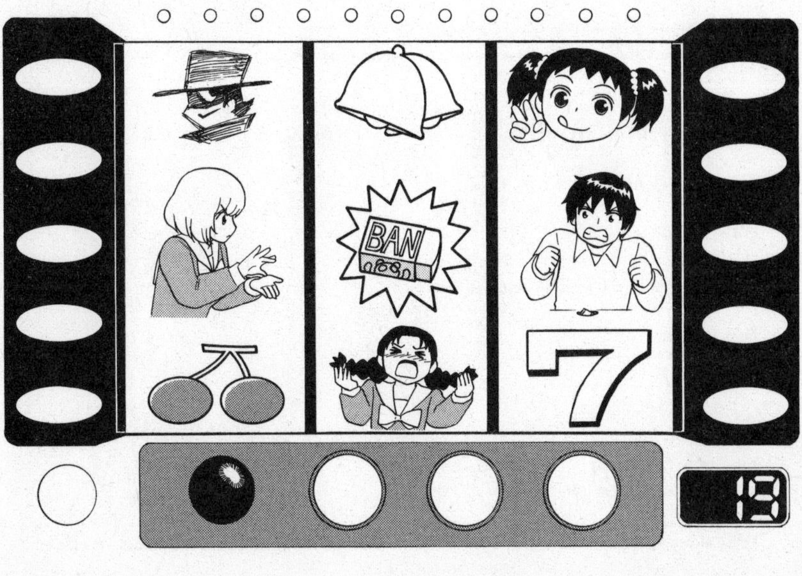
BAN
19

My Neighbor Seki, volume 9
Tonari no Seki-kun

A Vertical Comics Edition

Translation: Mari Morimoto
Production: Risa Cho
            Anthony Quintessenza

© Takuma Morishige 2016
First published in Japan in 2016 by KADOKAWA CORPORATION, Tokyo.
English translation rights reserved by Vertical, Inc.
Under the license from KADOKAWA CORPORATION, Tokyo.

Translation provided by Vertical Comics, 2017
Published by Vertical Comics, an imprint of Vertical, Inc., New York

Originally published in Japanese as *Tonari no Seki-kun 9* by MEDIA FACTORY.
Tonari no Seki-kun first serialized in *Gekkan Comic Flapper*, MEDIA FACTORY, 2010-

This is a work of fiction.

ISBN: 978-1-945054-01-3

Manufactured in the United States of America

First Edition

Vertical, Inc.
451 Park Avenue South
7th Floor
New York, NY 10016
www.vertical-comics.com

Vertical books are distributed through Penguin-Random House Publisher Services.